Inclusive Design

A UNIVERSAL NEED

OTHER BOOKS BY AUTHOR

Evidence-Based Design for Interior Designers
The Interior Design Intern

Inclusive Design
A UNIVERSAL NEED

Linda L. Nussbaumer,

Ph.D., CID, ASID, IDEC

South Dakota State University

FAIRCHILD BOOKS

NEW YORK

Executive Director & General Manager: Michael Schluter

Executive Editor: Olga T. Kontzias

Assistant Acquisitions Editor: Amanda Breccia

Development Editor: Rob Phelps

Assistant Art Director: Sarah Silberg

Production Director: Ginger Hillman

Associate Production Editor: Linda Feldman

Ancillaries Editor: Amy Butler

Associate Director of Sales: Melanie Sankel

Copyeditor: Susan Hobbs

Cover Design: Vanessa Han

Cover Art: Photograph © Tim Griffith; Project Name: Ed
Roberts Campus; Architects: Leddy Maytum Stacy Architects

Text Design: Alicia Freile, Tango Media

Page Layout: Alicia Freile, Tango Media

Photo Research: Avital Aronowitz

Illustrations: Precision Graphics

Library of Congress Catalog Card Number: 2011924731
ISBN: 978-1-56367-921-6
GST R 133004424
Printed in the United States of America
TP09

DEDICATION

To the innovators, leaders, and advocates of the past, present, and future who have dedicated their life's work to improving environments and products for everyone.

Table of Contents

Extended Table of Contents

Preface

Prior to the enactment of the Americans with Disabilities Act (the ADA), people with disabilities experienced discrimination in employment as well as access into public environments. Fortunately, the ADA of 1990, and amended in 2008, has drastically changed these concerns. However, many facilities are still not designed in a way that includes everyone, where attention is drawn to disabilities or where not everyone has similar accommodations. Thus, the purpose of this book is to help students understand why they should value and thus apply inclusivity into their designs.

Often books written on universal design are large handbooks and, frequently, most focus toward professionals. Several books have been written specifically about residential design, kitchens, and/or aging in place. However, none are designed specifically as textbooks. Because the Council for Interior Design Accreditation standards prescribes both the application of the ADA (accessibility) as well as universal design, it must be addressed in interior design education. Increasingly, colleges and universities are providing classes geared specifically to universal design; a textbook that focuses on universal design (or inclusive design) would be very helpful for these educators and students.

INCLUSIVE DESIGN: THE EVOLUTION OF UNIVERSAL DESIGN

Some books and organizations use the term "universal design" whereas others use the term "inclusive design." There are similarities and differences between these terms. Most often, the universal design term is used in the United States and inclusive design in Europe, Canada, and other countries. However, even in the United States, organizations and conferences have used inclusive design and some have used both terms in the same discussion.

Some researchers believe that inclusive design is a more appropriate term than universal design. Universal and inclusive have similar and yet different meanings. For example, "universal" means relating to the whole world and the universe, and something (e.g., product, device, environment) that is used by everyone. "Inclusive" means including many things but may be situational (e.g., a design specific for the hard-of-hearing or the visually impaired that allows the individual to be included), and including people of all kinds, i.e., nondiscriminatory. When analyzing these terms, it seems that inclusive fits better into the realm of design, and thus, inclusive design is more frequently used within this textbook. Further discussion is included in Chapter 3, "Inclusive Design," and Chapter 10, "The People."

SEQUENCE FOR LEARNING

This book is divided in three parts. Part I: Foundations for Inclusive Design, Part II: Inclusive Design for Products and Environments, and Part III: Advocates of Inclusive Design.

Part I includes Chapters 1 through 3. Chapter 1 provides a background of the ADA legislation prior to the use of inclusive or universal design. This is followed by a discussion of inclusive design in Chapter 2, as well as various terminology related to universal design. Additionally, further discussion of the difference between universal and inclusive design is included. Chapter 3 discusses the integration of inclusive design into the design process.

Part II includes Chapters 4 through 9. Chapter 4 discusses product design and inclusivity and provides examples of products that are inclusive. Chapter 5 focuses upon residential design that includes quality versus quantity, home modifications, lighting, and renovation, as well as designing an inclusive home. Also discussed in this chapter is housing for the aging populations that includes aging in place, the application of sustainable design and inclusive design, affordable housing with a brief discussion of cultural sensitivity along with a few examples of housing outside the United States. Chapter 6 provides an overview in the application of inclusivity for commercial design; then, specific information is presented on various commercial design typologies. Chapter 7 concentrates on office design; Chapter 8 focuses on healthcare and institutional design; and Chapter 9 centers on hospitality, retail, and other commercial designs.

Part III includes Chapter 10, "The People." This chapter's focus is the people who have experienced design (accessible, non-accessible, as well as inclusive design). Some use wheelchairs; one is blind; some have hearing limitations. They are designers, educators, professional people, and founders of organizations that promote inclusive design. Through their experiences and reflections, all clearly establish how inclusive design is a universal need.

PEDAGOGICAL FEATURES

For students to better understand how inclusive design is a universal need, various pedagogical features have been included. At the beginning of each chapter, objectives provide the learning focus, and key terms—bolded throughout the text—aid in a better understanding of the topic. At the end of each chapter, a summary recaps material presented and experiential- and application-type projects are included and can be used in the classroom or as additional self-taught learning experiences. The color inserts section provides an overview of important aspects of inclusive design and connects to chapter topics and case studies within the textbook.

Boxes provide additional material or various research summaries to emphasis a particular topic, and tables, charts, illustrations, and photographs lend a visual understanding for each topic. A glossary, bibliography, and index are also included at the end of the book as well as a basic metric conversion chart.

AN ESSENTIAL GUIDE FOR ALL CAREERS IN DESIGN

Universal design and accessibility are important in meeting CIDA accreditation standards. Within those colleges and universities that have separate courses on universal design, the book provides an excellent primary resource for these courses. In such a course, students learn background information about the ADA and the purpose of inclusive design. Then, as they progress through the course, students learn about products and various environments as well as apply this knowledge to projects.

For those who have incorporated universal design into many courses (e.g., an introduction to design, a codes course, or a design process or methods course), this book is important in the introduction of inclusivity, a universal need, and continues to be used as a source of information throughout the curriculum. For example, an introductory course or a codes course may introduce the topic and then apply inclusive design to projects within subsequent studio courses. With either method, this book offers students insight into ideas for application along with situations that may be used as case studies to enhance students' learning experiences.

Acknowledgments

Researching for and writing a textbook can seem like a daunting task. And yet, with the wonderful support of Condé Nast Publications and Fairchild Books' professionals, the task produces excitement and even enjoyment. First, I wish to thank Executive Editor Olga Kontzias for believing in my abilities, encouraging me, and connecting me to ideas and people. Thanks also to the professional staff: former Editorial Development Director Jennifer Crane; Senior Development Editor Joe Miranda; and Development Editor Rob Phelps. A special thanks goes to Rob for his great work as a reviewer and editor. I would also like to thank the talented production and art team of Associate Production Editor Linda Feldman; Associate Art Director Sarah Silberg; and Avital Aronowitz, photo editor. I am also grateful for the constructive criticism of acquisitions reviewers Janet Biddick, University of Oklahoma; Shauna Cory, University of Idaho; Betsy Gibb, University of Nebraska—Lincoln, and Shelley Mocchi, College of DuPage.

Expert contributions to this book have created a connection between information and reality. I would like to thank those experts who contributed to my book: Rosemarie Rossetti, Erik Weihenmayer, Tracy Bell, and Jenny Stenner, Shirley Confino-Rehder, Shashi Caan, Valerie Fletcher, and Gregg C. Vanderheiden. Their expert comments and advice give students and practitioners a real world perspective. Thank you to my friends and family who continually encourage and support me. Especially, thank you to my husband Jerry, who was my greatest fan and support in this endeavor.

I would like to dedicate this book to those who have endured environments that were not designed to be inclusive. It is my hope that designers (both present and future designers) will fully embrace inclusivity, apply its concepts to their design projects, and make life easier for those with special needs.

Part I

FOUNDATIONS FOR INCLUSIVE DESIGN

CHAPTER 1

Legislation that Precedes Inclusive Design

"Congress acknowledged that society's accumulated myths and fears about disability and disease are as handicapping as are the physical limitations that flow from actual impairment."

—*William J. Brennan, Jr.*

OBJECTIVES

- State the purpose of the Americans with Disabilities Act (ADA)
- Understand legislation that preceded the ADA
- Understand the organization of the ADA
- Explain the purpose and importance of the ADA
- Define disability as set forth in the ADA, amended 2008
- Define a reasonable accommodation
- Describe individuals protected by the ADA
- Explain the various possible accommodations for hearing and speech impairments
- Explain the purpose of the Americans with Disabilities Act Accessibility Guidelines (ADAAG)
- Explain the designer's role in complying with the ADA and applying ADAAG

KEY TERMS

- Air Carrier Access Act (ACAA)
- American National Standards Institute (ANSI)
- Americans with Disabilities Act (ADA)
- Americans with Disabilities Act Accessibility Guidelines (ADAAG)
- Americans with Disabilities Act Amendments Act of 2008
- Architectural Barriers Act (ABA) of 1968
- Civil Rights Act of 1964
- closed captioning
- disabilities
- Education for All Handicapped Children Act (EAHCA)
- Individuals with Disabilities Education Act in 1990
- impairment
- inclusive
- inclusive design
- International Classification of Functioning, Disability, and Health (ICF)
- limitation
- major life activities
- physiological impairment
- psychological impairment
- Rehabilitation Act of 1973
- telecommunications device for the deaf (TDD)
- Telecommunications Relay Services (TRS)
- text telephone (TTY)
- TeleTYpewriter (TTY)
- universal
- universal design
- Voice Carry Over (VCO)
- Video Relay Service (VRS)

Accessibility concerns everyone; therefore, design must be accessible to all.

Accessibility concerns people throughout the globe. In fact, as a part of the World Health Organization (WHO), the **International Classification of Functioning, Disability, and Health (ICF)** addressed the international standard for health and disabilities (Jones, 2010; WHO, 2010). However, creating designs that provide access to everyone is not international, particularly, in economically developing countries.

Countries that address access for everyone may also use different terminologies. For example, **universal design** is a term used in the United States whereas **inclusive design** is used in Canada, as well as Great Britain and other European countries.

However, these terms may even be interchangeably used in any one of the locations. For example, a 2007 symposium at the New York School of Interior Design entitled "Symposium on Inclusive Design: Understanding and Designing Accessible Residential Environments" offered presentations on universal design. The organization Concrete Change from Decatur, Georgia, discusses access into a residence in terms of **inclusive** as well as **universal**. The University at Buffalo addresses accessibility in their Center for Inclusive Design and Environmental Access. Additionally, on March 10, 2009, HR 1408, the Inclusive Home Design Act of 2009, was introduced in the U.S. House of Representatives.

Thus, there may be some confusion as to which term is correct or acceptable. To gain a better understanding of the similarities and differences between these terms, universal design and inclusive design are discussed in greater length in Chapter 2.

Prior to this discussion, however, it is important to understand the **Americans with Disabilities Act (ADA)** and, particularly, whom this act affects. By law, the ADA ensures equality for people with disabilities and allows them the same access as others have enjoyed, whether it be access to employment, a building, or communication. From this, inclusive design provides access to everyone regardless of ability and without drawing attention to a disability.

Equality for People with Disabilities

In the 1990s when the ADA law was signed, the number of people with disabilities was 48.9 million (U.S. Census Bureau, 2010). As of 2007, the number of people who had some level of disability is 41.2 million—15 percent of the population who are not institutionalized and are 5 years of age and older (U.S. Census Bureau, 2009). This number has fluctuated over the years and will continue to do so. The number of those with special disabilities such as eyesight and hearing, on-the-job concerns, impoverishment, military veteran status, and more are included in this number. On the other hand, this number does not include those with temporary disabilities as well as with arthritis or asthma—all of which can impair an individual's ability to function efficiently at work or home.

Understanding the distribution of disabilities among Americans helps us better comprehend the enormity of the problem and see that disabilities are not only about immobility and the elderly. (See Table 1.1, "Who's Disabled in America?," for the distribution of people with disabilities in America in 2007.) Clearly, an enormous number of people have some type of disability, and equality for people with disabilities remains a concern.

Historical Background for the Americans with Disabilities Act

On July 12, 1990, President George H. W. Bush signed into law the Americans with Disabilities Act (ADA), which went into effect on January 26, 1992 (ADA, 2008a). However, other preceding legislation paved the way for the ADA. Earlier legislation not only preceded but also influenced the enactment of the ADA. The four most significant acts were the Civil Rights Act of 1964, the Architectural Barriers Act of 1968, the Rehabilitation Act of 1973, and the Education for All Handicapped Children Act of 1975. Shortly after the ADA was signed into law, the U.S. Access Board developed and, in 1991, published the **Americans with Disabilities Act Accessibility Guidelines (ADAAG)**.

THE CIVIL RIGHTS ACT

The **Civil Rights Act of 1964** protects against discrimination based on race, color, national origin, gender, and religion. It prohibits discrimination in public facilities, governmental services, and employment (EEOCb). The difference between the Civil Rights Act and the ADA is that the ADA requires equal opportunity for people with physical and mental impairments (EEOCc), as opposed to race, color, and so on.

THE ARCHITECTURAL BARRIERS ACT

In 1961, the **American National Standards Institute (ANSI)** passed the first set of guidelines to ensure that people with disabilities were able to access and maneuver within public buildings. In 1968, Congress passed the **Architectural Barriers Act (ABA) of 1968**, the first accessibility law, which required that buildings and facilities designed, constructed, or altered with federal funds or leased by a federal agency must be accessible (Rhodes, 2010; U.S. Access Board, 2005) (see Figure 1.1). Although the ABA addressed architectural standards for new and

TABLE 1.1 Who's Disabled in America

As of 2007, there were 41.2 million Americans (noninstitutionalized civilians age 5 and older) with some level of disability; this table provides an overview of who they are, what they need, and how they fit into the overall U.S. population:

THE PEOPLE	THE NUMBERS
BY AGE:	
Ages 5–15	6%
Ages 16–64	12%
Ages 65 and older	41%
BY GENDER:	
Female	15%
Male	14%
BY NEED:	
Those (ages 6 and older) needing personal assistance for everyday activities such as getting into the home, taking a bath or shower, preparing meals, and performing light housework	11 million
Those (ages 15 and older) who use wheelchairs	3.3 million
Those (ages 15 and older) completely unable to see printed words or are partially blind	1.8 million
Those (ages 15 and older) completely unable to hear conversations or are partially deaf	1 million
Those (ages 15 and older) who have some difficulty having their speech understood	2.5 million
Those (ages 15 and older) completely unable to have their speech understood	431,000
ON THE JOB:	
Those (ages 16 to 64) with a medical condition making it difficult to find a job or remain employed	13.3 million
Those (ages 21 to 64) with some type of disability while employed during the past year	46% • 75% of those with a nonsevere disability to 31% with a severe disability • The employment rate for those without a disability is 84% for the same period
Those (ages 21 to 64) with difficulty hearing while employed	59%
Those (ages 21 to 64) with difficulty seeing while employed	41%
BY INCOME AND POVERTY LEVEL:	
Median monthly earnings for people with varied level of disability	• $1,458 (21 to 64) severe disability • $2,250 (21 to 64) nonsevere disability • $2,539 (21 to 64) no disability • $2,252 (21 to 64) difficulty hearing • $1,932 (21 to 64) difficulty seeing
Poverty rate for people (ages 25 to 64) with a nonsevere disability	12%
Poverty rate for people (ages 25 to 64) with a severe disability	27%
Poverty rate for people (ages 25 to 64) without a disability	9%
TRANSPORTATION ACCOMMODATIONS:	
Transit buses that were ADA lift- or ramp-equipped since 2006	98.5% (a 61.7% increase since 1995)

Source: U. S. Census Bureau. (2009). "Facts for Features: Americans with Disabilities Act: July 26." Retrieved on May 10, 2010, from http://www.census.gov/Press-Release/www/releases/archives/facts_for_features_special_editions/013739.html

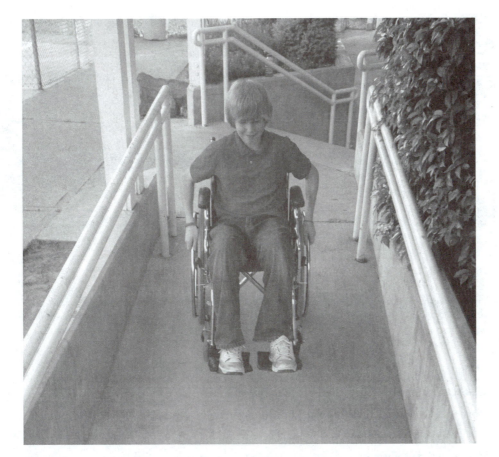

Figure 1.1

Passed in 1968, the Architectural Barriers Act (ABA) of 1968 required that buildings and facilities constructed with federal funds must be accessible. Ramps into buildings provide minimum accessibility.
© Ron Baily/istockphoto

renovated buildings and newly leased facilities, it did not address access to federal programs or activities that occurred within the buildings or facilities not federally funded or leased (US-DOJ, 2005).

THE REHABILITATION ACT

The **Rehabilitation Act of 1973** prohibited discrimination against people with disabilities in all federal agencies or programs receiving federal financial assistance and required affirmative action for people with disabilities. This act included:

- Reasonable accommodations for employees with disabilities
- Accessibility to programs
- Effective communication for people with hearing or visual impairments
- Accessibility into new constructions and alterations

However, each federal agency had the responsibility to comply on its own (US-DOJ, 2005). This act was the beginning of equality for people with disabilities in a governmental workplace (see Figures 1.2a–c).

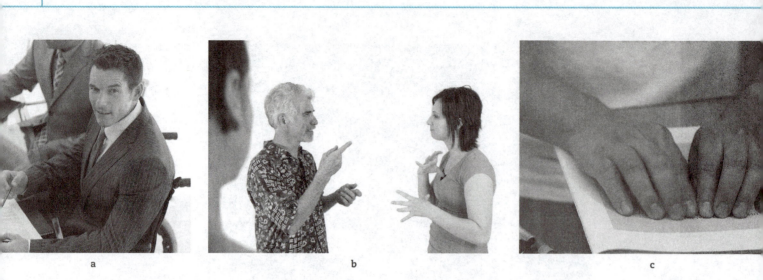

Figure 1.2a–c

Reasonable accommodations allow people with disabilities to be employed. Their disabilities include the (a) physical, (b) auditory, and (c) visual. A physical disability may mean that someone must use a wheelchair, a cane, or another assistive device. Those with auditory disabilities include the hard of hearing and the deaf. Interpreters and special assistive devices may be needed. Visual disabilities may require assistive devices such as a Braille writer, Voice Carry Over, and screen magnification. Wheelchair: © wavebreakmedia/istockphoto; conversation: © Loretta Hostettler/istockphoto; reading Braille: © Andres Balcazar/istockphoto

EDUCATION FOR ALL HANDICAPPED CHILDREN ACT

In 1975, the **Education for All Handicapped Children Act (EAHCA)** required all public school systems to offer equal access to education to children with a physical or mental disability. Schools were required to evaluate these children and provide an educational plan that would emulate the educational experience of children without a disability (see Figure 1.3). This act was revised and renamed **Individuals with Disabilities Education Act** in 1990 (US-DOJ, 2005).

THE AMERICANS WITH DISABILITIES ACT ACCESSIBILITY GUIDELINES

After the ADA became law, accessibility guidelines needed to be determined. Therefore, the U.S. Access Board developed. In 1991, the board published the first set of **Americans with Disabilities Act Accessibility Guidelines (ADAAG)** that addressed access into public buildings. On July 23, 2004, the U.S. Access Board revised guidelines to cover a wide range of facilities in the public and private sector. Then, in 2010, it was updated with guidelines for federal facilities covered by the ABA (U.S. Access Board, 2011). This update made the ADA and ABA guidelines consistent and addressed access issues in new construction and alterations as well. Revisions continue to meet the needs of people with disabilities and keep pace with technological advances. Also, the Access Board created the new ADAAG to be consistent with model building codes such as the International Building Code (IBC) and ANSI. The ADAAG is important for designers because it is used to determine appropriate clearance, access, and more (Rhoads, 2010). The guidelines may be viewed or downloaded online at http://www.ada.gov/regs2010/2010ADAStandards/2010ADAstandards.htm.

THE ADA AMENDMENT ACT OF 2008

September 25, 2008, President George W. Bush signed the **Americans with Disabilities Act Amendment Act of 2008**. The ADA, as amended, emphasizes that the definition of disability should be interpreted for broad coverage of individuals to the maximum extent permitted by the terms of the ADA and generally does not require extensive analysis (EEOCa). The remainder of this chapter provides background information on the ADA as well as includes updated material found in the ADA Amendment Act of 2008.

ADA Coverage

Clearly, the ADA recognizes and protects the civil rights of people with disabilities, and as previously noted, earlier acts paved the way for the ADA to become law. Prior to the enactment of the ADA of 1990, the general public isolated or segregated people with disabilities due to the lack of understanding and knowledge. Discrimination occurred in areas of "employment, housing, public accommodations, education, transportation, communication, recreation, institutionalization, health services, voting, and access to

Figure 1.3

Children must have equal access to an education regardless of their disability.
© Moodboard_Images/istockphoto

public services" (EEOCc, sec. 12101, para. 3). To alleviate discrimination, these areas were addressed through the ADA in 1990 and gave people with disabilities the same access as everyone else. In 2008, the ADA was amended and continues to protect people with disabilities against discrimination.

DISABILITY DEFINED

The ADA protects individuals with disabilities. The term *disability* can often be misunderstood; therefore, the ADA developed the following definition (ADATA, 2010c):

1. A physical or mental impairment that substantially limits one or more major life activities of such individual
2. A record of such an impairment
3. Being regarded as having such an impairment

The ADA Amendment Act of 2008 further clarified the various qualities of a disability. To better understand the definition that includes additions from 2008, the following various qualities (physical impairment, mental impairment, substantially limits, and major life activities) are further clarified.

Physical Impairment

A physical impairment is defined as any physiological disorder, cosmetic disfigurement, or anatomical loss affecting one or more body systems such as speech, hearing, and speech impairments, as well as mobility or dexterity loss (e.g., from arthritis). This may include medical conditions such as cancer and diabetes (ADATA, 2010c).

Mental Impairment

A mental impairment is defined as mental or psychological disorders such as emotional or mental illness, specific learning disabilities (e.g., identifiable stress disorders, dyslexia, and others), and more (ADATA, 2010c).

Substantially Limits

Substantially limits means that for an impairment to be considered a disability, it must cause the individual to be unable to perform, or be significantly limited in performing, one or more of the major life activities (ADATA, 2010c).

Major Life Activities

Major life activities are walking, talking, seeing, hearing, breathing, caring for oneself, and so on. For a disability to be covered by the ADA, the impairment must substantially limit one or more major life activities. With the ADA Amendment Act of 2008, major life activities may also include activities such as performing manual tasks, eating, standing, lifting, reading, and more. It may also include activities that relate to major body functions such as functions of the immune system, normal cell growth, digestive, neurological, respiratory, circulatory, and more. (See the complete list at the ADATA (2010c) website, http://www.adata.org/Static/Disability.aspx#1.)

Additional information was also included that provides clarification related to a person with a history or record of impairment and perceived to have an impairment.

People with a History or Record of an Impairment

A person with a history or record of impairment is protected under the ADA, whether or not the disability is no longer active. "For example, it protects people with a history of cancer, heart disease, or other debilitating illness, whose illnesses are cured, controlled, or in remission. It also protects people with a history of mental illness" (ADATA, 2010c).

People Rumored or Thought to Have an Impairment

A person rumored or thought to have an impairment is protected under the ADA from discrimination to the same extent as he or she would be if there was an actual disability. Thus, a person rumored to be HIV-positive cannot be discriminated against on the basis of that belief (ADATA, 2010c).

Exclusions to the Definition

The ADA provides exclusions that are not considered impairments. These relate to the illegal use of drugs, homosexuality and bisexuality, sexual and behavioral disorders, compulsive gambling, kleptomania, and more (ADATA, 2010c).

The ADA Amendment Act of 2008 also includes mitigating measures. For example, positive effects of mitigating measures (except for ordinary eyeglasses and contact lenses) are ignored to determine whether or not an impairment is substantially limiting. Some examples of mitigating measures include medication, medical equipment and devices, prosthetics, hearing aids, and many more. Additionally, ordinary eyeglasses and contact lenses are not used in an analysis because their lenses are "intended to fully correct visual acuity or eliminate refractive error" (EEOCc). For further details, see the ADA website at http://www.ada.gov/pubs/adastatute08.htm#12102.

The Americans with Disabilities Act, as Amended in 2008

The ADA is divided into five titles that address specific topics, and each title is further divided into sections. These titles include employment (Title I), public services (Title II), public accommodations and services operated by private entities (Title III), telecommunications (Title IV), and miscellaneous provisions (Title V). Of these, Title

III establishes design requirements for construction or alteration of facilities and is of greatest importance for designers. However, Titles I through IV are important areas to understand when designing for people with various disabilities. Title V does not relate to building design and constructions but includes information about ADA's relationship to other federal and state laws. Thus, only Titles I through IV will be briefly described here.

TITLE I EMPLOYMENT

Title I focuses on employment and establishes guidelines to be followed by employers (e.g., private employers, state and local governments employment agencies, labor organizations, and joint labor-management committees). According to the ADA (2009) and U.S. Access Board (2009), the law applies as follows.

- All employers of 15 or more may not discriminate against qualified individuals with disabilities. This number includes part-time employees who have worked for 20 or more weeks in the current or previous years.
- Foreign-based U. S. companies, their subsidiaries, and firms controlled by Americans must comply with the ADA in their employment of U.S. citizens unless such compliance would violate a foreign country's laws.
- Religious organizations must comply but are allowed to give preference in employment to individuals of a particular religion.

There are a few exemptions. Employers of fewer than 15 workers may be exempt from ADA compliance as well as the executive branch of the federal government. However, the Rehabilitation Act of 1973 may cover federal workers. Some are exempt provided they are exempt from taxation (ADA, 2008b). These include corporations fully owned by the U. S. government, an Indian tribe, and bona fide private membership clubs (except labor organizations) (U.S. Access Board, 2009).

People affected by Title I Employment

The ADA protects any qualified individual with a disability from discrimination in employment. The changes in the ADA Amendment Act of 2008 clarified the statements related to the definition of a disability (discussed earlier in this chapter). The ADA also states that a qualified individual with a disability is one who has the skills, experience, education, and other job-related requirements of a position, whether or not the individual needs reasonable accommodation and can perform the essential functions of the position he or she holds or desires (ADA, 2008b). To more clearly understand this statement, the ADA (2008b) defines reasonable accommodation as follows.

1. Any modification or adjustment to a job or the work environment that will enable a qualified applicant or employee with a disability to participate in the application process or to perform essential job functions.

2. Also includes adjustments to assure that a qualified individual with a disability has rights and privileges in employment equal to those of employees without disabilities (ADA, 2008b, question 9).

The ADA provides a question and answer section to help understand the ADA. Within this section, the ADA (2008b) provides examples of reasonable accommodations to a facility accessible and usable by:

1. restructuring a job
2. modifying work schedules
3. acquiring or modifying equipment
4. providing qualified readers or interpreters
5. appropriately modifying examinations, training, or other programs

However, employers are not required to lower quality or quantity standards to make accommodation, and they are not obligated to provide personal use items (e.g., glasses, hearing aids, wheelchairs, prosthetic limbs). Appropriate accommodations are based on circumstances of each case, and the key is "effectiveness, i.e., whether the accommodation will provide an opportunity for a person with a disability to achieve the same level of performance and to enjoy benefits equal to those of an average, similarly situated person without a disability" (ADA 2008b).

Title I and the Work of Designers

Although an original design of an office may provide accessibility, it is possible that a new employee (or a current employee) will need different reasonable accommodations due to hearing or visual impairments, size, or another diverse need. In this case, designers may be involved in the redesign of an office to provide reasonable accommodations. This section of the ADA helps the designer understand the reason an individual may have his or her space or the facility reconfigured to provide reasonable accommodations (see Figure 1.4).

Modifying Existing Facilities to Make them Accessible

An employer is obligated to provide access for an applicant to participate in a job application process and for an employee with a disability to perform the essential function of the job. This includes access to a building, work site, needed equipment, and all facilities (e.g., break room, lounge) used by employees (ADA, 2008b).

The Job Accommodation Network Modifying facilities to accommodate those with disabilities may seem overwhelming. For this reason, the U.S. Department of Labor's Office of Disability Employment Policy (ODEP) created the Job Accommodation Network (JAN). It assists the individual (applicant or employee) as well as the employer in creating workable solutions that will accommodate any

Figure 1.4

The ADA requires reasonable accommodations for job applicants, employees, and those taking exams. Individuals who have difficulty reading a document (on paper or a computer screen) must be given reasonable accommodations by providing a larger print document or other options, such as this video-magnifier for a Braille document. Photo supplied by Bosma Enterprises

number of disabilities, and their services are available by phone or Text Telephone (TTY). Information is located at http://askjan.org/ (JAN).

TITLE II PUBLIC SERVICES

Title II focuses on access to public services—general state and local government services as well as public transportation.

Regulations for State and Local Government

Title II requires that services and programs of local and state governments and non-federal government agencies provide equal access to qualified individuals with a disability. Facilities are not required to remove physical barriers (e.g., stairs) in all existing buildings as long as programs are made accessible to everyone. However, facilities are required to provide appropriate auxiliary aids for those who have hearing, vision, or speech impairments. Additionally, safety requirements may be imposed to operate a program as long as there is an actual risk (ADATA, 2010a).

Title II and ADAAG

In 2004, the ADAAG was revised; it contains scoping and technical requirements to create accessible facilities and buildings. Access begins in the parking lot and an accessible route to the building. It continues throughout the building and includes interior elements such as drinking fountains, sinks, and more. Compliance requires that application occurs during the design, construction, and alteration of facilities and buildings for public and private entities. The ADAAG also contains specific requirements for restaurants, cafeterias, medical care facilities, and others, and new 2010 guidelines affect new constructions and alterations (U.S. Access Board, 2009, 2011). The ADAAG is an important tool for the designer as they layout spaces for new construction or alterations.

Title II and Transportation

Title II also applies to public transportation provided by public entities that are regulated by the U.S. Department of Transportation (DOT). This includes the National Railroad Passenger Corporation (NRPC) and other commuter authorities as well (ADATA, 2010b). This title covers public transportation other than aircraft (ADA, 2009). Although air carriers are covered under employment title, aircraft is not covered by the ADA. However, the **Air Carrier Access Act (ACAA)** covers access for people who are disabled (ADA, 2008b). For more information about the ACAA, go to http://www.disabilitytravel.com/airlines/air_carrier_act.htm (Accessible Journeys, 2011). The purpose of Title II is to ensure that such systems be made available to individuals with disabilities (ADA, 2009; ADATA, 2010b).

With the Amendment Act of 2008, all existing Amtrak stations were required to be accessible by July 26, 2010. The Department of Transportation (DOT) also requires public entities to use ADAAG as the accessibility standard for new construction and alterations of transit facilities and for transit vehicles (U. S. Access Board, 2009).

TITLE III PUBLIC ACCOMMODATIONS AND SERVICES OPERATED BY PRIVATE ENTITIES

Title III focuses on public accommodations for individuals with disabilities. The ADA (2009) states that these individuals must have "full and equal enjoyment of goods, services, facilities, privileges, advantages, or accommodations" from entities (private or public) that accommodate the public (ADA, 2009, sec. 12182). This includes every business within the private and public sector that offers services to the public. Even some private entities are considered public accommodations by the ADA (2009).

Various entities include places of entertainment, lodging, recreation, exercise, education, public gathering, and public display; establishments serving food or drink, for sales or rental, providing service, and social service; and public transportation. Exemptions are given to private clubs or establishments and religious organizations including places of worship. The Amendment Act of 2008 did not change any portion of this section of the ADA.

Title III and ADAAG

Title III affects the majority of work for designers, and the ADAAG provides the basic rules for enforcement; therefore, designers must comply with the ADA as it relates to public accommodations and services by private entities. New ADAAG revisions provide changes for compliance with the ADA (U.S. Access Board, 2011). Figure 1.5 shows an example of a hotel registration counter that is made accessible to meet the ADA's guidelines that cover the needs of a person in a wheelchair—one of the basic rules within the ADAAG.

New Construction and Alterations

Whether new construction or alteration of a public accommodation and commercial facility, accessibility must be included to the maximum extent possible (ADA, 2009). When alterations affect regular access, an accessible path of travel must be provided to the altered areas and to the restrooms, drinking fountains, and telephones with **telecommunications device for the deaf (TDD)**. New construction and alterations must, at a minimum, meet the ADAAG design standards (U.S. Access Board, 2009).

Figure 1.5

This hotel registration desk meets the needs of someone sitting or standing. Thus, it is accessible to someone in a wheelchair—one of the basic rules within the ADAAG. Photo courtesy Linda L. Nussbaumer

Elevators in New Construction or Alterations

Elevators are not required in newly constructed or altered buildings under three stories or having less than 3,000 square feet per floor; however, an elevator is required in a professional office of a healthcare provider, shopping mall, shopping center, depot or terminal, or airport passenger terminal (U. S. Access Board, 2009).

Access to Examinations and Courses

Examinations and courses related to licensing, certification, applications, or credentialing for professional and trade purposes must be offered in accessible buildings, or alternative accessible arrangements must be made (U.S. Access Board, 2009). This relates to physical impairments as well as hearing or visual impairments. In these cases, special accommodations must be made for equal access.

Title III and Transportation

Transportation in Title III refers to buses and other vehicles (except aircraft and automobiles or vans with a capacity of less than eight) purchased by private entities to provide public transportation. These vehicles must be accessible except for historical or antiquated vehicles in which alterations would compromise their authenticity (ADA, 2009). As noted earlier, aircraft are covered under the ACAA and, therefore, excluded from the ADA. However, it would be difficult to design and provide adequate room for a wheelchair in automobiles and vans with a capacity of less than eight.

TITLE IV TELECOMMUNICATIONS

Title IV of the ADA requires all telecommunications companies provide telecommunications relay services to allow individuals with hearing impairments the ability to communicate through a telecommunications device for the deaf (TDD) or **text telephone or TeleTYpewriter (TTY)** or other nonvoice devices (ADATA, 2010a). Although the Amendment Act of 2008 did not affect this section of the ADA, technology has made various telecommunication methods available as noted in the following.

Other Telecommunications Methods

Title IV also led to the development of dual-party relay services now known as **Telecommunications Relay Services (TRS)**. TRS is a telephone service that uses operators called *communications assistants* to facilitate telephone calls between people with hearing or speech impairment and a person without the impairment. There are other forms of TRSs. Some use a special text telephone (TTY-based TRS). Some use a **Voice Carry Over (VCO)** that allows the person with a hearing impairment to use his or her own voice to speak directly to the called party but receive text responses. Some use an Internet-based form such as a TRS-mediated call or **Video Relay**

Figure 1.6

Telecommunication devices for the deaf (TDD): The text telephone (TTY) with text answering machine and built-in printer is an advanced communication device for deaf and hard-of-hearing people.
© Clarity, a division of Pkantrinics. Inc.

Figure 1.7

The Voice Carry Over (VCO) telephone is a text telephone that is designed to be used by individuals who have difficulty hearing or are deaf. Incoming sounds may be amplified to 26 decibels and the device has an adjustable tone control.
© Clarity, a division of Pkantrinics. Inc.

Figure 1.8

Videophone (above monitor) captures the image and allows communication through sign language and/or an interpreter. Photo courtesy Linda L. Nussbaumer

Service (VRS) call. Other forms are available depending upon the individuals needs (FCC, 2010). Figure 1.6 shows an example of a TDD/TTY device and Figure 1.7 show a VCO phone. Videophones (VRS) are also commonly used in offices and allow two people to communicate using sign language or through an interpreter and sign language (see Figure 1.8).

Closed Captioning

Title IV also requires **closed captioning** for all television public service announcements produced or funded in whole or in part by the Federal Government (ADATA, 2010a). Closed captioning allows the person with a hearing limitation to access the audio portion of television programming as text on the television screen. Closed captioning can be turned on through the remote control or on-screen menu (FCC, 2010).

Differing Views Regarding Building Access

The ADA has enforced equal access for people with various disabilities. Clearly, their lives have improved. Designers must comply with the ADA using the ADAAG. However, even though there are accessibility guidelines, those with disabilities and designers may differ in what they feel appropriate access is.

The study "Issues of Disability and Building Access" (InformeDesign, 2003, November 1) looked at groups that use, access, and design the built environment. The study revealed differences of opinions related to accessibility. It also resulted in suggestions to improve future accessibility. For a closer look at what this study revealed, see Study Sketch 1.1: "Issues of Disability and Building Access."

Historical Buildings and Accessibility

City programs, services, and activities are often provided in city- or government-owned buildings; these may be considered historic buildings. City governments may also assume that, because it is an historic building, they are not obliged to alter and improve the building to become accessible for people with disabilities. The problem is that people with disabilities would be unable to access the building or its programs (US-DOJ, 2008). Study Sketch 1.2: "Issues: Historically Significant Facilities" provides further detail regarding this type of situation.

Since the ADA was enacted, much progress has been made to provide access for those with disabilities. However, societal attitudes often hamper its advancement. Therefore, summarized by InformeDesign (2003, November 1), a study was conducted using focus groups to determine barriers that compromised activities for people with disabilities.

Method

A three-year research project focused on discovering barriers and facilitators that people with physical limitations encountered in the built environment.

There were seventeen focus groups that consisted of the following:

- Five groups of people with mobility limitations and their significant others
- Five groups of physicians and therapists
- Two groups of architects and planners.

Data were collected through life history interviews, key informant interviews, and focus groups. Open-ended questions were used in focus groups; discussion was recorded by audiotape and a note-taker. After the audiotapes were transcribed, notes were analyzed by counting "the number of times participants discussed areas of participation, environmental barriers, and environmental facilitators."

Findings

Each group interviewed provided the following information:

- People with disabilities and their significant others found problems more frequently than the building professionals anticipated
- Key areas for improvement were housing design and transportation systems
- People without disabilities may view the necessary level of access differently than designers.

Criteria

Findings suggest the following criteria:

- When designing the built environment, other types of mobility limitations should be considered as well as the wheelchair.
- Early in the design process, communication should occur among the disabled, their significant others, healthcare providers, designers, planners, and other building professionals, which can result in practical solutions to access issues.

Litigation

The ADA is a law. This means that individuals who believe discrimination exists can file lawsuits and obtain court orders to stop discrimination. Individuals may also file complaints with the U.S. Attorney General, who is authorized to bring lawsuits in cases of general public importance or an alleged pattern or practice of discrimination. In these cases, the Attorney General may seek both monetary damages and civil penalties. Such cases do not exceed $55,000 for a first violation or $110,000 for subsequent violations (ADA, 2010).

Many cases have been documented and can be found on http://www.ada. gov/aprsep09.htm#litigation. The following example describes a case settled in Pennsylvania and can be found under ADA's (2010) "Other Settlements: Title II."

> An individual with a mobility disability complained that a Pennsylvania county theater did not have enough designated wheelchair spaces. The county has agreed to add additional wheelchair seating spaces to the theater, including accessible spaces in the balcony section. Additionally, the existing accessible seating closest to the stage will be made level (para. 2).

The following example describes a case in which the U.S. Attorney obtained an informal settlement in Rhode Island. This case is also found under ADA's (2010) "Other Settlements: Title III."

> As a result of a compliance review, a national chain hotel has agreed to increase the number of accessible rooms it offers to individuals with mobility disabilities by providing five new accessible rooms dispersed among the room types it offers to the public. In addition, the hotel will ensure that it offers at least 11 accessible rooms to individuals who are deaf or hard of hearing. The hotel agreed to purchase five portable visual alarms to be used for hearing-accessible rooms and will ensure that the balance of six additional portable visual alarms are provided through a sharing program with nearby hotels in the area (para. 13).

Clearly, when the law is not followed and people with disabilities are not allowed equal access, lawsuits will occur and settlements can be costly. Therefore, designers must carefully design spaces to have equal access.

Summary

Since 1990, the ADA has created a better environment for many, including both persons with disabilities and the general public. For persons with disabilities, passage of the ADA became the catalyst in alleviating discrimination and has legalized equal access for employment, public accommodations, public services, and more. For the general public, the ADA requirements created not only an awareness of disabilities but also a genuine concern for equal access and opportunities for everyone.

With the ADA Amendment of 2008, the definition of persons with disability has been clarified and removes the need for a lengthy analysis—particularly for employers.

The changes to the ADAAG have brought together various factions such as ANSI and, in the future updates, the IBC. These combined forces assist designers as they conduct a code search for both ADA compliance as well as fire and building codes.

For designers, Titles II and III of the ADA are particularly important as they address accessibility guidelines for buildings of public accommodation, commercial facilities, state and local government facilities, and vehicle guidelines. By law, designers must comply with the ADA by using the ADAAG—the design standards. Through their projects, designers have the opportunity to alleviate discrimination by not only providing accessibility but also providing access to everyone—an inclusive design for the built environment.

Inclusive Design Projects

EXPERIENTIAL PROJECTS

1. What are challenges faced by someone with limited physical mobility?

Limited physical mobility comes with many challenges. To better understand these challenges, work in teams of three to experience the world of someone who has limited mobility. To complete the tasks, use one of the following physically limiting techniques: remain in a wheelchair, tape one arm to limit use, or use crutches and do not use one leg. Team members will perform different tasks: Team member #1 has limited mobility and uses a device to become mobile; #2 documents by photographing or videotaping the experience; and #3 ensures the safety of everyone. If possible, roles may be switched.

Experience the classroom building:
- Move through the classroom.
- Leave the classroom and move about other areas of the building.
- Enter and use a restroom.
- Use a fountain.
- Use the building exit and enter another building on campus.

Have a meal in the campus cafeteria:
- Enter the building.
- Maneuver throughout this space.
- Pick up your tray and silverware.
- Order food and place it on a tray.
- Pay for food at cash register.
- Locate a place to sit.

Next, analyze this experience in the following areas by noting the problems and possible solutions concerning:
- Entrance
- Path of travel
- Ability to conduct task

2. What are the challenges faced by someone with visual limitations?

Having **visual limitations** comes with many challenges. To better understand these challenges, students will work in teams of three and experience the world of someone who is blind or has difficulty seeing. To complete the tasks, use one of the following visual limiting techniques: blindfold, eye-glasses covered with Vaseline (cataracts), eye-glasses with an opening only in the center (glaucoma), or eye-glasses with the center or pupil area covered (age-related macular degeneration). Team members will perform different tasks: Team member #1 has limited vision and uses the visual limiting technique; #2 documents by photographing or videotaping the experience; and #3 ensures the safety of everyone. If possible, roles may be reversed.

Experience the classroom building:
- Move through the classroom.
- Leave the classroom and move about other areas of the building.
- Enter and use a restroom.

- Use a fountain.
- Use the building exit and enter another building on campus.

Have a meal in the campus cafeteria:
- Enter the building.
- Maneuver throughout this space.
- Pick up your tray and silverware.
- Order food and place it on the tray.
- Pay for food at the cash register.
- Locate a place to sit.

Next, analyze this experience in the following areas by noting the problems and possible solutions concerning:
- Entrance
- Path of travel
- Ability to conduct task

3. What are challenges faced by someone with hearing limitations?

Limited hearing ability comes with many challenges. Some people with limited hearing ability are also challenged with visual limitations. To better understand these challenges, students will work in teams of three and experience the world of someone who has limited hearing and/or visual ability. To complete the tasks, use one of the following limiting techniques: earphones that deaden sound completely, earplugs that mute sound, or earphones that deaden sound completely with eyeglasses covered with Vaseline (cataract). Team members will perform different tasks: Team member #1 has limited hearing and/or visual; #2 documents by photographing or videotaping the experience; and #3 ensures the safety of everyone. If possible, roles may be reversed.

Experience the classroom building:
- Move through the classroom.
- Leave the classroom and move about other areas of the building.
- Enter and use a restroom.
- Use a fountain.
- Use the building exit and enter another building on campus.

Have a meal in the campus cafeteria:
- Enter the building.
- Maneuver throughout this space.
- Pick up your tray and silverware.
- Order food and place it on the tray.
- Pay for food at the cash register.
- Locate a place to sit.

Next, analyze this experience in the following areas by noting the problems and possible solutions concerning:

- Entrance
- Path of travel
- Ability to conduct task

APPLICATION PROJECTS

1. Does everyone have the same opportunities?

After participating in the hands-on experiences in Project 1.1, a question may be "Does everyone have the same opportunities?" The following exercise examines this question.

With knowledge gained through the textbook, locate the section regarding reasonable accommodations in the ADA. In written format complete the following:

- Develop a scenario from one of the three limitations (physical, hearing, visual, and mental) in which reasonable accommodations are needed. In the scenario, describe the task to be completed and the limitation or limitations (an individual may have more than one limitation). To create this scenario, you may use hands-on experience or interview someone with any of these challenges.
- Describe ways to accommodate the individual in this scenario. Include images of assistive technology that may be used as applicable.
- Cite sources, and create a reference list.

2. What happens when the ADA laws are broken?

Although the ADA has been in force since 1992, violations occur. To enforce these laws, someone with a limitation generally files a lawsuit. This exercise answers the question, "What happens when the ADA laws are broken?"

Locate the ADA website (http://www.ada.gov/aprsep09.htm#litigation) that describes litigation. Select and read three cases. In written format, complete the following:

- Describe each case.
- Explain what section of the ADA was violated in each case.
- Explain how each case was resolved.
- Compare these cases for similarities and differences.

Inclusive Design

"The golf car has opened the eyes of Americans to the need for more truly universal design that not only improves the lives of people with disabilities, but the lives of us all."

–U.S. President George H. W. Bush

OBJECTIVES

▼ Define accessible design

▼ Define lifespan or transgenerational design

▼ Explain the phrase "designing for all"

▼ Define inclusive design

▼ List the principles of inclusive design

▼ List the criteria for inclusive design

▼ Explain the difference between inclusive and universal design

▼ Explain the connection between the ADA and inclusive design

▼ Explain the purpose of the Eden Alternative®

▼ List the Eden Alternative® Principles

▼ Describe wayfinding

▼ Explain the connection between wayfinding and inclusive design

While the ADA was designed and becoming law in the early 1990s, efforts were underway to create a design with all people in mind. Advocates of accessibility had already established a Center for Universal Design (CUD) at the College of Design, North Carolina State University, and today, the CUD continues to function as a resource for research, education, publications, and much more. Since then, other centers have developed using the name **universal design** or the term **inclusive design**.

Over the years, the concept of designing for all has taken the front row along with sustainable design in the design world. Designers talk about and apply designs that include all people of varying ages and abilities. Many products and environments comply with the ADA requirements that ensure ease for anyone to use or maneuver.

But do these accessible designs also draw attention to the disabilities they are meant to assist?

The best answer to this question requires a clear understanding of the terms that relate to designing for everyone.

Understanding the Terms Related to Designing for Everyone

Various terms have emerged that relate to designing for everyone. The most common terms include **accessible design, lifespan design, transgenerational design, designing for all,** universal design, and inclusive design. Within the description of these terms, the word "impairment" has been dropped and **limitation** used. Unless it refers to the ADA law, those with disabilities refer to impairment as limitation. Limitation is also the term preferred by those affected by a limited ability.

ACCESSIBLE DESIGN

Accessible design means that products and environments are designed and constructed so that people with disabilities may access and use them (Pirkl, 1994). Thus, with this terminology, though all barriers have been removed and access is allowed, the design is geared towards a specific group of people—those with disabilities.

LIFESPAN AND TRANSGENERATIONAL DESIGN

Transgenerational design is similar to lifespan design and refers to making products and environments compatible for physical and sensory limitations that may restrict major life activities. Lifespan and transgenerational design are virtually synonymous;

both terms refer to the design of products and environments that accommodate and appeal to people of all ages and abilities. Both reject the idea that products should be targeted to older consumers strictly because they're compatible with physical and sensory limitations that may restrict major life activities. Lifespan and transgenerational design advocates the design of products that transcend all populations from young to old (Pirkl, 1994).

DESIGNING FOR ALL

Designing for all targets products, environments, and services that can be used by many people without the need for adaptation. It relates to human diversity, social inclusion, and equality. The phrase *designing for all* has been used in Europe and seeks to provide a user-friendly term acceptable to the general public. Several organizations advocate its use (e.g., designforall.org, edean.org, dfaei.org, and others).

UNIVERSAL DESIGN

Universal design has various definitions. The founder of the Center for Universal Design, Ron Mace (1941–1998), who coined the term *universal design*, defined it as "the design of products and environments to be usable by all people, to the greatest extent possible, without the need for adaption or specialized design" (CUD, 2008). To clarify the definition, the intent of universal design is to simplify life for everyone by making products, communications, and the built environment more usable by as many people as possible at little or no extra cost. Universal design benefits people of all ages and abilities.

Some designers have raised concerns regarding the definition "because it has no practical limits" (Vanderheiden, 2009, p. 3-13), and implied an ideal goal of designing things that everyone could use. "For example, building a $2,000 Braille display into every electronic device with a visual display is not generally practical" (p. 3-13).

To create a more practical definition, Gregg C. Vanderheiden (1996), a University of Wisconsin-Madison professor of engineering, proposed another definition: "the process of creating products (devices, environments, systems, and processes) which are usable by people with the widest possible range of abilities, operating within the widest possible range of situations (environments, conditions, and circumstances)" (Vanderheiden, 1996, para. 3; 2009, p. 3-13). This definition acknowledges that every product cannot be designed for all people but rather for those with the widest possible range of abilities who are most likely to use the product. This is a more practical and logical approach.

In addition to Vanderheiden's definition, the CUD developed seven principles of universal design, which are also referenced in articles and books. See "Seven Principles of Universal Design."

Seven Principles of Universal Design

The Center for Universal Design (CUD) at the College of Design, North Carolina State University, developed the following seven principles of universal design:

1. Equitable Use: The design is useful and marketable to people with diverse abilities.
2. Flexibility in Use: The design accommodates a wide range of individual preferences and abilities.
3. Simple and Intuitive Use: Use of the design is easy to understand, regardless of the user's experience, knowledge, language skills, or current concentration level.
4. Perceptible Information: The design communicates necessary information effectively to the user, regardless of ambient conditions or the user's sensory abilities.
5. Tolerance for Error: The design minimizes hazards and the adverse consequences of accidental or unintended actions.
6. Low Physical Effort: The design can be used efficiently and comfortably and with a minimum of fatigue.
7. Size and Space for Approach and Use: Appropriate size and space is provided for approach, reach, manipulation, and use regardless of user's body size, posture, or mobility.

Source: Center for Universal Design (CUD). (2008). *What is universal design: Principles of universal design*. North Carolina State University: The Center for Universal Design. Retrieved on June 17, 2010, from http://www.design.ncsu.edu/cud/about_ud/udprinciples.htm

INCLUSIVE DESIGN

Inclusive design is similar to universal design. The term began in the United Kingdom where it referred to providing quality of life and independent living for the aging population (Waller & Clarkson, 2009, 19-1). The term was coined to describe products or environments that maintain quality of life and independent living for an aging population and because assistive or medical devices had become expensive, stigmatizing, and undesirable.

Then, going beyond this concept of design for the older population, the British Standard Institute defined inclusive design as "the design of mainstream products and/ or services that are accessible and usable by people with the widest range of abilities within the widest range of situation without the need for special adaptation for specialized design" (Waller & Clarkson, 2009, p. 19-1 and 2). As with universal design, various definitions have emerged for inclusive design.

English Partnership (2008b) defined inclusive design as "a way of designing products and environments so that they are usable and appealing to everyone regardless of age, ability, or circumstance by working with users to remove barriers in the social, technical, political, and economic processes underpinning building and design." English Partnership (2008a) is now part of the Homes and Communities Agency (HCA), a national housing and regeneration agency in England—an agency that supports affordable housing and sustainability. Together, they partner with local authorities, the Housing Corporation, regional development agencies, and the Commission for Architecture and the Built Environment (CABE).

An English governmental commission related specifically to the design community, CABE provides their interpretation of inclusive design. It states that it is "the process by which places are planned, designed and built, managed and used, with people like us in mind. It creates places which we can all use with ease and dignity and where we have a sense of belonging" (CABE, n/d). CABE's definition relates to the design process as well as creates environments that are **inclusive** to all people (see Figure 2.1a and b).

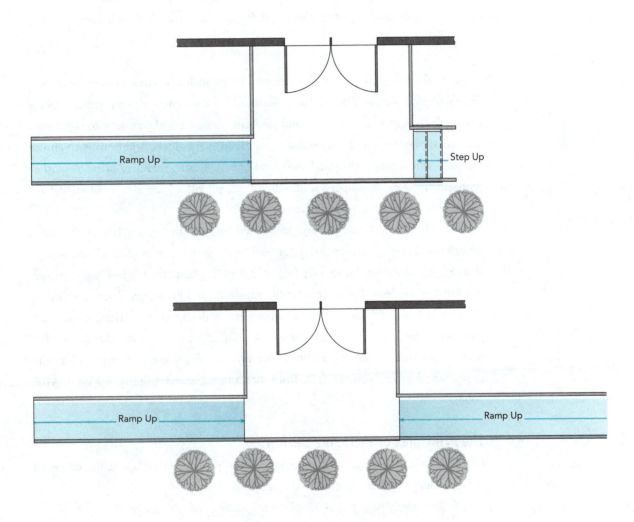

Figure 2.1a and b

These two drawings demonstrate the difference between accessible design and other types (e.g., universal, designing for all, transgenerational, inclusive). In (a) the first drawing, to make the entrance accessible a ramp is added with steps available for those who are able to use them. For the entrance to be inclusive in (b) the second drawing, ramps, which are appropriate for everyone, are added on both sides, and no steps are necessary. © Precision Graphics/based on a drawing by Linda L. Nussbaumer

Focus or Purpose of Inclusive Design

Inclusive design means more than catering to the needs of people with disabilities. Inclusive design is about designing places that everyone can use. If designed inclusively, everyone can move, see, hear, and communicate effectively. According to CABE (2008), inclusive design's purpose is to

> remove the barriers that create undue effort and separation. It enables everyone to participate equally, confidently, and independently in everyday activities. An inclusive approach to design offers new insights into the way we interact with the built environment. It creates new opportunities to deploy creative and problem-solving skills (p. 3).

CABE (2008) states that the creation of an inclusive environment involves a variety of professionals. Those related specifically to the design are surveyors, designers (e.g., architects, interior designers, and landscape designers), planners, building control surveyors, engineers, access consultants, and facilities managers. Additionally, to ensure that an environment is designed, built, and operated using inclusive principles, other professionals (e.g., developers, landlords, service providers) are also involved. All are responsible for creating an inclusive environment.

Providing access to everyone should be integral to design. But at the same time, it should be applied creatively, be innovative, provide individual solutions (e.g., Braille application for the visually impaired, a videophone for the hearing impaired, or push-button doors for the physically impaired), and be designed for everyone—all their variability. When a built environment is designed inclusively, it not only provides access for people with various disabilities, those who are elderly, families with small children, and others, but it also provides everyone with the opportunity to interact; thus, everyone benefits from such an environment in many ways (CABE, 2008).

The Principles of Inclusive Design

CABE (2008) developed the following five key principles that are at the center of inclusive design and are specific to the design field:

1. Inclusive design places people at the heart of the design process:
   - Everyone connected to the design of the product or environment should be involved in the design process from the beginning.
2. Inclusive design acknowledges diversity and difference:
   - Diversity relates to various ages, abilities, limitations, and more.
   - Early identification of barriers provides the opportunity for inclusion for a successful design.

3. Inclusive design offers choices where a single design solution cannot accommodate all users:

   ■ One solution cannot address everyone's needs.

   ■ Choices are necessary.

4. Inclusive design provides for flexibility in use:

   ■ Products and environments adapt to changes of various users from toddlers to those in wheelchairs.

5. Inclusive design provides buildings and environments that are convenient and enjoyable to use for everyone (p. 7–15):

   ■ Considers roads, parking, walkways, entrances, and other routes.

   ■ Considers signage, lighting, visual contrast, materials, and more.

Refer to the condensed version of the "Five Principles of Inclusive Design."

Inclusive Design Clarified in Laymen's Terms

Clearly, inclusive design is a type of design that includes everyone in planning, designing, building, and managing as well as those using the product or environment. With input from the users (e.g., homeowner, receptionist and sales staff, waitress and guest, nurse and patient, or others) along with the design team, the design will not bring attention to one specific type of person when a product is used or an environment is navigated. With everyone's input in a design, the product or environment will function easily for everyone.

IS ONE TERM (UNIVERSAL OR INCLUSIVE) BETTER THAN THE OTHER?

Either the term *universal* or *inclusive* may be used to describe a design that is intended to meet the needs of many people. However, two questions remain: Does one fit the definition better than the other? Or are these terms entirely interchangeable? In the literature and on websites, one or two or even a mixture of terms may be used. Many believe that these terms mean the same or nearly the same.

However, according to Dr. Scott Rains (2009), a consultant and researcher on universal design, inclusive design can be interpreted as broader than universal design because it also embraces diversity in social and economic circumstances. The Digital Accessibility Team (DAT) (2009) influences the research and development of new technologies for people who are blind and partially sighted. The DAT points out that the definition of inclusive design includes the concept of responsibility—involving people who are responsible for the design. Director of the Helen Hamlyn Centre at Royal College of Art, Jeremy Myerson, (2007) also notes that the universal design principles seem somewhat prescriptive in design thinking, but at the time they were developed the seven principles of universal design (1997) were practical as a criteria and an aid for evaluation.

Discussions have and probably will continue to occur on whether the term used should be universal or inclusive design (Rains, 2009). Even a United Nations adhoc committee that developed the new Convention on Human Rights of Persons with Disabilities grappled with this very question—which one to choose (IHCD, 2010). Interestingly, within this document, universal design is defined and **universal** or universality is used in two other instances whereas **inclusive** is used in four instances as a descriptor, and in two of the four, it is used to describe environments that are "inclusive and accessible" to persons with disabilities.

It seems that *inclusive* refers to including (rather than excluding) people in using a product or environment whereas *universal* considers the global aspect—occurring everywhere or available to everyone. With this knowledge, the terms inclusive and universal are used where each fits most appropriately within this text. To provide a context for the use of inclusive design, a revised set of criteria has been developed and is used to describe products and/or environments throughout the book.

Revised Criteria for Inclusive Design

As noted earlier in this chapter, the principles of universal design need updating. To do so, examining both principles (universal design and inclusive design), a set of criteria that is easier to use is suggested here. To begin this process, refer to "Comparison of Principles of Inclusive Design and Universal Design," where each universal design

How the Principles of Universal Design Fit within the Principles of Inclusive Design

The following list compares key terms in the five inclusive design principles developed by CABE to the seven universal design principles developed by CUD.

1. *People*
   a. All seven principles of CUD for universal design apply to CABE's Inclusive Design Principle 1; however, the intent of the inclusive design principle is to involve all people (users, contractors, surveyors, and others) in a project during the entire design process.
2. *Diversity*
   a. **Equitable Use:** the design is useful and marketable to people with diverse abilities.
3. *Choice*
   a. **Simple and Intuitive Use:** The design is easy to understand.
   b. **Low Physical Effort:** The product or environment can be used efficiently, comfortably, and with minimal fatigue.
4. *Flexibility*
   a. **Flexibility in Use:** The design accommodates a wide range of individual preferences and abilities.
5. *Convenience*
   a. **Perceptible Information:** Necessary information is communicated effectively to the user.
   b. **Tolerance for Error:** The design "minimizes hazards and the adverse consequences of accidental or unintended actions."
   c. **Size and Space for Approach and Use:** "Appropriate size and space is provided for approach, reach, manipulation, and use regardless of user's body size, posture, or mobility."

principle developed by CUD is listed under an inclusive design principle developed by CABE to which it best corresponds.

THE RESULTS OF THE COMPARISON

Although the comparison between inclusive and universal design should be easy to see, some of the similarities and differences between their principles are not so obvious. Take a closer look at the following phrases from the "Principles of Inclusive Design." Within this list, the terms that emerged most often are italicized:

- **People at the heart of the design process**
  - *Responsive* to the people involved
- **Acknowledges diversity and difference; useful and marketable to people of diverse abilities**
  - *Adaptable* and *accessible* addresses differences in people—age, abilities, ethnicity
- **Offers choice**
  - *Adaptable* provides options
- **Easy to understand**
  - *Adaptable* and *accessible* addresses ease of use and understanding

- **Low physical effort; used efficiently and comfortably and with a minimum of fatigue**
  - *Adaptable* and *accessible* addresses ease of use and minimal effort
- **Flexibility in use**
  - *Adaptable* and *accessible* addresses flexibility
- **Convenient and enjoyable to use for everyone**
  - *Adaptable* and *accessible* addresses convenience and enjoyment
- **Communicates necessary information effectively to the user**
  - *Adaptable* and *accessible* addresses information that is easy to understand
- **Minimizes hazards**
  - *Secure* addresses health, safety, and welfare
- **Appropriate size and space**
  - *Accessible* addresses the ADAAG

The italicized terms are *responsive, adaptable, accessible,* and *secure.* Because these terms emerge most frequently, they were developed into the criteria to analyze a design project relative to inclusivity. See "Inclusive Design Criteria," which lists the criteria with descriptors. A definition of each of these essential terms follows.

Definition of Responsive

Responsive refers to everyone involved in the project. This includes both daily and occasional users as well as surveyors, developers, architects, interior designers, access specialists, engineers, contractors, installers, maintenance crews, and others from the pre-design through occupancy stages. It also must respond to the daily users' needs, which may be specific needs for the present (e.g., being accessible, providing supportive products such as canes and wheelchairs) as well as for the future (e.g., being adaptable to aging changes). For inclusive design, being responsive means that accessibility must be invisible and not draw attention to a disability.

Definition of Adaptable

Adaptable refers to flexibility for people of various ages, abilities, ethnicity, and more. To be adaptable, the product or environment must be convenient and easy to use with minimal effort; its directions should be easy to understand. With adaptability, the user should be able to enjoy the product or environment in the same way as everyone else. Being adaptable also means there are options (e.g., choice of entrances rather than only one for someone in a wheelchair).

Definition of Accessible

Accessible is similar to adaptable except that being accessible means the product or environment must comply with the ADA and use the ADAAG.

Inclusive Design Criteria

The terms that emerged most often from "How the Principles of Universal Design fit within the Principles of Inclusive Design" are listed as follows and developed into criteria with descriptions that apply to both universal design principles and inclusive design principles:

1. *Responsive*—relates to needs and wants of all involved
   a. People involved from pre-design through occupancy
   b. Daily user's needs
   c. Invisible accessibility
2. *Adaptable*—relates to diversity and differences
   a. Differences in people
   b. Easy to use and understand; flexible, convenient, and enjoyable
   c. Providing options
3. *Accessible*—relates to the ADA and the ADAAG
4. *Secure*—relates to health, safety, and welfare
   a. Physical health: ergonomics; indoor air quality; safety; security
   b. Psychological health: feelings of security and safety

Definition of Secure

Secure relates to health, safety, and welfare—a standard that is important to all interior design professionals. Minimizing hazards, providing good indoor air quality, selecting nonslip or nonglare products, and providing fire alarms and secure entrances are examples of the secure criterion.

The Challenge of Inclusivity

It is impossible to design every product or environment to fit everyone every time. No design is used by everyone, regardless of how many or how severe the disability. Neither universal design nor inclusive design can create a product or environment that everyone can use all the time.

Inclusivity can occur, however, as appropriate for the individual (Vanderheiden, 2009). The challenge of inclusive design, therefore, is to match the product or environment to its users, each with their individual needs. To do this, the designer must choose what must be included and what may be excluded for each particular design.

EXAMPLES OF EXCLUSION

Chairs are perfect examples of **exclusion** (or not including everyone). For example, a toddler-sized chair is not appropriate for an adult, and vice versa. In the same way, an office chair that is adjustable can work for several individuals; however, because individuals' sizes vary greatly (short to tall or small to large), the amount of adjustability may be extreme. To illustrate, an individual who is five-foot tall and weighs 100 pounds may need an entirely different chair design than an individual who is seven-foot tall and 300 or more pounds.

EXAMPLES OF INCLUSION

Although not every product can be designed for everyone to use, the concept behind inclusive design is to create products and environments that are adaptable, accessible, and secure for the person using them. The advantage of inclusive design is that it considers the person who is tall or short, large or small, left-handed or right-handed. It also includes persons who have arthritic hands, slight loss of sight or hearing, and more. In other words, it considers areas not covered under the ADA. Some examples follow, and others can be found throughout the book.

Although one chair cannot be adjustable for every body type, an ergonomically designed office chair is adjustable for differing needs. Adjustment can be made in a variety of ways:

- The height and depth of the seat is adjustable.
- The tilt of the back is adjustable.
- The armrest height and width are adjustable and, therefore, the armrest is designed to fit the wide ranges of sizes, postures, and activities.
- Narrow backs allow the arms to move freely.
- Backs are designed to fit to the curvature of the spine and body.

The Embody office chair by Herman Miller has many adjustable parts and, therefore, is characterized as inclusive design (see Figure 2.2). Ergonomic design can also be utilized in the home, where people also come in different sizes and require support for their bodies. Throughout this book, illustrations of products for both office and home are offered as examples of inclusive design. With home offices, the same careful design can be applied at home.

Another example that applies inclusive design would be designing a slightly inclined approach with a zero-step threshold at the entrance. If this approach and entrance were also well designed and landscaped, it would be inclusive of all who want to enter. Figure 2.3 shows a circular well-landscaped ramp that is the main entrance and demonstrates inclusivity in design.

Application of Inclusive Design

By complying with the ADA and also applying revised inclusive design criteria in a design project, everyone has opportunities and obligations in all aspects of society.

When design features are appropriate for almost everyone, people come first (not the design), and everyone benefits.

EXAMPLES THAT APPLY INCLUSIVE DESIGN CRITERIA

Criteria for inclusive design—responsive, adaptable, flexible, and secure—will be referenced periodically throughout this text. The following includes some examples of how designers apply these criteria to achieve inclusive design.

Responsive—Considering the Needs and Wants of All People Involved

The responsive criterion involves many people during the data collection and the use of various methods of collection data. Examples of responsive criteria include interviews, surveys, and focus groups and should include everyone affected during the design process. In a focus group, designers use interview sessions to collect evidence for a design project. Using knowledge acquired from these methods of information gathering, the design can better respond to people's needs and wants.

Adaptable—Making the Product or Environment Easy to Use with Minimal Effort

The adaptable criterion applies to designs that require simple movement to use and are easy to understand without much effort. Examples of the adaptable criterion include:

- Clear floor space and floor paths that are free of obstacles help prevent accidents.
- Entrance doors that are opened with a lever handle, which are easy to use, particularly for small children, people with arthritis, and those with their arms full of books, packages, and so forth (see Figure 2.4).
- Various easy- and convenient-to-use hand-held products for the kitchen, garden, office, and cleaning, such as those by OXO International. These products are designed to be usable by many people (e.g., young and old, male and female, left- and right-handed, those with arthritic hands, as well as those with special needs). Grip handles provide a secure grip, especially for those with limited mobility or strength. Figures 2.5a and b show two products used in the kitchen with grip handles that make the tools easier to use.

Adaptable Means Flexible

Adaptable criterion includes built-in flexibility. With flexibility, products and environments adjust and adapt to people of various age, size, ability, and ethnicity. Adaptable products include:

- Software programs that allow a computer to display text in varying fonts and sizes and are useful for people with visual limitations
- Ergonomic chairs that are adjustable and adaptable to various sizes (refer to Figure 2.2)

Arm width adjusts by pushing arm pads in or out with elbows (proper position of arm aligns elbows with shoulders)

Button (under arm) to adjust arm height

Joystick to adjust seat height (proper seat height requires less than 90-degree angle between thighs and calves)

Chair back inspired by human spine; adapts to an individual's shape and movement

Knob to adjust backfit for spine support

Tilt Limiter level; limits recline angle to one of four positions from reclined to upright

Lever to adjust the Tilt Limiter

Handle to adjust seat depth (proper seat depth requires two fingers of clearance between the back of knees and seat edge)

Figure 2.2

The Embody Office Chair by Herman Miller has many adjustable parts and has an ergonomic design that can be utilized by many people of different size and body types. Courtesy of Herman Miller, Inc.

- Adjustable workstations that are designed to meet a variety of needs
- Keyboard trays or desks that adjust to varying heights for keyboards, laptops, and monitors
- Workstations that are designed to accommodate varied height users (i.e., sitting or standing; see Figures 2.6a and b)

Adaptable Means Providing Options

Adaptable criterion provides options to users of a product or environment. It also presents the designer with the opportunity to expand his or her design in a variety of creative ways; for example:

- Varied height counters provide options for use.
- The use of various wayfinding methods provides option for audio instructions, maps, written directions, or other methods.

Above and Beyond ADAAG Standards for Accessibility

Accessible criterion relates to the ADA and the application of the ADAAG, which requires (at a minimum) an accessible environment; however, inclusive design goes beyond the minimum standards of the ADAAG. To provide access for everyone—people of various ages, sizes, and abilities—consider the following:

- The use of various wayfinding methods accommodates various needs.
- Gradual inclines to an entrance and zero-step thresholds provide accessibility (refer to Figure 2.3).
- Varied or lower counter heights provide access to people of various heights (sitting or standing).
- Electronic doors sensor provides easier access.
- Duplex outlets at 18 inches above the finished floor mean less bending.
- Wider doors provide more room for a wheelchair as well as for anyone maneuvering with packages and furnishings.

Quality appliances or storage units should be chosen mindful of easy access for all (see Figures 2.7a, b, and c).

Secure Addresses Health, Safety, and Welfare

Secure criterion addresses aspects of a design that consider physical and psychological health as well as the safety and well-being of occupants and users of a space. Reliable design features that ensure security include the following:

- Nonslip finishes within an interior are safe for everyone.
- Nonglare finishes are especially important for the safety of a person with visual limitations.

Figure 2.3

The main entrance is a circular entrance ramp that demonstrates an inclusive design—a design for everyone to use that does not draw attention to anyone with a disability. Courtesy of Herman Miller, Inc.

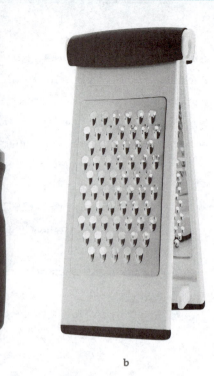

a   b

Figure 2.4

Lever door openers for interior and exterior doors, such as this one by Schlage, are a universal design because those who lack strength in their hands and arms will have less difficulty opening doors with the lever handle than grappling with a traditional knob handle. Photo provided by Schlage

Figure 2.5a and b

With their grip handles, both the (a) peeler and (b) cheese shredder are easy to use by many people and especially for those with minimal dexterity due to impairments that range from arthritis to a wrist fracture from a sports injury. Image provided by OXO

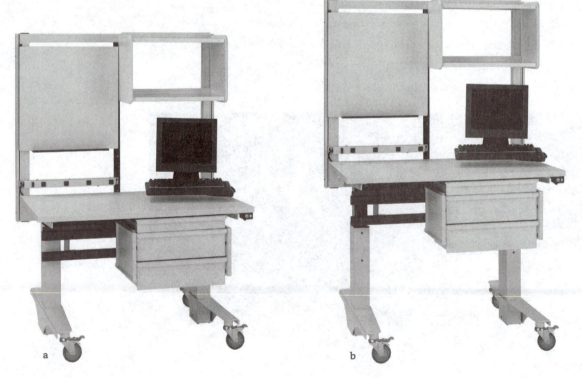

a   b

Figures 2.6a and b

Height adjustable workstation, such as this Co/Struc System by Herman Miller, allow the user to (a) sit or (b) stand as they use the computer. These are being used in hospitals and other areas where a variety of people use the same workstation. Courtesy of Herman Miller, Inc.

a b c

Figures 2.7a–c

Refrigerators with (a) side-by-side doors or (b and c) below counter-level drawers provide easy access for people of all statures and abilities. Courtesy of Maytag (a and b); Photo courtesy of Kitchenaid

Advantages of Inclusive Design

Inclusive design has many advantages in today's society. It is economical, attractive, and marketable. It also makes choices easier for people of various ages and abilities. For example, a mall directory may provide visual and voice-activated options to locate a store, or an entrance door may provide two options—a push button as well as a lever handle to open the door.

ECONOMICAL AND INCLUSIVELY DESIGNED PRODUCTS AND ENVIRONMENTS

Products and environments that everyone can use are more economical. To explain, a registered architect and assistant director of the Inclusive Design and Environmental Access (IDEA) Center, Danise Levine (2003), states that buildings designed to be usable by everyone from the beginning will need fewer renovations in the future. If any renovations were required later, they would be less expensive. "Many universal design features cost nothing, and those that have marginal additional costs may have a value that exceeds their expense" (p. 10).

Products and environments that meet the criteria (e.g., responsive, adaptable, accessible, and secure) are marketable to many people, which make them more economical as well. Because consumers prefer more inclusive environments at work and home, spaces are being designed for easy access for, and inclusive of, many people. Additionally, products and environments designed with many people in mind standardize and create inclusivity. For example, if all doors were standardized at three feet wide, they would not only accommodate wheelchairs or walkers but would also save time and money for builders, designers, and manufacturers because of the consistent size of the doors. A wider door is also more convenient for people who need to move furniture through doorways (Null & Cherry, 1996, p. 30).

ATTRACTIVE AND INCLUSIVELY DESIGNED PRODUCTS AND ENVIRONMENT

A misconception about inclusive design is that it is unattractive, institutional, and unappealing, and that such designs are considered only for people who are older or have a disability. If only accessibility (the ADAAG) is considered, a product or the environment may have an institutional look; however, when applying inclusive design, the opposite is true. To be inclusive, the design must blend in as though it were intended for people without disabilities (Null & Cherry, 1996, p. 31). The examples in Figures 2.8a and b demonstrate the attractiveness of grab bars as well as the shower chair attached within the shower itself.

MARKETABLE AND INCLUSIVELY DESIGNED PRODUCTS AND ENVIRONMENTS

Millions of Americans, **baby boomers** as well as individuals with disabilities, are eager to buy products and live in environments that are flexible, comfortable, and accommodate their needs—now and in the future.

Baby Boomers

With baby boomers retired or retiring, they are in the market for economical, accessible, and aesthetically pleasing products and environments. Many baby boomers are and continue to be independent (Leibrock, 2011; Null & Cherry, 1996). They plan to live in their homes (aging in place) as long as possible and have the same accommodations when they travel as well.

People with Disabilities

The ADA compliance ensures people with disabilities access to and inclusion into many places. Many public environments are now designed with equal access; auto-

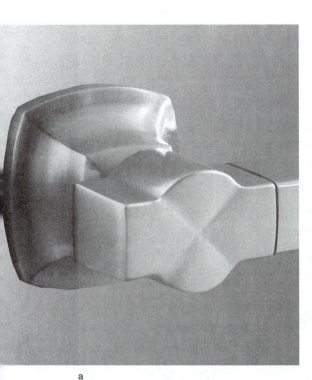

a

b

Figures 2.8a and b

To be inclusive, the design must blend in as though it were intended for people without disabilities; for example: (a) this grab handle at the end of a towel bar and (b) this shower unit with its built-in shower seat and a decorative grab bar that resembles a towel bar. Photo courtesy of Kohler Co.

matic door openers are provided for anyone to easily enter or exit; a variety of light sources are selected to provide security and to accommodate various abilities to see; and colors are carefully chosen for those with visual limitations.

On the other hand, some places still separate those with and without abilities by placing ramps in out-of-the-way areas or providing wheelchair seating in tight or inconvenient areas. Designers must be the advocates and make changes to these types of situations in order to provide equal access to, and inclusion of, everyone.

Fortunately, the stereotypes of the past are diminishing. People in general interact with a broader population that includes those with physical or mental limitations. Also, more people want to live in their homes as long as possible and be able to entertain friends with disabilities. This makes inclusive design a universal or global need and thus very marketable.

The Little People

When hearing the term *little people*, many think of children. However, little people, or dwarfism, relates to people who are short in stature. Their world is as challenging as it is for the very tall or large, and few pieces of furniture or environments are designed for them.

However, products are being designed or can be adapted for little people. One example, discussed in Chapter 6, is Sitmatic, which designs the chair to the person (Sitmatic, n/d). Others include office furniture by The Little Office (The Little Office, 2006) and the ErgoChair by Adaptive Living (Adaptive Living, n/d). Although products are available for little people, there is a market for products and environment that can be adapted to their needs. (See Figures 2.9a and b.)

Inclusive Design for Everyone

From baby boomers to people of various sizes to people with disabilities, there is a market for inclusive design. Many products (e.g., chairs, refrigerators) and environments (i.e., easy access, wider opens, security) meet inclusive design criteria while being economical and attractive. Thus, products that are easy for everyone to use are becoming the norm.

Figure 2.9a

For people of small stature, normal height of door handles are too high. In this example, an additional door handle has been added to accommodate an employee of smaller stature. Photo courtesy of Robyn Farris

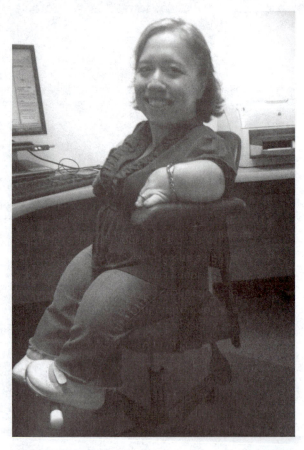

Figure 2.9b

The combination of a lower height desk and an ErgoChair for Little People designed with a special foot rest accommodates a person of small stature. The chair is produced by Adaptive Living. Photo courtesy of Robyn Farris

Inclusive Design and People of the Older Generation

The number of people who are older (65 and up) has steadily increased. Reasons range from better health to the number of baby boomers who are entering retirement age. In fact, as we look ahead to 2050, the estimated population of 65 and older will be greater than 20 percent of the total population (AoA, 2009).

Because baby boomers have been great consumers and very independent, they may find it difficult to lose their independence and identity as well as admit that their bodies are changing. To understand the changes that take place during the aging process, refer to "Characteristics of Aging."

As people age, and because of the characteristics of aging, their housing needs to change. Baby boomers, however, may have different preferences than past generations.

Characteristics of Aging

Changes in vision
- Inability to adapt to changing light levels
- Susceptible to veiling reflections (i.e., reflective glare—light or glare bouncing off of a task with shiny or glossy surface and into the eyes)
- Yellow tinting of the human lens
- Reduced amount of light perceived
- Reduced ability to discern detail
- Restricted depth perception
- Reduced perception of contrast

Changes in hearing
- Difficulty hearing high frequencies
- Difficulty hearing with ambient or background noise

Changes in cognitive ability
- Decrease in ability to make judgments
- Reduced attention span
- Depression
- Disorientation

Changes in mobility
- Reduced mobility
- Fear of falling
- Reduced bone density and weakened joints

Source: Leibrock, C. A. & Harris, D. D. (2011). *Design details for health: Making the most of interior design's healing potential, (2nd Ed.).* New York: Wiley.

HOUSING PREFERENCES OF BABY BOOMERS

Housing preferences of baby boomers vary. This was revealed in a survey of consumers and buildings in 2009 conducted by the National Association of Home Builders and the MetLife Mature Market Institute. The survey divided the participants into two groups. The older group was 65 and over, and the young group was 55 to 64-year-olds. Both groups had similar housing preferences with amenities that would allow time for an active lifestyle. The greatest difference was that the younger group showed greater interest in technology features. On the other hand, the older group expressed the greatest interest in having a single-story floor plan, or at least with a first-floor master bedroom and various inclusive features.

The survey also revealed that the majority (79 percent) preferred a single-story house. Some preferred a two-story house (15 percent), and a few preferred a split-level house (7 percent). The top five inside features were (in order of importance) washer and dryer in the unit or house, storage space, windows that open easily, master bedroom on the first floor in a two-story home, and easy-to-use climate-controlled thermostat. From the survey, it seems that most baby boomers are planning ahead and prefer easy access. They may also be planning to age in place rather than live in long-term care facilities.

ALTERNATIVES TO LONG-TERM CARE FACILITIES

With the increase in the older population, there will be a need for long-term care facilities. But many people, as they age, would rather not live in a long-term care facility such as a nursing home, a place where a person is perceived to exist rather than to live.

In the past, older people had only one choice when they were unable to care for themselves, or their families were no longer able to care for them; that choice was a nursing home (now called long-term care facilities). With aging baby boomers, long-term care may not be their preference and they will prefer alternatives. Thus, Dr. William Thomas developed the Eden Alternative® Principles in 1991 to provide living environments for our aging population rather than offering institutional living. Many long-term care facilities are now using his principles to develop living environments (Eden Alternative®, 2009). See "Eden Alternative® Principles" for more information.

Applying Eden Alternative® Principles to Design Projects

The Eden Alternative® Principles (2009) can be applied to projects and create living environments. Such projects could create facilities that include a variety of activities, provide green spaces, and include opportunities for various ages to interact. To include a variety of ages, the facility might have a children's day care, adult day care, assisted living, residential apartments for all ages, dining facilities for everyone, interactive spaces, and shops that include a hair salon, coffee shop, library, and more. This

Eden Alternative® Principles

The Eden Alternative® (2009b) mission is to improve the well-being of elders and their care-givers by the transformation of communities where they live and work. Its vision is to eliminate loneliness, helplessness, and boredom. For this reason, the Eden Alternative® (2009a) developed the following principles:

1. The three plagues of loneliness, helplessness, and boredom account for the bulk of suffering among our elders.
2. An elder-centered community commits to creating a human habitat where life revolves around close and continuing contact with plants, animals, and children. It is these relationships that provide the young and old alike with a pathway to a life worth living.
3. Loving companionship is the antidote to loneliness. Elders deserve easy access to human and animal companionship.
4. An elder-centered community creates opportunity to give as well as receive care. This is the antidote to helplessness.
5. An elder-centered community imbues daily life with variety and spontaneity by creating an environment in which unexpected and unpredictable interactions and happenings can take place. This is the antidote to boredom.
6. Meaningless activity corrodes the human spirit. The opportunity to do things that we find meaningful is essential to human health.
7. Medical treatment should be the servant of genuine human caring, never its master.
8. An elder-centered community honors its elders by de-emphasizing top-down bureaucratic authority, seeking instead to place the maximum possible decision-making authority into the hands of the elders or into the hands of those closest to them.
9. Creating an elder-centered community is a never-ending process. Human growth must never be separated from human life.
10. Wise leadership is the lifeblood of any struggle against the three plagues. For it, there can be no substitute.

Sources:
Eden Alternative®. (2009a). *Eden Alternative®: Our 10 principles.* Retrieved on June 17, 2010, from http://www.edenalt.org/our-10-principles
Eden Alternative®. (2009b). *Our mission, vision, values.* Retrieved on March 20, 2011, from http://www.edenalt.org/mission-vision-values

type of facility encourages transgenerational interaction as well as promotes a living environment that responds to user needs. This type of facility will be described as a student project in Case Study 8.1.

Wayfinding

Wayfinding is a term that describes methods people use to navigate through unfamiliar territory (Salmi, 2007). Although signage is an important part of wayfinding, its purpose is to direct people through a primary circulation path (corridors, aisles) that lead to various destinations. Successful wayfinding is inclusive and provides everyone with the same access to products and activities within an environment and throughout a community (Salmi, 2007; Nussbaumer, 2009).

An important part of wayfinding is cognitive mapping (mental map of a three-dimensional space), which provides a spatial representation to orient oneself (Salmi, 2007; Nussbaumer, 2009). Wayfinding should include a variety of ways to move users through a space.

WAYFINDING METHODS

Designers create wayfinding using several methods; these include:

- Examining the circulation path through spatial organization or building layout
- Providing visual cues such as landmarks
- Providing direction through signage
- Providing directories to assist in wayfinding
- Designing maps that are easy to read
- Using color and lighting to reinforce the pathway (Salmi, 2007; Nussbaumer, 2009)

By using various methods to create wayfinding, designers include many people in the design. To find their destination, some may need to read directions, some may need to locate a landmark, some may need maps, some may need to hear the directions, others may need the use of lighting or color, and some may prefer a combination of wayfinding methods. Thus, providing various wayfinding methods accommodates everyone.

Summary

This chapter has provided an overview of inclusive design and pointed out that it goes beyond complying with the ADA. By using new inclusive design criteria, attention is not drawn to any one person, and everyone has the same opportunity to use a product or navigate an environment. Inclusive design products and environments are responsive, adaptable, accessible, and secure. They are also economical, attractive, and marketable to many people, but most importantly, they provide advantages to those with disabilities as well as for those who are aging. By using a variety of wayfinding methods, everyone can easily navigate unfamiliar environments. Subsequent chapters address inclusive design for specific environments.

Inclusive Design Projects

EXPERIENTIAL PROJECTS

1. How does an entrance affect an overall environmental experience?

Entering a building is where individuals with limitations experience whether or not a space is accessible; however, an inclusively designed space may provide a more positive experience for everyone. This exercise compares an accessible entrance with an inclusive entrance. Locate two different types of entrances: one that meets the minimum ADA requirements and one that is inclusive. Photograph and create a poster that includes a description of each.

2. How can inclusive design criteria help create better designs?

The inclusive design criteria guide designers as they design products and environments. This project is intended to help better understand these criteria. Locate examples of each of the following criteria, and describe how the example meets each criterion as:

1. Responsive
2. Adaptable
3. Accessible
4. Secure

APPLICATION PROJECT

1. How can inclusive design criteria help create better environments?

Complying with the ADA is required; however, designing inclusive products and environments is not. For that reason, some environments follow only minimum requirements. Unfortunately, this draws attention to those with disabilities. Thus, for this exercise, locate a space that meets both the ADA minimum and inclusive design criteria. The procedure is as follows:

1. Locate a space that meets the minimum ADA requirements.
2. Locate another space that is designed inclusively.

For each space, take photographs that demonstrate the category. Write an analysis of these spaces that includes drawings. For the space meeting minimum requirements, sketch ways to create an inclusive space; and for the inclusively designed space, use a sketch to highlight areas that meet inclusive design criteria.

CHAPTER 3

Integrating Inclusive Design into the Design Process

KEY TERMS

- analysis
- case study
- content analysis
- contract document phase
- contract administration phase
- design development phase
- design process
- evidence
- evidence-based design
- experiment
- fact finding
- FF&E (furniture, fixtures, and equipment)
- focus group
- InformeDesign
- interview
- observation
- participatory design
- population
- post-occupancy evaluation
- programming phase
- punch list
- research
- role-playing
- schematic (or concept) development phase

OBJECTIVES

- ▼ Explain the design process
- ▼ Describe each phase of the design process
- ▼ Provide examples of tasks that occur during each phase
- ▼ Provide a brief scenario using the design process
- ▼ Explain how inclusive design criteria are implemented throughout the process
- ▼ Explain the importance of conducting research
- ▼ Briefly describe various data collection methods
- ▼ Explain ways that more than one data collection method is used in research
- ▼ Provide examples of various resources for research
- ▼ Describe how the information can be used in a project

A design solution incorporates a logical systematic process as well as creative thinking. An important part of this process includes collecting information about those who use the products and environments so their needs are met. Because designers and other professionals use a process to solve problems, the design process is briefly described in this chapter, and within a scenario, inclusive design is integrated into the discussion.

The Design Process

The **design process** is divided into five phases: (1) programming, (2) schematic (or concept) development, (3) design development, (4) contract documentation, and (5) contract administration. Prior to beginning the design process, an initial contact is made with the client. At this time the designer recognizes the problem and decides whether or not to commit to and accept the project. When accepted and a contract prepared, the design process can begin (see Table 3.1).

THE PROGRAMMING PHASE

Solving a design problem is not about beauty, but rather about the data and research collected to create a successful design. This occurs during the **programming phase,** which consists of information gathering. This phase begins by identifying the problem and the client's needs and desires—especially, any special needs and concerns. Much of this information is gathered by locating **evidence**; conducting **interviews**, surveys and questionnaires, **observations, focus groups**; participating in **role-playing**; and reviewing **post-occupancy evaluations**. These data collection methods create **evidence-based design**. These will be discussed later in this chapter as they relate to applying inclusive design. For examples that demonstrate a variety of research methods, see Case Study 3.1: "The Importance of the Programming Phase" later in this chapter.

THE SCHEMATIC (OR CONCEPT) DEVELOPMENT PHASE

With all information gathered, the **schematic (or concept) development phase** consists of analyzing the facts and generating ideas, brainstorming possibilities, and developing alternative solutions to the problem. Integrated into this phase is the development of the design concept or idea that drives the design. To incorporate the design concept into the project as well as analyze the problem, designers develop schematics drawings, conceptual sketches (e.g., bubble diagrams, plans, and illustrative sketches). With various options at hand, those selected are based on the client's

TABLE 3.1   The Design Process

DESIGN PROCESS PHASES	PROGRAMMING		SCHEMATIC (CONCEPT) DEVELOPMENT
	INITIAL CONTACT WITH CLIENT	*PROGRAMMING*	
Scope of services and/or tasks	Recognize problem;	Define problem;	Continue to analyze facts;
	Commit to project	State the goals and objectives	Generate ideas and brainstorm
	Accept the project	Gather information: the facts	Sketching of ideas, plans, details, etc.
	Contract written	Interview client, use surveys, questionnaires, conduct observations, etc.	Develop preliminary plans
	Retainer obtained	Research to develop a strong Evidence-Base	
		Analyze facts	
		Organize the information and develop program requirements	
	ANALYSIS		

DESIGN DEVELOPMENT	CONTRACT DOCUMENTATION (CDS)		CONTRACT ADMINISTRATION
	IMPLEMENTATION TAKE ACTION		
Select and Refine	*BIDDING PROCESS*	*ORDER/ CONSTRUCTION*	*EVALUATE*
Develop drawings, details, specifications	Construction drawings	Ordering Process	Create Punch List during Walk-through
	Specifications written	Construction	After approx. 3 months:
		Supervision	Conduct POE
	SYNTHESIS		

budget, needs, objectives, and desires. Finally, by refining the sketches, schematic drawings are developed into preliminary drawings.

THE DESIGN DEVELOPMENT PHASE

In the **design development phase**, designers begin with preliminary drawings from which they develop final design drawings, details, sections, and elevations. Schedules are also created that include the major tasks, activities, people, materials, and time-frames to execute the design.

Thorough data collection and research during the programming phase provides a solid base for a successful project, whether a restaurant, hotel, medical facility, apartment, or private residence. As you view these examples, keep in mind that these only touch the surface of research; providing a design that is inclusive for everyone into a building and its spaces takes a great deal more study throughout the entire process.

After a designer has accepted the project and contracts are signed, data collection may begin. The following examples demonstrate a variety of research methods; these include providing individual questionnaires, conducting interviews (individual and focus groups), participating in observations and role-playing, building study models, viewing and analyzing the site, and reviewing an older or similar set of construction documents.

Questionnaires

Individual questionnaires may be different for a manager than a waitress or housekeeping staff member. The reason is that each may have different perceptions, which will be important in your design. Interviews are also conducted with one or more people to provide greater insight into any issues or concerns not addressed in the questionnaire.

Observations

Observations can be made through various methods. One method called *behavioral mapping* allows designers to not only observe the users but also to note problems that need to be addressed. Case Study Figure 3.1a demonstrates using a computer

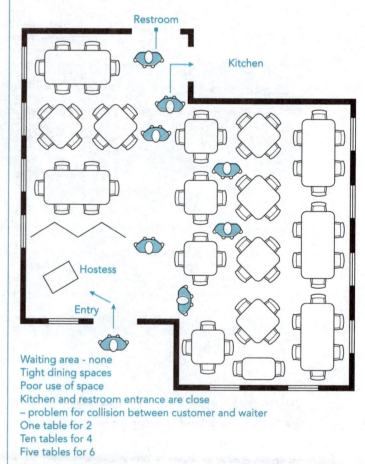

Waiting area - none
Tight dining spaces
Poor use of space
Kitchen and restroom entrance are close
– problem for collision between customer and waiter
One table for 2
Ten tables for 4
Five tables for 6

Case Study Figure 3.1a

This plan was produced using a computer application in a sketch mode. The designer prepares the plan prior to visiting the space and then may add or adjust the plan as well as make notes while observing the space. © Precision Graphics/Based on a drawing by Linda L. Nussbaumer application in a sketch mode. In this case, the designer has prepared the space prior to the visit and then may add or adjust the plan as well as make notes while observing movement of people within the space. Turn to Color Plate 5 to see a hand sketch that notes where important areas are located and where movement takes place. Dots are added to Color Plate 6 to indicate where employees and guests are found. Their interaction as well as areas of congestion can be noted. Color Plate 7 shows an interior designer observing and making notes during an observation.

Participant Observation

Participant observations or role-playing provides interior designers first-hand knowledge of workers, users, or others that use a space. Case Study Figure 3.1b shows an interior designer participant observer acting as a waitress. Through this experience, she learns about the challenges of working behind the scenes with the chef and in the dining area with various customers. Customers may even include a person who is blind, has hearing loss, or suffers from mental limitations. Like an actor or an actress, the interior designer participant observer must learn as much as possible about their role—even working in that position to understand it better. In this way, an interior designer can better understand a worker's challenges and issues within the position.

Study Models

Designers may even create study models at various stages of a project. A model created early in the design phase helps envision an appropriate space plan.

Case Study Figure 3.1b

A designer can take a service job, such as waiting tables in a restaurant, to better understand the issues and concerns of an environment's users—both its clients and staff. Fotosearch/SuperStock

Site Visit and Documentation

Another important aspect of data collection is visiting the site. Such a visit will aid understanding of the topography, location of other buildings, and more. Additionally, if a building is to be replaced or remodeled, a set of documents should also be viewed and analyzed.

Goal = Insight

These methods as well as others suggested in the text provide you with greater insight into issues of accessibility as well as a stronger ability to create an inclusive environment.

THE CONTRACT DOCUMENT PHASE

The **contract document phase** consists of preparing construction drawings (e.g., plans, elevations, and sections) and writing specifications. Construction drawings provide all necessary information to implement the project. This includes structural, architectural, mechanical, and electrical aspects of the design as well as finishes and furniture. Specifications (technical documents) are "written instructions to the general contractor and vendors for materials, performance standards, and methods of construction or installation" (Nussbaumer, 2009, p.7).

THE CONTRACT ADMINISTRATION PHASE

The **contract administration phase** includes the selection of the contractor and subcontractors, the placement of orders, construction and installation, and the supervision of work. Evaluations take place as the project nears or is at completion. These include a walk-through (site inspection) to look for any omissions or errors. During this walk-through, notations are made on a form called a **punch list**.

Shortly after the client has moved in, a **post-occupancy evaluation** (POE) should also be completed. Designers use the POE to identify and evaluate a completed project as well as identify problem areas. It may also be helpful to review conceptual development, evaluate data-gathering methods, and examine space utilization. This type of follow-up evaluation is "important to the client and the design to improve present and future projects" (Nussbaumer, 2009, p.7).

Brief Scenario: Using the Design Process

As an example, decisions surrounding the furnishing of a home office with a workstation, chair, and storage equipment require a creative act. First, in the programming phase, information is gathered about the client and the space. The designer examines the space (e.g., existing furnishing, color scheme, lighting), and learns the client's preference for style, materials, and furnishings. The designer also discovers the client's specific needs and desires for the use of the space (e.g., reading, writing, drafting, computer use), and ascertains budgetary constraints. To accomplish this, various research methods are used, such as interviewing the client, measuring the space, taking inventory of existing furnishings and lighting, researching new products, and gathering evidence to create an inclusively designed space. To ensure this occurs, the ADAAG guidelines must be the minimum application, and to move beyond the minimum, inclusive design criteria are used to analyze the data. This creates an invisible accessibility—a type of accessibility that is not obvious, such as a ramp that everyone uses. Invisible accessibility is important for inclusivity.

In the schematic development phase, sketches for the space are generated as well as a design concept. Schematic drawings are developed, and from these, preliminary drawings for spatial layout, lighting, color, and furnishings are presented to the client. During this presentation, the client has the opportunity to determine whether or not the space meets his or her specific needs for invisible accessibility (see Figure 3.1).

In the design development phase and after the client approves the preliminary drawings, design drawings can be completed and schedules developed to provide the designer and client with the timeframe toward completion. In this case, the design drawings include a floor plan, furniture plan, elevations, and sections as well as wall and floor covering plans and a finish schedule. Once again, as these documents are developed, they must be reviewed for application of the ADAAG and inclusive design criteria. (See Figure 3.2.)

Next, in the contract document phase, construction drawings are prepared, and specifications are written. In this case, if any structural changes are taking place, a demolition plan, construction plan, and electrical plan are drawn. With this phase and the next phase, a continual review of the ADAAG and inclusive design criteria ensures its application during the construction phase. (See Figure 3.3.)

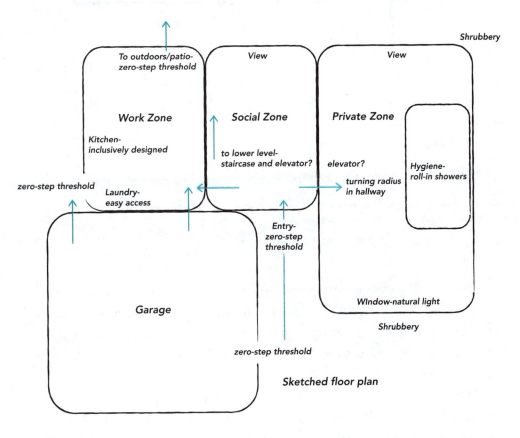

Figure 3.1

A variety of sketches and diagrams generate ideas for a design. This bubble diagram includes notations necessary for the creation of an inclusively designed project. © Precision Graphics/Based on a drawing by Linda L. Nussbaumer

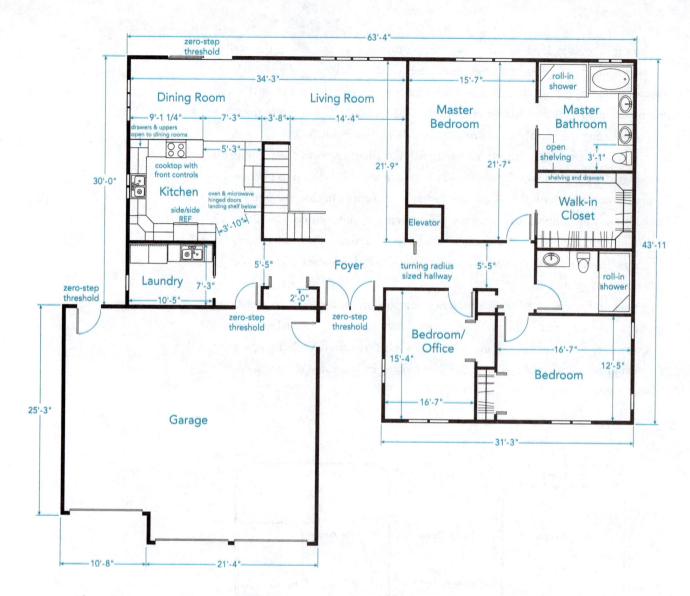

Figure 3.2

Using the bubbles diagram in Figure 3.1, the designer created several preliminary drawings. When the general plan was selected, drawings such as this were developed for final approval. © Precision Graphics/Based on a drawing by Linda L. Nussbaumer

In the contract administration phase, contractors are selected and orders are placed for all products and materials. Contractors should be selected based on the knowledge or willingness to learn and participate in creating an inclusive space. As construction and installation take place, work is supervised to make sure the client's needs and desires are met (see Figure 3.4).

When the project is nearing completion, the space is examined for those items that must be completed, repaired, or are missing. It must also be examined for its application of inclusivity. Finally, after the project is completed and the client has had time to use the space, conducting a POE provides evidence for areas of improvement for this and future projects. With an emphasis on inclusivity, the POE must

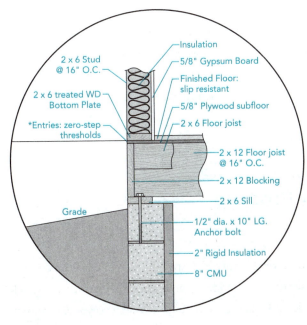

2 x 6 Stud @ 16" O.C.
2 x 6 treated WD Bottom Plate
*Entries: zero-step thresholds
Grade
Insulation
5/8" Gypsum Board
Finished Floor: slip resistant
5/8" Plywood subfloor
2 x 6 Floor joist
2 x 12 Floor joist @ 16" O.C.
2 x 12 Blocking
2 x 6 Sill
1/2" dia. x 10" LG. Anchor bolt
2" Rigid Insulation
8" CMU

Figure 3.3

Construction documents are created during the contract design phase. Detail drawings take the drawing one step further to indicate to a contractor that zero-step thresholds and slip-resistant floor coverings are required. © Precision Graphics/Based on a drawing by Linda L. Nussbaumer

Finish Schedule

No.	Room Name	Dim	Dim	SqFt	Perimeter	Flooring: Carpet C1	Wood-WD1	Quarry Tile-QT 1	Tile-CT 1	Base: Rubber Base-RB 1	Wood Base WB 1	Tile-CT 1	Walls North: Paint-P1	Tile-CT 1	East: Paint-P1	Tile-CT 1	West: Paint-P1	Tile-CT 1	South: Paint-P1	Tile-CT 1	Ceiling: Paint-P4	Acoustical Tile-AT 1	Hgt	Remarks	Description
	Foyer	8'8"	7'9"	67.43	32'11"	•				•			•		•		•		•		•		12	Low VOC paint	
	Living Room	17'0"	21'9"	349.62	76'	•				•			•		•		•		•		•		12	"	
	Dining Room	18'2"	9'9"	177.63	55'11"	•				•			•		•		•		•		•		9	"	
	Kitchen	16'1"	11'10"	101.6	56"			•				•	•	•	•	•	•	•	•	•	•		9	"	slip resistant flooring covering
	Laundry	11'9"	7'2"	83.7	37'-9"			•				•	•	•	•	•	•	•	•	•	•		9	"	slip resistant flooring covering
	Back Entry	13'0"	7'9"	99.55	41'2"			•				•	•	•	•	•	•	•	•	•	•		9	"	slip resistant flooring covering
	Hallway	15'11"	7'9"	123.8	47'5"	•				•			•		•		•		•		•		9	"	
	Bedroom/Office	12'5"	13'4"	164.7	51'4"	•				•			•		•		•		•		•		9	"	
	Bedroom	17'11"	13'4"	238.9	62'5"	•				•			•		•		•		•		•		9	"	
	Bathroom	11'11"	7'5"	86.7	38'3"			•				•	•	•	•	•	•	•	•	•	•		9	"	slip resistant flooring covering
	Master Bedroom	15'7"	22'3"	346.1	75'7"	•				•			•		•		•		•		•		9	"	
	Master Bathroom	11'11"	12'9"	147.8	48'6"			•				•	•	•	•	•	•	•	•	•	•		9	"	slip resistant flooring covering
	Walk-In Closet	11'11"	9'0"	107.1	41'10"	•				•			•		•		•		•		•		9	"	

Figure 3.4

Schedules are prepared and specifications written during the contract document phase. It is important to indicate and specify materials that will be inclusive such as low-VOC or no-VOC paints, slip resistant floor coverings, low-VOC adhesives, and many more. This example indicates two important inclusive elements related to paint and floor coverings. Courtesy Linda L. Nussbaumer

examine the project based on the ADAAG and the application of inclusivity—not drawing attention to a disability. Thus, it is important to review and analyze for the application of inclusive design criteria when conducting a POE. Table 3.2 includes notations regarding the use of the ADA and inclusive design criteria throughout the design process.

Applying Inclusive Design into the Design Process

When designers and other professionals apply inclusive design to their projects, they consider assistive devices and supportive products (audible alarms, computers, wheelchairs, and more) and accessible and healthier environments for everyone. Designers may also work with employers as they establish policies to work in home office spaces or to create reasonable accommodations within a corporate office environment (Null & Cherry, 1996). Thus, whether working in a home or corporate office, creating an inclusive space accommodates everyone.

CONDUCTING RESEARCH

One of the most important aspects of the programming process is conducting research. To create an inclusively designed environment, product and application research as well as study of other environments is essential. Data collected during the programming phase occurs through **fact finding**, or **research**, or a combination of both. To help us understand the difference between fact finding and research, Wang (2004) defines fact finding as "dealing with facts that already exist (e.g., the number of chairs at the table), whereas research (e.g., placement of a chair or chairs related to psychological needs) seeks to produce new knowledge in recognizable ways that can usually be applied regardless of locale" (p. 35). As information is gathered and analyzed, only facts and new research evidence relating and pertaining to the project goal should be considered, In particular, when emphasis is placed on inclusive design, research related to its application must be a priority.

INCLUDING THE PEOPLE IN THE DESIGN PROCESS

The responsive criterion discussed in Chapter 2 takes into account what people say they need and want. Thus, users or occupants working in or otherwise using a workplace or another environment, as well as others, must be actively involved in the design and decision-making process. When creating an inclusive design, it's important to involve everyone with a vested interest in the environment. This is called **participatory design** (CPSR, n/d). (See Figure 3.5.)

| TABLE 3.2 | Application of Inclusive Design Criteria within the Design Process |||

DESIGN PROCESS PHASES	PROGRAMMING		SCHEMATIC (CONCEPT) DEVELOPMENT
	INITIAL CONTACT WITH CLIENT	*PROGRAMMING*	
Scope of services and/or tasks	Recognize problem *Note accessibility needs*	Define problem; State the goals and objectives *Set inclusive design goals*	Continue to analyze facts
	Commit to project	Gather information: the facts *Determine present and future needs for accessibility.*	Generate ideas and brainstorm
	Accept the project		Sketching of ideas, plans, details, etc.
	Contract written	Interview client, use surveys, questionnaires, conduct observations, etc. *Include questions related to inclusivity (home or work)*	Develop preliminary plans
	Retainer obtained		*Use ADAAG and include inclusive design criteria in all of the above*
		Research to develop a strong Evidence-Base *Include inclusive design in research*	
		Analyze facts *Include inclusive design criteria to analyze facts*	
		Organize the information and develop program requirements *Include ADAAG and Inclusive Design criteria in program requirements*	
	ANALYSIS		

DESIGN DEVELOPMENT	CONTRACT DOCUMENTATION (CDS)		CONTRACT ADMINISTRATION
	IMPLEMENTATION TAKE ACTION		
Select and Refine	*BIDDING PROCESS*	*ORDER/ CONSTRUCTION*	*EVALUATE*
Develop drawings, details, specifications	Construction drawings	Ordering Process	Create Punch List during Walk-through
	Specifications written	Construction	*Examine for application and use of ADAAG and inclusive design criteria*
Develop using ADAAG and inclusive design criteria	*Develop using ADAAG and inclusive design criteria*	Supervision	
		Examine the application of ADAAG and inclusive design criteria	After approx. 3 months:
			Conduct POE *Ask questions related to ADAAG and inclusive design criteria*
	SYNTHESIS		

Figure 3.5

People from various backgrounds come together to provide input into a design project.
© WendellandCarolyn/istockphoto

STRATEGIZING DATA COLLECTION FOR INCLUSIVE DESIGN

At the beginning of the design process, and within the programming phase, various data collection methods are used. Data collection includes research as well as interviews, surveys, questionnaires, or other methods. Strategies to accomplish these tasks must be set.

1. Establish goals and objectives: Keeping the inclusive criteria in mind, determine what the client wants to accomplish and how it can be achieved.

2. Gather and analyze the data: Gather information regarding the client as well as their needs and desires; consider the client's need for creating an inclusive space for now and the future.

3. Conduct research for new evidence: Using the inclusive criteria, look for data that can be applied to the design.

4. Specify needs: Determine needs related to the structure and budget constraints as well as those related to human factors (anthropometrics and ergonomics, and the ADAAG along with inclusive design criteria).

5. Evaluate the collected data: Determine the importance and value of the data collected and evaluate based on the ADAAG along with inclusive design criteria.

6. Organize and decide: Organize the parts into a meaningful whole and decide information (based on the ADAAG and inclusive design criteria) relevant only to the project.

7. Present conclusions: Examine and determine if findings address the goals; then present to the client.

Data Collection Methods

Inclusive design criteria must be considered throughout the entire process, but particularly during this programming phase and when collecting data. With all participants included in some way, clients' needs and desires will become clear during interviews, through surveys and questionnaires, through observations, from case studies, through experimentation, and by conducting research for new evidence.

SURVEYS AND INTERVIEWS

By conducting surveys and interviews, clients' goals and objectives are clarified (Pile 2003). The more participants involved, the more specific needs, desires, and even concerns become clear.

Participants in Surveys and Interviews

Design projects typically are either residential or commercial. For residential spaces, all occupants as well as the owner are interviewed. For commercial spaces, data are collected for various groups and for specific information; these include:

- Management: Executives, managers, supervisors, and others in managerial positions (Pile, 2003; Rayfield, 1994)
- Other personnel: Staff, laborers, administrative assistants, and clerical workers
- Typical users: Customers, diners, hotel guests, patients, and other users (Nussbaumer, 2009; Pile, 2003)

Including various users allows people who will be affected by decisions to play a significant role in shaping the design. As suggested by CABE (2008), as many people as possible should be involved in the design. This may include people with specific disabilities as well as those who have worked on similar projects, such as surveyors, architects, engineers, facility managers, and access consultants.

The **InformeDesign** research summary (2007, March 17) "Nursing Staff Involvement in Design" demonstrates the importance of involving everyone in a design project. The summary points out that since healthcare facility design impacts nursing staff and patient care for the long-term, nursing staff should be engaged in the design process. Nursing staff has daily insight into the present and future care of patients and could provide visions for future nursing care within the building design (e.g., space for patient rooms, storage areas, support spaces, and so on).

Conducting Surveys with Written Questionnaires

A written questionnaire (paper or electronic) is often used to collect data. These can be designed for various categories of users. Questions may be very specific as well as open-ended to allow for greater insight. Answers to questions may provide special needs–related data that can help meet reasonable accommodations as well as create an inclusive space. See Study Sketch 3.1: "Neighborhood Open Space Impacts Older Adults' Quality of Life" for a successful example of this method of data collection.

Conducting Surveys of Existing Conditions and FF&E

The survey of existing conditions begins with a review of existing plans as well as a tour of the existing facility. During the tour, physical measurement of the space and all objects—**furniture, fixtures, and equipment (FF&E)**—within the space must be taken (Nussbaumer, 2009; Piotrowski, 2002). This helps determine if the existing space and furnishing will accommodate all users (daily or occasionally) of the space.

Conducting Interviews

Survey questionnaires are entirely written and do not allow for verbal input; therefore, live interviews provide greater detail. Interview questions assess individuals' emotions, attitudes, beliefs, and opinions about the space. Individual needs may become clearer as well and allow for a fully inclusively designed space. Interviews allow the opportunity for users to provide a verbal response; however, interviews take time, and responses may lack full disclosure or may even be embellished (Guerin & Dohr, 2005; Nussbaumer, 2009). Proper training and preparation for interviews may eliminate such response issues (Nussbaumer, 2009; (Rayfield, 1994)).

Conducting Focus Groups

Focus groups are a type of interview in which people are interviewed as a group (Leedy & Ormrod, 2005). These user groups may be composed of management and other personnel, typical users with varied needs or usages, or architects, designers, and/or project managers along with psychologists and sociologists (Null & Cherry, 1996). From these varied groups, rich data are collected and/or provide great insight for the project.

The survey and interview methods can be applied to one research project. In the InformeDesign research summary (2010, April 5), "Neighborhood Open Space Impacts Older Adults' Quality of Life," the survey data collection method (written questionnaire) and focus interviews were used. This study also demonstrates the importance of involving various participants.

OBSERVATIONS

Observing people's behavior is a data collection method that provides information about circulation, interaction, routines, issues, and much more to better understand a project. Observations can be accomplished in several ways:

1. Structured observation: preplanned observations
   - Systematic observation: carefully planned observation using a predesigned score sheet for recording data.
   - Behavioral mapping: creating a map or drawing similar to a floor plan; observing the people who use a space and their activities as well as the location of the activities (Guerin & Dohr, 2005; Nussbaumer, 2009).
2. Unstructured observations: unplanned observations
   - Casual observations: observing through intentionally planned visual inspections or recalling from life's experiences (e.g., a past shopping experience)
   - Participant observation: observing as a participant (role-playing)
   - Trace observations: observing or looking for physical traces of evidence such as worn carpet, stacks of paper, chairs used for storage, and more.

Photographs or videos can provide additional trace observations as well as observe patterns of behavior within the space (Guerin & Dohr, 2005; Nussbaumer, 2009).

Role Playing

Role playing is a participant observation method (noted previously). It allows designers to collect data while acting as the user. Examples may include acting as a patient in a hospital or staff in a corporate office. Such an experiment helps designers better understand users' needs.

Technology can be used to simulate role playing by digitally placing people within the space. Animated technology such as the Second Life program can place individuals into a space. This program may be better utilized during earlier stages of the design to evaluate circulation within the space.

EXPERIMENTATION

Experimentation is defined as systematically testing ideas (or hypotheses). In others words, the researcher is trying to discover what action causes what result. In an experiment, variables are elements that are manipulated and compared. The most common method of experimentation includes a pretest, treatment, and post-test. With this type of **experiment**, the subject is given a pretest followed by the treatment; then a post-test is administered (Guerin & Dohr, 2005; Nussbaumer, 2009).

"The treatment may be an activity, a learning situation, a condition, or an event" (Nussbaumer, 2009, p. 49). Groups may also be compared: an experimental group receives the treatment whereas a control group does not. Test results determine whether or not the treatment had an effect on the experimental group (Nussbaumer, 2009).

Researchers from higher education or research institutes may conduct experiments by employing a specific teaching method in higher education or using a designed space in a public environment. These types of studies give insight to needs or concerns for teaching within the academic community or comfort or satisfaction with a spatial design for the general **population**.

The InformeDesign research summary (2008, October 8) "Confusing Images Made Clear for Colorblind Individuals" is an example of an experiment that relates to the application of universal design. See "Study Sketch 3.2: Confusing Images Made Clear for Colorblind Individuals" for a description of this study.

When studies employ the experimentation method, they may also include other data collection methods. The InformeDesign research summary (2009, April 15), "Supportive Classrooms for Children with Autism" is an example that used online questionnaires as well as behavioral mapping, researcher and teachers observation, and video observation. See Study Sketch 3.3: "Supportive Classrooms for Children with Autism" for a description of this study.

Experiments can be conducted by testing an interior material such as wallcovering, fabrics, carpet, and so on for specific properties or contaminants. Figure 3.6 shows an experiment conducted on the wallcovering to test for mold levels and types found inside a home. Such a test would probably not be conducted by the designer but, rather, a chemist who specializes in mold testing.

Figure 3.6

This experiment demonstrates the testing of a product for mold levels in various materials on the walls and flooring. In this photo, a section of the wall covering is selected. Using a special mold/dust collect nozzle, the section of the material framed within a cardboard square is vacuumed. The particles are analyzed for mold spore counts. © D. Hurst/Alamy

STUDY SKETCH 3.3: Supportive Classrooms for Children with Autism

For some studies, a variety of data collection methods is necessary. The InformeDesign research summary (2009, April 15) "Supportive Classrooms for Children with Autism" is an example that used online questionnaires as well as behavioral mapping, researcher and teacher observation, and video observation.

The purpose of the study was to review primary design guidelines for the autistic user and test its theory within a classroom. A total of 83 primary caregivers and teachers of autistic children (58 primary caregivers, 25 teachers) completed voluntary online questionnaires. Respondents ranked architectural features (e.g., colors and patterns, textures, olfactory issues, acoustics, and lighting) and spatial arrangement from the most to least effect on autistic behavior.

Based on the survey, design interventions were implemented. For each intervention, an experiment was conducted in which "a control group and study group were observed at the Advance Society for Developing Skills of Special Needs Children in Cairo, Egypt for one school year." Two design interventions were implemented.

- To investigate how acoustics affected autistic behavior in a speech and language acquisition classroom, the floor, walls, and ceilings were soundproofed to reduce echoing and external noise.
- To investigate how spatial arrangement affected autistic behavior, the other classroom was divided into spatial zones with one escape zone—one with fewer stimuli.

From February to June 2003, observations of 45 minutes each were conducted "at three-week intervals over a period of 12 weeks." Data collection methods used included "behavioral mapping, direct observation by researcher and teacher, and video observations." Researchers measured progress based on behavioral patterns such as attention span, response time, and behavioral temperament.

- Attention span: Number of seconds a child stayed on task before becoming distracted.
- Response time: Number of seconds a child took to respond to a question or command.
- Behavioral temperament: How often self-stimulating actions (e.g., rocking, hand biting, head banging) occurred—a decrease in frequency indicated progress.

This study provided feedback on the design intervention and showed that changes to the architecture may be helpful in creating a better environment. However, there are still wide-range challenges and needs among children with autism that make it difficult to create comprehensive guidelines.

Source: InformeDesign. (2009, April 15). "Supportive classrooms for children with autism." Retrieved on June 21, 2010, from http://www.informedesign.umn.edu/Rs_detail.aspx?rsId=3296

Modeling

Modeling is a type of experiment that uses three-dimension full- or small-scale models or two-dimension visual models. Models test an idea by using the physical (e.g., new product mock-ups) or visual (e.g., concept maps or mathematical forms). Some models are used:

- to bring out problems that were invisible or hidden
- to test a new design idea
- to conduct experiments in a laboratory to test materials for tensile strength or flame resistance
- as concept maps (e.g., bubble diagrams) to test ideas during the schematic development phase

CONTENT ANALYSIS FROM WRITTEN OR VISUAL SOURCES

Data may be collected from written or visual sources. New evidence may be collected from written sources such as academic journals, case studies found in trade publications, post-occupancy evaluations, online databases, manufacturers' literature, and product specifications as well as past experience. New evidence may also be collected from visual sources such as photographs (Nussbaumer, 2009). See Figures 3.7 and 3.8 for examples of various written and visual sources.

The data collection method—analysis of visual content, or **content analysis**—was used in the InformeDesign research summary (2010, April 5) "Outdoor Accessibility Preferences of Assisted Living Residents." See Study Sketch 3.4: "Outdoor Accessibility Preferences of Assisted Living Residents" for further details regarding the process used to implement this research project.

Academic Journals

Academic journals provide articles on research projects that uncover new evidence. (Nussbaumer, 2009) notes that academic journals are found in university libraries and online. "The *Journal of Interior Design* is specific to interior design, and the *Journal of Facilities Management* is specific to facility management" (p. 10). Articles relative to interior design may be located in journals such as *Journal of Sociology, Ageing and*

Figure 3.7

Trade publications and academic journals are sources for research of evidence. Photo courtesy Linda L. Nussbaumer

Figure 3.8

Visual sources for evidence may include photographs provided by the client or taken by the interior designer of existing conditions. Photo courtesy Linda L. Nussbaumer

Society, *American Journal of Alzheimer's Disease and Other Dementias, American Journal of Infection Control, Architecture and Behavior, Children and Schools, Building and Environment, Applied Ergonomics, Design Issues, Housing and Society, Human Factors, Environment and Behavior, Journal of Housing and the Built Environment, Journal of Housing for the Elderly, Journal of Visual Impairments and Blindness, Occupational Ergonomics, Space and Culture,* and *Urban Studies.*

Other journals can be found through search engines such as scholar.google.com and pubmed.gov. "Additionally, InformeDesign, which is described later in this chapter, has summarized articles from many of these journals, drawing key points of interest to interior designers and omitting material irrelevant to design and technical jargon" (p. 10).

Case Studies

Some of these written sources are called case studies. The **case study** method is used to systematically solve a problem and investigate a single occurrence such as one involving an individual, a group, or an entire community. It may involve various data collection methods by using a visual and written analysis and observations. Case studies may also compare characteristics of one project to another. Designers may develop and publish case studies of their project in trade magazines so that others may learn from their experience (Nussbaumer, 2009).

Trade Publications

Trade publications provide articles about completed projects (e.g., case studies). The most common trade publications include *Interior Design, Interiors and Sources, Metropolis, I.D. (International Design), Visual Merchandising + Store Design (VM+SD), Fine Homebuilding, Lighting Dimensions, Home Furnishings News (HFN),* and *Healthcare Design.* These publications include articles that describe design projects as well as provide visuals (Nussbaumer, 2009).

Post-Occupancy Evaluation

Post-occupancy evaluation (POE) is a case study method tool. A POE is used to assess completed projects using various data collection methods such as questionnaires or onsite surveys. It is also used to collect data concerning the positive and/or negative effects about the design and generally occurs after the product or space has been used or occupied for approximately one to three months. The evaluation helps researchers assess how well the product or space performs for the occupants relative to various predetermined criteria such as function and, for a space, circulation.

ASID or IIDA Knowledge Centers

The American Society of Interior Designers (ASID) and International Interior Design Association (IIDA) offer "knowledge centers" on their websites. ASID (2005) (www.asid.org) provides professional interior design news, research, and information through its Knowledge Center. Its resource sections include a variety of topics such as sustainable design, aging, and accessibility. The IIDA Knowledge Center (http://knowledgecenter.iida.org) provides abstracts from a variety of research articles. Research may be conducted by topic, resource type, and client type.

InformeDesign

Scholarly journals publish articles that provide evidence for designers on today's issues. However, these articles are not easily accessible to designers, are geared toward research and academics rather than practice, and thus, are not user friendly. To create more user-friendly articles, the InformeDesign database was created and contains more than 1,100 research summaries of these articles. Thus, this website (http://www.informedesign.org) has become an important sources of new evidence for designers.

Summary

Understanding the design process and what takes place at each phase is essential for all designers. Integrating research throughout the design process will provide a richer, more successful project. All users should also be involved during data collection, while conducting experiments, and more. Most importantly, the application of inclusive design criteria begins with data collection and in the research of new evidence explaining what others have done. It must continually be evaluated through the project to be appropriately applied.

Inclusive Design Projects

EXPERIENTIAL PROJECT

1. Can being a participant observer produce self-awareness?

Return to Chapter 1 and Experiential Projects 1, 2, and 3. Choose one exercise that was not conducted. Follow the instructions and complete the exercise.

APPLICATION PROJECT

1. What can a designer learn through observations?

Making observations can produce valuable information about areas of concern. Choose a busy public space such as a shopping mall, restaurant, hotel lobby, or another public area. Select a location to observe within this space that provides a view of the entrance and main activities that would occur in the space. Complete the following:

1. Create a sketch of the area.
2. Observe movement of people and the general pattern.
3. Observe where the majority of people congregate.
4. Note those who are working in the space and those who are guests.
5. Note problems observed.

2. What problems are revealed during a hunt for evidence?

Hunting for evidence (good and bad) can reveal problem areas or those that are well designed. To locate evidence, a camera and a notepad are needed. Both good and bad examples must relate to the following:

1. Entering and exiting
2. Wayfinding
3. Task based
4. Safety

After these examples are located and photographed, create a poster and describe the reason why each is good or bad. Good examples must be inclusive in design.

Part II

INCLUSIVE DESIGN FOR PRODUCTS AND ENVIRONMENTS

CHAPTER 4

Product Design and Inclusivity

"The real questions are: Does it solve a problem? Is it serviceable? How is it going to look in 10 years?"

—*Charles Eames*

OBJECTIVES

- Analyze products (small to large) for their fit to inclusive design by using the criteria of *responsive, adaptable, accessible*, and *secure*
- Analyze new technologies to determine their inclusive fit
- Discuss challenges of new technologies to inclusive design
- Explain the connection between ergonomics and inclusive design
- Describe the connection between sustainable design and inclusive design
- Locate and describe a product or material that incorporates ergonomics, sustainability, and inclusive design

KEY TERMS

- assistive technologies
- bariatric(s)
- Braille
- ergonomics
- formaldehyde
- global positioning system (GPS)
- iChat
- indoor air quality
- iPhone
- iPods
- ischial tuberosity
- musculoskeletal disorders (MSD)
- sink
- sustainable design
- toxins
- trackpad
- VoiceOver
- volatile organic compounds (VOCs)

To this point, our focus has been on ADA law, various terms related to inclusive design, and how to incorporate inclusive design criteria into the design process—necessary background for the remaining chapters. In this chapter, a variety of products are described, including medicine bottles, faucets, chairs, electronics, furniture, and more. Their features consider one or more limitations (e.g., hearing, vision, mobility, or cognition. Additionally, they are described and analyzed using inclusive design criteria (e.g., responsive, adaptable, accessible, and secure). Connections are also made among **ergonomics**, **sustainable design**, and inclusive design.

Product Design

Many popular new products on the market are designed for various ages and abilities. Their design may be traditional or technologically advanced for easy use. Whether large or small, contemporary or traditional, there are many new and innovative ideas applied to the creation of inclusive products.

Exemplary Products

Although designers do not specify all the products that follow, many are excellent examples that take various impairments into consideration. The design of these products (e.g., medicine bottle, computers, phones, and more) makes for easier use for those with physical, vision, and/or hearing difficulties.

MEDICINE BOTTLE DESIGN

Although interior designers do not specify the medicine bottles, designers do create unique products. The medicine bottle provides an overview of issues and solutions related to various physical limitations (e.g., arthritic or weak hands, or weak vision). Target Corporation considered inclusion of many in the creation of their medicine bottle. According to Target (2010), their new Clear Rx bottle design started with a strong dose of common sense. Its features reduce the chance of taking the wrong dose or confusing medications among family members. This concept also improves medication packaging and design as well as making prescription and health information easier to use. Here is a list of its features:

- Clear, simple, and easy to read labels with larger type and clear instruction
- Personalized color rings for each member of the family

- Clear, simple, and easy-to-read patient information to help the patient understand the details
- Convenient top label that identifies the prescription it holds
- Larger print used and "cautions" visible at a glance
- A blunder-proof dispenser that precisely measures liquids into an oral syringe that also eliminates a mess
- A handy label magnifier that fits behind the patient care information— provided on request, free of charge

As is shown in Figure 4.1, this medicine bottle provides convenience, safety, and readability for the patient. It is safe for the user, adapts to any age group. Thus, it meets the criteria (adaptable and secure) for an inclusive product.

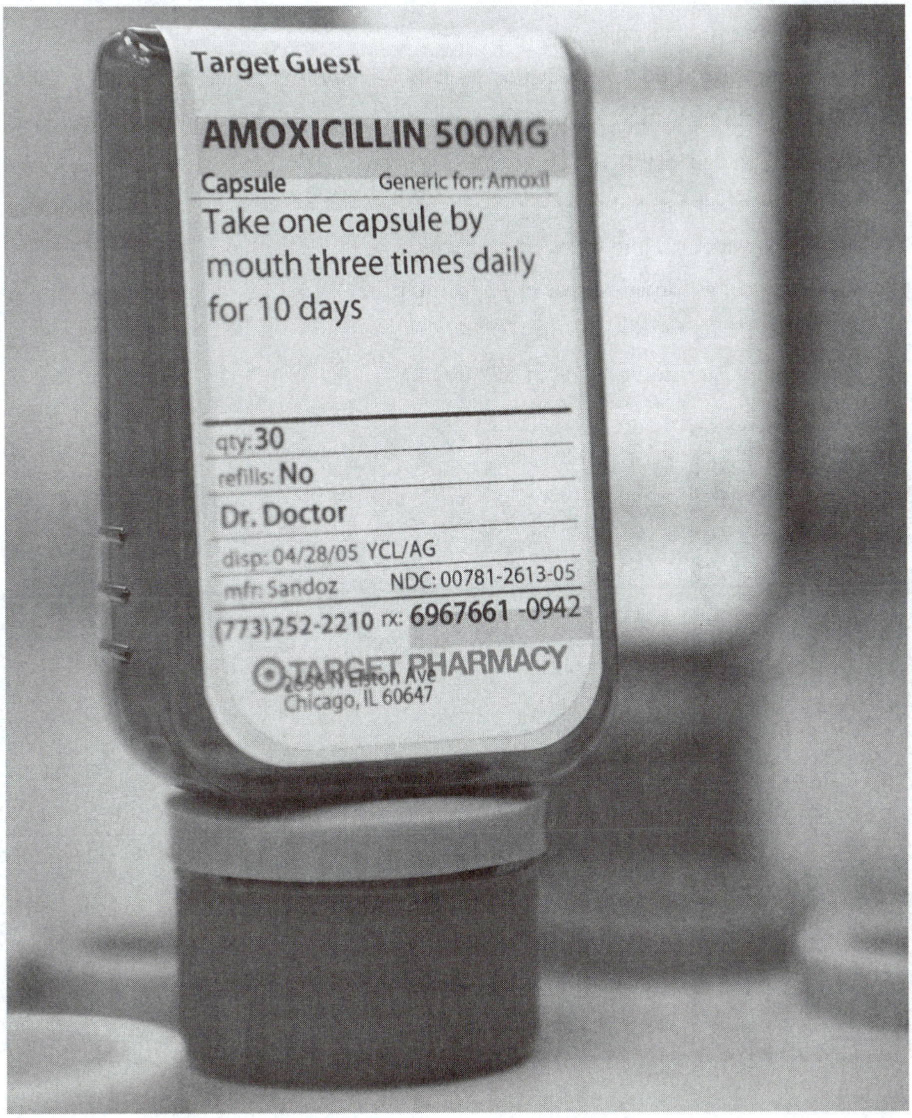

Figure 4.1

Target's flat-faced medicine bottle is easy to read, use, and is safe. Scott Olson/Getty Images

FAUCET DESIGN

As designers research and specify products for various environments, they must be inclusive of everyone who may use that product. Faucets must be accessible to all, whether at home or work or in a public environment.

The Delta Single Hole Electronic Lavatory (2010a) faucet for the bathroom complies with the ADA and includes (or is inclusive of) everyone. It senses movement and eliminates the need for a user to turn the faucet on or off, which is easier for those with physical impairments (see Figure 4.2a). The Delta (2010b) Pilar® Pull-Down with Touch20™ Technology faucet exhibits accessible qualities that works like a handle—by touching part of the "hand," or spout, the water will turn on or off (see Figure 4.2b). The handle is used to adjust to temperature and flow rate. Users do not need to touch the handle when washing dishes or when turning the water on and off. It can even turn itself off. This method conserves water and reduces the potential for cross-contamination from messy hands.

The Delta Pilar® Pull-Down with Touch20™ Technology faucet has many features that coincide with inclusive design criteria: it is responsive (it responds to an individual's various needs) and adaptable (it is easy to use and has convenient features).

- Convenient functions
- Turns water on and off with a touch
- Turns off automatically after a specific time
- Appropriate for any décor
- Anyone can use with touch features

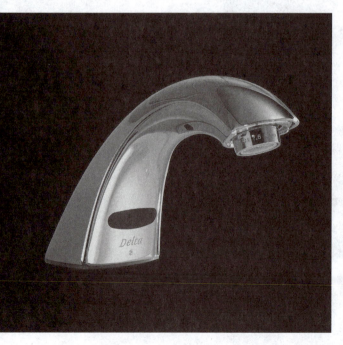

Figure 4.2a

This Delta Single Hole Electronic Lavatory faucet complies with the ADA. It senses movement that eliminates the need to turn the faucet on or off. © Delta Faucet

Figure 4.2b

A Delta Pilar® Pull-Down with Touch20™ Technology faucet that turns on and off by touching the faucet or handle. © Delta Faucet

- Temperature controls and amount of water controlled by handle that is easy to adjust
- Allows just a touch to start the flow of water
- Touch of the forearm or wrist starts the flow of water, which reduces the potential for cross-contamination from messy hands

As is shown in Figure 4.2a and 4.2b, these faucets have a basic design that fits many décors and are adaptable for various users; thus they both meet important criteria for an inclusive product.

Creating an Easier Way of Shopping

Individuals who must depend on wheelchairs to move from place to place often find shopping difficult. Designed by MIT's engineering students, the Grocery Mate makes shopping easier. Turn to the color pages of this book, where "Wheelchair Shopping with the Grocery Mate" describes the reason, purpose, and operation of their invention.

Changes Due to Technology

Technology, particularly electronic technology, has changed the face of our society with computers, cellphones, **iPods, global positioning systems (GPS)**, and more. As technology companies offer consumers more choices, the opportunity is created to integrate inclusivity into each product (Stephanidis, 2009). Computers are one example of creating access to all.

COMPUTERS

In the early 1990s, accessibility to computers for those with special needs was generally provided through add-ons. At that time, only Apple computers had built-in access features such as Sticky Keys and Mouse Keys, which were designed for those with physical or motor skill difficulties. Also, at that time, computers played an important role in education and employment, but it wasn't until the mid to late 1990s when they became more common in homes and offices. It was not until the development of Windows 95 that regular accessible features were introduced into a PC operating system (Vanderheiden, 2008). Today, computers are everywhere—in schools, homes, offices—and hand-held devices such as cellphones and iPods provide connection to the Internet and email as well. For this reason, many computers and hand-held devices provide some assistive technologies that make them usable for everyone.

The Apple computer (Macintosh) comes with a wide range of assistive technologies. In other words, a Mac works for everyone regardless of ability, and its inclusive access features are built into the computer. The following are a few examples found on the website for Apple, Inc. (2010a).

Vision

As part of many Apple computers, a variety of built-in tools and technologies help people with visual impairments (2010e). These include:

- Built-in screen reading called **VoiceOver** controls the computer for those who are blind or have low-vision (see Figure 4.3)
- Braille mirroring enables multiple **Braille** devices along with the VoiceOver feature
- Screen magnification can increase items up to 40 times for those with low-vision.
- Video display can be adjusted (e.g., increase and decrease contrast, switch to grayscale, changing the screen to white-on-black, black-on-white)

Hearing

A variety of features are designed to assist individuals who have difficulty hearing computer speech, sound, and alerts (2010a). These include:

- **iChat**, a communication tool that uses Internet-based text, audio, and video conferencing
- Open- and closed-captioning
- Screen flashing that serves as an alert

Physical and Motor Skills

A variety of features are designed to help individuals navigate the computer if they have difficulties using the keyboard and mouse or **trackpad** (2010d). These include:

- Slow keys to help avoid typing errors and multiple key strokes
- Mouse keys on the numeric keyboard that can control mouse pointer (see Figure 4.4)
- Complex, routine tasks that can be automatically performed or with the aid of voice activation
- Custom keyboard shortcuts

Literacy and Learning

Features are provided that simplify tasks as well as make them easy to learn (2010c). These include:

- Simple finder
- Built-in dictionary

Figure 4.3

To aid someone with visual limitations, the VoiceOver (e.g., computer voice) describes items on the screen. The keyboard can also be used to control the computer.

Figure 4.4

For those with difficulty using a mouse or trackpad, the mouse keys can be used to control the mouse pointer using keys on a numeric keypad. You can even click the mouse button and hold it down to drag and drop items on the screen and navigate menus, the dock, windows, toolbars, palettes, and other controls.

INCLUSIVE DESIGN CHOICES AND COMPUTERS

From this example, it is clear that today's computers are inclusive—designed for all. However, not all computers provide equal access.

Microsoft also provides various types of assistive technology products. These products are designed to provide additional accessibility to people who have physical or cognitive difficulties, limitations, and disabilities. In selecting the appropriate product, it must be compatible with the computer operating system and program on the computer. Some, but not all, accessible features are built into Windows and other Microsoft products; therefore, Microsoft suggests working with a Microsoft Accessibility Resource Center. These centers are located throughout the country and will help identify the correct assistive technology. However, Windows 7 operating system now features the Ease of Access Center to add assistive features. Thus, internal features for new operating systems have simplified access to assistive technology.

OTHER ELECTRONIC DEVICES

The Apple **iPhone** 4 features VoiceOver for the visually impaired, video for the hearing impaired, magnifications, high contrast, and support for closed captioning (Apple, Inc., 2010b). This electronic device used some assistive technologies in its design.

Other cellphones such as the Motorola DROID, BlackBerry, Samsung cellphones, and others have features that provide assistive technology, but some have limited capabilities. Standard features include volume control and a speakerphone.

The Motorola DROID also includes text telephone (TTY) compatibility, hearing-aid compatibility, and a touch screen (Motorola, 2010) (Figure 4.5).

GPS or navigation systems are designed to make traveling from place to place easier. These systems are voice activated as well as provide visual directions. Particularly helpful is the voice that tells the driver the appropriate lane changes to prepare for a turn. Often, the voice gives three reminders prior to a turn so the driver has time to make the transition from one lane to another. Some GPS units also have touch screens to make them easier to operate (Garmin, 2010). These features are inclusive of many people.

DISADVANTAGES TO ELECTRONIC DEVICES

Designing electronic devices with **assistive technologies** varies from many features to very few or none. Even though many companies know these devices are needed, they may or may not implement them because it is not profitable to make products more accessible (Vanderheiden, 2009). To remedy this problem, manufacturers need to consider ways to create accessibility for these products in the design phase as well as at a reasonable cost to the wholesaler and the consumer.

For the consumer, these electronic devices—computers or handheld—with assistive technologies often come at a higher cost. This means that those with disabilities may not have the same access as others, thus creating a division between those who can afford the device and those who cannot. Additionally, there is not only the cost of the device but also access to services such as Internet connections (Vanderheiden, 2008).

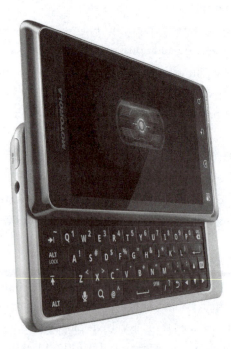

Figure 4.5

Features on this Motorola DROID allow for universal access such as volume control, speakerphone, text telephone (TTY) compatibility, hearing aid compatibility, and a touch screen. © Motorola Mobility, Inc.

Some communities, on the other hand, provide free Internet access in public libraries or other public areas, wireless Internet service throughout the city, and community education courses on how to use these devices. If affordable, devices such as the DROID run on their own network and, thus, external Internet access is not needed. However, to be inclusive, everyone should have access wherever they are located (public building or private residence) and communities should also provide free public education on operating various electronic devices (e.g., computers, software, and so on).

Furniture

Furniture with inclusive design features is also available. Just as with other product designs, furniture may also have an up-to-date or traditional design, or it may include advanced technology for easy use.

LIFT CHAIR

People whose legs and/or arms are weak need assistance getting out of some chairs. Lift chairs have been designed for that purpose; however, some manufacturers tilt the entire chair, which does not look like a regular piece of furniture in the lift position. The Risedale (2010) seat-lift chair has remedied this by designing a chair that is stylish with the seat only functioning as the lift. Because only the seat rises rather than the entire chair, it has a universal look that could be used in a residential setting—homes, apartments, and assisted living. (See Figure 4.6.)

The seat-lift chair is designed for easy movement upward and gives the sitter a safe, secure feeling because of the flexible seat that is designed to move up and down while staying on a level plane. While seated, the sitter is on a level surface during all stages of lifting and avoids a dumping action that may occur if the entire chair lifts and tilts.

The lift chair has many features that coincide with inclusive design criteria of adaptable (easily and safely aids function and maintains dignity of user) and accessible (removes barriers) design, including:

- A classic design with an open-legged, wingback look that lends itself to most interior designs and, thus, gives the user a feeling of inclusion
- A traditional design that is appropriate for most interior uses
- An available ottoman
- Availability in four colors
- A durable 100 percent polyester upholstery fabric
- A flexible seat
- A simple and uncomplicated power lever
- A hidden power lever that makes it impossible to know it is a lift chair
- A power lever that lifts the sitter up, while a simple pull lowers the sitter down

- A power lever that may be placed on both sides
- A seat that lifts up and forward rather than just forward
- A seat that avoids an unsafe dumping action
- Adjustable legs that lower 1.5" for users under 5'1"

As shown in Figure 4.6, the chair has a classic design that fits many décors and is adaptable to many people. Thus, it meets the criteria for an inclusively designed product.

ARMCHAIR

The lift chair is one solution when individuals have difficulty lifting themselves out of a chair, but using the arms of an armchair is another more traditional solution. In this case, the individual must have greater arm strength than one needing a lift

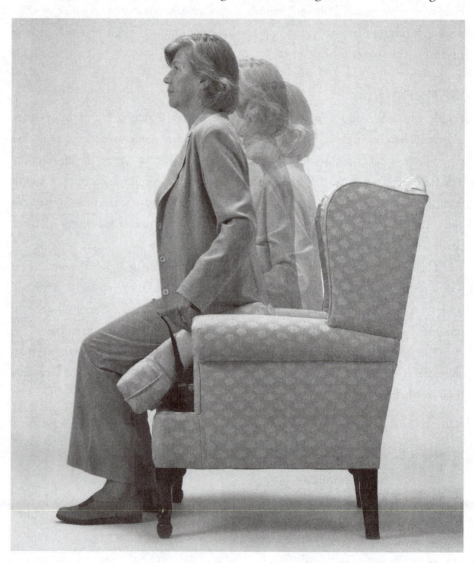

Figure 4.6

The Risedale Seat Lift Chair is a traditional and stylish solution that easily raises and lifts the sitter. The power lever lifts the seat up and forward preventing a dumping effect. It is appropriate with a variety of design concepts with its classic open-legged, wing-chair look. Photo courtesy of Uplift Technologies Inc.

chair. Thus, the chair's arms provide support for those who need to push themselves up from the chair.

FURNITURE IN COMMERCIAL SETTINGS

Ergonomics is an applied science that studies the relationship between human beings and their functions within their environment—the way bodies work efficiently in space. "Ergonomics applies anthropometric data in order to give users comfort and efficiency in completing tasks while sitting standing, or walking" (Nussbaumer, 2009).

In observing humans in their environment, it is often easy to tell whether ergonomics did or did not play a role in the selection of products or furniture. For example, if the sitter's feet are dangling or the knees are high above the seat, individual users were not considered in the design process. Rather, furniture was selected for the comfort of the average-sized human.

Waiting Room or Lobby Furniture

Furniture in areas such as waiting rooms or spaces in which people congregate is often selected for the average person. It is possible, however, to select furniture that provides seating for various sizes within large waiting rooms or lobbies. For example, selections may include **bariatric** furniture for large individuals, a few adjustable pieces for short and tall individuals, and the majority for average individuals. The problem is that adjustable seating in these locations (e.g., waiting rooms and lobbies) may be more costly, but if the waiting time is lengthy within these spaces, providing pieces in a variety of sizes will offer comfort to everyone. Hill-Rom® has designed waiting room chairs that provide bariatric and regular seating. In Figure 4.7, both are included in one tandem section, and thus comfortable seating is provided for many (Figure 4.7).

Figure 4.7

Hill-Rom® has designed waiting room chairs that provide bariatric and regular seating. © 2011 Hill-Rom Services, Inc. Reprinted with permission—all rights reserved

Office Furniture

In an office, furniture selection must take into account individuals using the space on a daily basis. Whether in an office or a classroom, adjustability and flexibility of chairs, keyboards, or workstations provide an ergonomically designed environment. To analyze a product for ergonomics, the inclusive design criteria are the same; however, an emphasis should be on physical health and comfort (criteria: responsive, adaptable, secure).

For example, many jobs require extended periods of time on the computer and are, therefore, often associated with upper-body **musculoskeletal disorders**. Alternative keyboards help prevent uncomfortable upper-body postures; however, it is unclear how these keyboards reduce stress on wrist and arm posture. The research summary "How Alternative Keyboards Affect Arm Position" from InformeDesign (2007, April 30) describes a study that evaluated the effect of six keyboard types on wrist and forearm posture and typing speed as well. This study found that each individual should be provided a choice of keyboards to determine which is most comfortable. Thus, the keyboard selected must respond to an individual's needs. For further details on this study, see Study Sketch 4.1: "How Alternative Keyboards Affect Arm Position."

A variety of keyboard supports are common; however, improvements are continually being made to provide healthy work conditions. For example, Steelcase has designed a keyboard platform with a mouse pad at the same horizontal plane, but the mouse surface adjusts for the left or right hand (Figure 4.8).

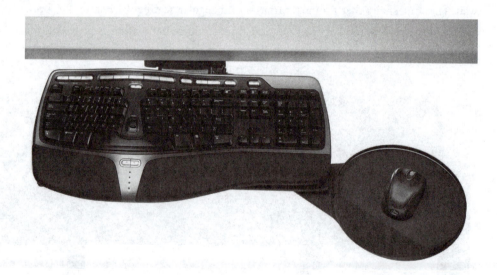

Figure 4.8

Steelcase has designed a keyboard platform with a mouse pad at the same horizontal plane; the mouse surface adjusts for the left or right hand. © Steelcase

STUDY SKETCH 4.1: How Alternative Keyboards Affect Arm Position

Many jobs require working at a computer for an extended period of time, thus some people develop upper-body muscular disorders. Alternative keyboards may solve this problem. A study was conducted to evaluate "the effect of six keyboard types on wrist and forearm posture" as well as typing speed.

Subjects

A total of 105 subjects (67 female and 38 male with an average age of 30.9) were selected from a university campus (47 participants) and a local temporary employment agency (58 participants). Subjects were given a practice session on the alternative keyboards prior to performing the randomized touch-typing test at a workstation under controlled conditions, which included work surface positions, chair type and position, monitor, and keyboard. Six keyboard designs were evaluated:

1. A conventional keyboard
2. A conventional laptop
3. A fixed, split keyboard with 6-degree split, but no gable
4. A fixed, split keyboard with 12-degree split and 8-degree gable
5. A fixed, split keyboard with 12-degree split, 14-degree gable, and zero-degree slope
6. A fixed, split keyboard with 12-degree split, 14-degree gable, and negative 7-degree slope

Testing

During the test, researchers measured subjects' postures and collected motion analysis using an infrared light-emitting diode that recorded typing speed. After finishing the typing test, subjects completed the comfort questionnaire for the keyboard in which they selected their first choice keyboard and ranked all keyboards using five categories (ease of use, speed, accuracy, comfort, and overall) from best to least favorable.

Criteria

From this study, design criteria were identified:

1. The keyboard type influences wrist and forearm postures regardless of other workstation features (e.g., chair or work surface).
2. Keyboard users with hand or arm pain should be advised to select keyboards and workstations that maintain neutral wrist and forearm postures, reduce shoulder strain, and provide comfort for the user.
3. An alternative keyboard contributes to a neutral wrist and forearm posture and gives comfort to the user.

Implications

Although this study was conducted among a large number of subjects (105), the brief exposure to alternative keyboards prior to testing may have impacted subjects' preference. This, however, may indicate that each individual should have a choice of keyboards to determine which is most comfortable.

Source: InformeDesign (2007, April 30). "How alternative keyboards affect arm position." Retrieved on July 2, 2010, from http://www.informedesign.umn.edu/Rs_detail.aspx?rsId=2758

Environmentally Friendly Products

Sustainable design is a type of design that concerns the environment and its impact on humans. This type of design specifically applies conservation of natural resources and promotion of good outdoor and indoor air quality; therefore, if a product or material is safe for the global and interior environment, it is safe for all. Additionally, such a product or material will meet inclusive design's secure criteria related to health, safety, and welfare.

INDOOR AIR QUALITY

An important concern is the effect of **indoor air quality** on human health. Many products and materials affect indoor air quality; they may include building materials, interior finishes, furniture, fabrics, cleaning products, cosmetics, personal hygiene products, and more. These products may emit gases into the air from **volatile organic compounds (VOCs)**, **formaldehyde**, or other chemicals. When installed or used, products and materials containing these chemicals may continue to affect the interior. "**Toxins** from various chemicals are absorbed into other materials and later desorbed back into the interior; this is called the **sink** effect… Therefore, materials must be carefully researched, selected, and specified to minimize indoor air pollution" (Nussbaumer, 2009, p. 121). Clearly, products that support good IAQ are inclusive of all occupants.

Research and Development

Products have been studied for a variety of reasons. Researchers at universities, research institutes, and corporations conduct research that can significantly change the way a product is designed. The following are examples of research projects conducted to improve products as they relate to inclusive design.

TESTING PRODUCTS FOR INCLUSIVE DESIGN FEATURES

Corporations test products in the design phase, but often researchers will also test products or even develop surveys to test products. In the research summary "Designing Usable Products for Everyone" from InformeDesign (2006, April 12), a survey instrument was developed and tested on a small group. The survey was then tested on a larger group of subjects of varying ages and abilities. Results indicate that that many products are not designed with everyone in mind. See Study Sketch 4.2: "Designing Usable Products for Everyone" for further information about this study.

REACHING ABILITIES WHILE SEATED

People who use wheelchairs often have difficulty reaching to the front, side, and back; therefore, the purpose of the research study summary "Understanding Seated Reaching Abilities" from InformeDesign (2010, February 11) was to measure how far people could reach without losing their balance. This study replicated someone sitting in a wheelchair while trying to reach. The study determined that some individuals need counterbalancing supports (e.g., a handle for the nonreaching hand) to ensure safety in a reaching task. This information is helpful when designing wheelchairs that are safe for everyone (i.e., meeting the accessible and secure criteria). See Study Sketch 4.3: "Understanding Seated Reaching Abilities" for further information about this study.

RESEARCH AND DEVELOPMENT

Many corporations use research to create new products. Some have research and development (R&D) teams within corporations. These R&D teams conduct research and then use their research to develop new materials and products.

STUDY SKETCH 4.3: Understanding Seated Reaching Abilities

This study indicated that previous studies have not identified standard averages for the distance that people can safely reach while sitting based on age and body measurements. This is important to identify because average reach distances are used to determine placement of shelving or products. The purpose of this experiment was to measure the distance that seated people could reach without losing their balance. This study replicated someone sitting in a wheelchair while trying to reach.

There were 38 subjects (20 male and 18 female; ages 21 to 74 and healthy; 4'7" to 5'll" tall; 110 to 293 pounds with 12 of the 38 obese). The subjects were tested while sitting on a platform with their feet off the ground. Subjects were asked to reach to the side, forward at a 30-degree angle, and backward at a 30-degree angle. "Each reach was completed twice" with the longer reach recorded. A pressure-sensitive pad was attached to the platform to locate the **ischial tuberosity**, or bony area that bears the weight of the body while sitting.

Results

The study determined that the ischial tuberosity affects balance and, thus, reach. The uppermost and outer portion of the thighbone provided more balance support. "Taller and younger people had a longer center of pressure than shorter and older people." The center of pressure aids balance. Subjects with larger hip widths had shorter maximum center of pressure. The larger hip width occurred with those who were obese and had a larger amount of soft tissue. Thus, the hip breadth as a predictor for reach may be misleading.

Implications

The study determined that some individuals need "counterbalancing supports (e.g., a handle for the nonreach hand) to ensure safety in a reaching task." This information is helpful when designing wheelchairs that are safe for everyone.

Source: InformeDesign. (2010, February 11). "Understanding seated reaching abilities." Retrieved on July 2, 2010, from http://www.informedesign.umn.edu/Rs_detail.aspx?rsId=3388

Height-Adjustable Desk

Steelcase, Inc. (2010) used research to develop a new desk. Research showed that "changing position through the day increases blood flow, decreases lower and upper body discomfort, and increases productivity" (para. 2). From this information, Steelcase developed a desk (Airtouch Height-Adjustable Desk) that promotes healthy ergonomics (secure criterion) by allowing the user to change positions from sitting to standing—(adaptable and responsive criteria). See Figure 4.9.

Seating

Haworth, the office furniture manufacturer, spent two years in research and development that led to new product innovations for Zody seating. The Human Performance Institute at Western Michigan University (WMU) was commissioned by Haworth to conduct the research.

The WMU research study evaluated and quantified the comfort of the lower back while sitting in a task chair. Haworth also conducted research and development on specific components of the chair. Throughout the research, great care was taken to ensure that the chair's comfort components were consistent with the intended design. Results from both studies were applied to the design of the Zody chair's lumbar support, pelvic support (PAL™), and mesh upholstery. The end result of their research was a chair that works with the body; the chair is "ergonomically advanced, exceptionally comfortable, sleek, and stylish" as well (Bellingar, Beyer, & Wilkerson, 2009, p. 5). From this, it is clear that this chair fits several inclusive design criteria: it is responsive to individual needs, adaptable to the user, and secure for the physical health and well being of the sitter.

The Zody chair is also environmentally friendly in ways that have a positive effect on indoor air quality because it is a low-emitting product. It also meets other sustainable criteria by using renewable energy sources during manufacture; it has up to 51 percent recycled content; and it is nearly 98 percent recyclable.

Many products are being created—as is the Zody chair (see Figure 4.10)—that incorporate adaptability (an inclusive design criterion) and ergonomics with sustainable design features. This will only continue as the demand increases.

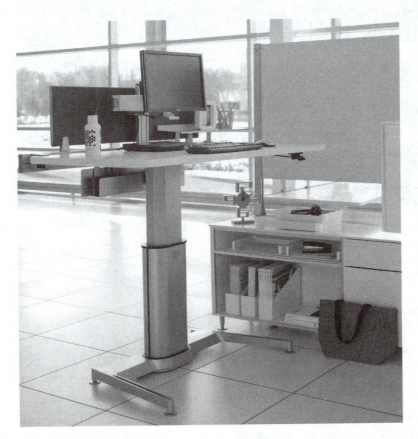

Figure 4.9

The Airtouch desk requires no electric power and easily adjusts up and down with an ergonomic lift handle in about 1 second from 26″ to 43″ with infinite increments. © Steelcase

Figure 4.10

The Zody chair by Haworth is ergonomically advanced, comfortable, sleek, and stylish. Courtesy of Haworth

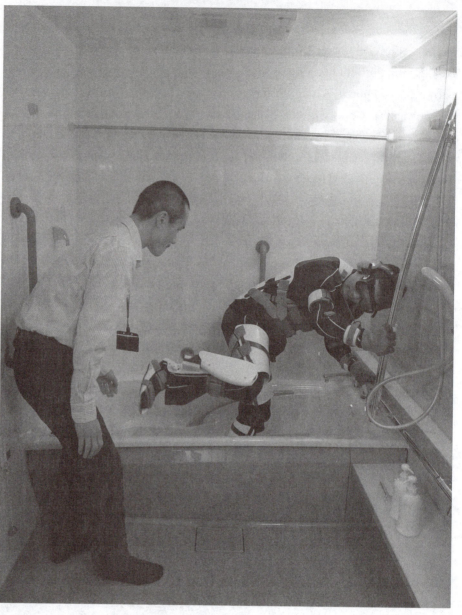

Figure 4.11

The TOTO Universal Design Center in Japan conducts simulations to reproduce limited range of motion experienced by older bathers. © TOTO USA, Inc.

Bath Products

TOTO, a Japanese-based manufacturer of bath products, has established the Universal Design Research Center in Japan—the only such center in the world. TOTO monitors 280 people in various situations to develop products that are inclusive. In their research, they study human movements as well as consider the use and purpose of the products. Their goal is to create balance between elegance and usefulness, beauty and accessibility, unobtrusiveness and flexibility as well as creating products that are easy and safe to use (TOTO, 2010, October 4). Figure 4.11 shows a test in progress.

Summary

Any product or material can be analyzed for inclusive design criteria (responsive, adaptable, accessible, and secure), as was demonstrated in this chapter. For the product to be inclusive it must meet more than the basics of accessibility. Many of today's technologies provide some access, but not necessarily to everyone and not with all criteria met.

Products must also be ergonomically correct and comfortably fit the body while the user conducts various tasks. This is important when meeting adaptability and being responsive to the individual. Additionally, meeting secure criteria requires attention paid to ergonomics to keep the physical body healthy and safe from injury.

Inclusive Design Projects

EXPERIENTIAL PROJECTS

1. How does product design meet inclusive criteria?

Analyzing and comparing products increases an understanding of inclusive design. For this exercise, locate two similar products (e.g., two types of kitchen utensils, kitchen or bathroom fixtures, task chairs, dining chairs, desks, or other products) and list characteristics of each that meet (or do not meet) inclusive design criteria (responsive, adaptable, accessible, and secure); then compare and analyze their similarities and differences related to the criteria.

2. Technologies are inclusive—or are they?

Technology is important in today's society, and for this reason, technologies need to be inclusive. The question is, "Are all technologies inclusive?" The following exercise investigates this question.

1. Locate two types of communication technology (cell phones, computers, mouse, or another technology).
2. List the characteristics of each that meet (or do not meet) inclusive design criteria (responsive, adaptable, accessible, and secure).
3. Compare and analyze their similarities and differences as they relate to the criteria.
4. Explain how the technologies can improve to become more inclusive.

APPLICATION PROJECT

1. How are ergonomics, sustainability, and inclusive design incorporated into one design?

Often products have characteristics of inclusivity as well as ergonomics and sustainability. Today, many designers and clients require ergonomically designed products that are sustainable. This exercise is intended to have students consider all three (ergonomics, sustainability, and inclusivity) in one. Complete the following:

1. Locate and describe a product or material that incorporates all three (ergonomics, sustainability, and inclusive design).

2. Using the product or material, consider the type of interior environment where ergonomics, sustainability, and inclusive design will be used.

3. Describe that type of interior environment.

CHAPTER 5

Residential Design

"It used to be that designers made an object and walked away. Today the emphasis must shift to designing the entire life cycle."

—*Paul Saffo*

OBJECTIVES

▼ Explain the difference between quality and quantity in housing

▼ Describe ways an accessibility specialist or occupational therapist can assist in creating an inclusively designed home

▼ Describe issues related to the aging eye and ways to create a supportive environment for the older adult

▼ Explain ways to renovate an historic building and still preserve its historic integrity

▼ Explain how visitability relates to inclusive design

▼ Describe how an existing home can become inclusively designed

▼ Explain ways that a kitchen can be designed to be inclusive

▼ Explain ways a bathroom can be designed to be inclusive

▼ List the advantages and disadvantages of various housing options for older adults

▼ Explain how Fair Housing Act (FHA) applies to accessible housing

▼ Discuss the advantages and disadvantages of aging in place

▼ Describe how sustainable and inclusive design can be applied in housing

▼ Discuss issues related to the application of inclusive design in affordable housing

▼ Explain why understanding other cultures is important in design

▼ Explain what is meant by cultural regionalism

A private residence should reflect the person or family who inhabits it. It should also adapt to guests who enter. Unfortunately, very few residential environments are accessible to all, and the majority of those that are have not applied inclusive design criteria. In fact, most residential design is not designed for various stages in the lifecycle (i.e., small children to the aging adult). To do so, apply the following to the design or renovation of a residential environment:

- Consider the quality of an environment rather than spatial quantity.
- Use an accessibility specialist or **occupational therapist** along with designers for home modifications.
- Plan appropriate lighting for the aging eye.
- Use inclusive design criteria to renovate historic buildings.
- Apply inclusive design criteria and good indoor air quality to all types of residential housing.

For older adults, various housing options are available as they age. They may choose to move from a single-family home to an apartment, condominium, a retirement community, congregate housing, or another type of dwelling. Even with these options, many older adults will choose to **age in place** (i.e., remain in long-term housing—a place with which they are familiar). In this case, if the home was not designed for various life stages, retrofitting may be necessary to accommodate changing needs.

Quality Versus Quantity

For several decades, many people aspired to own a **McMansion**. But in the last decade and, more recently, due to economic conditions, more people are interested in smaller homes—less square footage and volume. With the change to smaller homes, there is also a change in lifestyle that translates into the overall home layout. Although kitchen and bath remodeling continues, some homes are designed with fewer bathrooms, and there is also a decrease in property improvements such as formal landscaping with decorative water features, gazebos, and tennis courts (Peachy Green, 2011).

With decrease in size, some are opting for quality rather than quantity. Architect Sarah Susanka (2001) coined the phrase "the not so big house" and wrote a book by the same title. Her inspiration for writing the book came from a concern that interiors of large suburban houses lacked character and psychological warmth. She suggests that a house represents more than square footage with a specified number of bedrooms and baths. It should express the owner's personality and provide comfort for all occupants. If this is the case, a house must be designed for all of life's stages and, thus, be inclusive for all. To do so, an interior designer as well as an accessibility specialist or occupational therapist that specializes in accessibility can provide assistance in renovation or modification as well as in new construction.

Occupational Therapy

When a person's physical mobility changes, he or she may find it difficult to maneuver into and throughout the home as well as complete daily tasks. These changes may happen as a person ages, from injury or surgery, or from other life-changing occurrences. Occupational therapists are trained to recommend and implement strategies for every room to help a person perform daily tasks in an effective and efficient manner. Their involvement is in addition to the design team and residents.

According to the American Occupational Therapy Association (AOTA) (2007), an occupational therapist can recommend the following:

- In the bathroom:
  - Replace the toilet with a higher model or a longer seat for people in wheelchairs or with limited hip movement.
  - Install handheld showerheads, large shower and bath controls, and grab bars around the bathtub walls.
  - Install faucets with a lever control for people with a weak grip.
  - Identify design features that will promote safety and comfort.
- In the kitchen:
  - Lower sinks and countertops to accommodate wheelchairs.
  - Store often-used items in easy-to-reach places.
  - Design workspace to accommodate seated activities, such as lower countertops with beveled, rounded corners.
- In hallways and doorways:
  - Create clear, unobstructed openings that a person in a wheelchair or with a cane can pass through easily.
  - Create entryways and hallways with a 32-inch clearance.
  - Ensure that thresholds are level with the floor.
  - Install secure carpets or runners in hallways or stairwells to provide traction.
  - Install handrails for gripping.
- In the living room and bedroom:
  - Arrange furniture so that it creates open space and clear passage.
  - Place the bed where it is easily accessible to a person in a wheelchair.
  - Place the telephone where it is easily accessible.
  - Install locks on exit doors, if a person is likely to wander.
  - Increase home security if a person is likely to wander (para. 2).

Home modifications provide the opportunity for a person who is aging or has a disability to remain in his or her home as long as possible (AOTA, 2007). As suggested through the inclusive design criteria, being responsive is to involve everyone in the design process. In this case, it includes the individual needing the home modification, family members, designers, occupational therapists, contractors, electricians, and others such as those involved in the person's care.

Families, in particular, can be involved with the occupational therapist and aid the person who is aging or has a disability in several ways. AOTA (2007) suggests that they can:

- Investigate and suggest resources to remain independent.
- Help facilitate his or her independence by assisting with access to community resources.
- Introduce changes slowly to incur as little disruption as possible.
- Ensure the contractor and builder are licensed and insured.

Case Study 5.1: "Design for Dwarfism" describes a design project for dwarfism that utilizes the occupational therapist, interior designers, and industrial designers in one project. For more information regarding home modifications using the occupational therapist, view the American Occupational Therapy Association website (http://www.aota.org/) for more detail (AOTA, 2007).

Lighting and the Aging Eye

The eye allows a person to see by detecting light. When a person ages, there is a reduction in pupil size and, thus, a reduction in the amount of light entering the eye. This means the quality of vision changes (*The Eye Digest*, 2009).

As a person ages, elasticity of muscles is reduced. This means that eyes adjust more slowly to changes in light levels. This can reduce the person's ability to discern details, which makes it difficult to see edges, changes in flooring, or even food on a plate. Issues with light level changes may also result in a "dazzle effect called **contrast glare** that makes it more difficult to focus when moving between light levels" (Leibrock, 2000, p. 78).

Contrast glare is a great concern when designing for people as they age. If a person is unable to focus from one light level to another, it affects the ability to see changes in a walking surface (e.g., heights, material changes, corners), and the person could more easily fall and be injured. For example, moving from a dark, low-lit interior to bright outdoor light can cause contrast glare. Also, the use of wall-mounted fluorescent fixtures on the head wall (above the bed) in a hospital room can cause contrast glare (Leibrock, 2000).

As a person ages, the eye lens thickens and makes a person more susceptible to **veiling reflections** (or **veiling glare**). Veiling reflections can be experienced when looking at shiny paper or shiny flooring. Veiling reflections on a shiny floor surface, for example, may read as water to the aging eye. When a person with an aging eye experiences veiling reflections, it may cause him or her to fear falling (Leibrock, 2000).

As a person ages, the pupil becomes smaller and the lens denser. This restricts depth perception and causes problems with spatial orientation and mobility. "For example, a strip across a hallway could be perceived as a stair or a change in elevation. Shadows from high-contrast lighting may have the same effect" (Leibrock, 2000, p. 81). To eliminate shadows, lighting levels should be kept even. However, some contrast is needed in specific areas to distinguish between flooring and walls. Contrast also is helpful for those with poor peripheral vision.

About 85 percent of older people experience a yellow tinting of the eye lens. Cool colors (e.g., blue-green and blue-violet) become grayed, which makes it almost impossible to see the edge of a blue sofa, chair, or ottoman placed on a blue carpet. Thus, this can cause an older person to fall (Leibrock, 2000).

Because the aging eye may experience glare, problems with depth perception, or the graying of colors, extreme care must be taken in choosing colors, materials, and lighting for interiors used by older adults.

Other issues in aging relate to eye diseases such as **cataracts, glaucoma, age-related macular degeneration**, and others. A cataract progressively clouds the eye lens, and thus, vision becomes blurry and totally cloudy. **Cataracts** occur as the result of aging; however, they can occur from unhealthy lifestyles such as smoking. Cataract surgery is common, and with cataract removal, vision greatly improves (National Eye Institute, 2010b).

Glaucoma is an eye disease that can damage the optic nerve and result in vision loss and blindness. When pressure within the eye increases, it damages the optic nerve because of the buildup of fluid inside the eye. The result is blind spots in the field of vision. If detected in the early states, glaucoma can be treated; however, if left untreated, it can cause irreversible blindness (Improve Your Vision.com, 2009; National Eye Institute, 2010c).

Age-related macular degeneration (AMD) is the leading cause of blindness and a disease that blurs the sharp, central vision needed for frontal activities such as reading, driving, and sewing. AMD affects the part of the eye that allows a person to see fine detail (Improve Your Vision.com, 2009; National Eye Institute, 2010a).

With this knowledge, it is clear that designing for older adults must consider visual changes related to age and/or disease. Great care in the selection and placement of materials, colors, and lighting is crucial to the well being of the aging person.

Design for Dwarfism

MJ Divino, Mary Falzarano, and Matt Johnson from Kean University

"What if we designed a house specifically for a person with dwarfism and a person of average height living together?"

From that one simple question, a design studio assignment was developed, but it would become so much more than an isolated theoretical design problem. To design for people with such unique characteristics, interior design students would be asked to delve into the "client's" needs to a point which they had never experienced. In addition, specific products would need to be developed to use in the design of a living space for this client. To remedy this, the Interior Design program at Kean University (Union, New Jersey) was able to take advantage of the expertise of two other programs within the University: Occupational Therapy and Industrial Design.

Occupational Therapy

XYZ Design Company has been contracted to redesign a home for a mixed height couple.

The job was to redesign a living space based on a universal and inclusive design that was accessible and usable for the two clients: Sue, a person with dwarfism, and her new husband, Joe, a man of average height. The home was a five-room, two-story small house.

Given the XYZ design firm had not had a request to redesign a home for a couple with these different needs, they researched the issues of a person with dwarfism to understand generalized issues that would impact the design of the home for usability and inclusion for the husband of average height. Case Study Figure 5.1a shows students conducting research.

The designer found that people with dwarfism comprise approximately 5 percent of the population; however, there are more than 200 diagnoses and variations of short stature. People with dwarfism typically present with short stature (under 4'10") and with shorter than typical arms and legs. Some people have short fingers and smaller than average hands whereas others may be proportionate in the size of their head and hands, yet short trunk, legs and arms.

To further evaluate the needs of a person with dwarfism, and to completely

Case Study Figure 5.1a

Research is an integral part of the design process and promotes a successful design solution. Additionally, having all parties participating in the design process is also important. Here, as part of the learning process, students are conducting research for a design project. © Shutterstock

understand any physical issues that the husband of average height may present, the services of an occupational therapist (OT) were contracted. Occupational therapy is a science-driven, evidenced-based healthcare profession that uses meaningful and purposeful occupations as the agent of change for people of all ages with physical, psychosocial, and emotional limitations or impairments to participate in everyday life (AOTA, 2009). The OT utilized client-centered standardized evaluations to assess the physical abilities of the couple and to determine their living, work, and leisure interests.

Findings from the evaluation of the couple concluded the following. Sue is a 52-year-old woman who is 3'10" tall with spondyloepiphyseal dysplasia congenital (SEDc). She utilizes a motorized scooter for 95 percent of her mobility but can independently transfer off and on the scooter to other surfaces (car seat, bath, bed, toilet).

SEDc is an inherited disorder of bone growth, and because skeletal dysplasia is a lifelong condition Sue may require adaptations to her living space and items to decrease the amount of wear and tear on her joints. She may require the use of a power wheelchair as she ages. Sue had a surgical fusion of the cervical spine and bilateral total hip replacements. She has limitations in both shoulders and elbows, which limits her reach to no higher than eye level. Additionally, an arthritic condition and muscle weakness limits Sue's overall upper body strength. She is unable to stand for long periods of time and has less range of motion in her right hip than her left, thus she must always step up

stairs using her left leg first. She is able to ascend and descend stairs but requires the assistance of a cane and rail, and if the steps are over 4 inches high, she is unable to enter a building.

Joe is a 54-year-old man who reported that he had recently been diagnosed with multiple sclerosis (MS) that results in a mild neuropathy in both hands and feet. He shared that he is now only able to tolerate ambient lighting due to his diagnosis of MS. Joe further reports that he experiences occasional left hip pain.

Interior Design

Fourteen interior design students (in three teams) took on the challenge of designing a living space that was inclusive to both a person with dwarfism and a person of average height. Although the situation was fictitious, two individuals represented both clients. They were able to use general information about people with dwarfism from one client, and detailed information about the needs of both from the surveys conducted by the occupational therapy students.

All three teams developed unique and beautiful designs. Their goal was to create a living space that not only accommodated the functional needs of two different people who stressed the need for independent lifestyles but was also aesthetically pleasing to the point that "anyone" would want to live in the house. The students used further interviews of the clients to develop color palettes and material and furniture selections that were pleasing and comfortable. In the end, they were able to devise solutions with a combination of existing selections that were accommodating to people with dwarfism without making it look as if the home was designed specifically for people with dwarfism. Resale value of the home was a strong consideration for the project as well.

In the color pages of this book, Color Plates 23a and b show an example of one floor plan. Color Plate 15 shows a perspective of the kitchen and Color Plates 17 through 22 show greater details of the kitchen. These images demonstrate how the design is inclusive of both clients and appropriate for resale.

The value of the project for the interior design students was not only in the researching and learning of new aspects of design through the study of people with dwarfism. They learned that in addition to legislation such as the Americans with Disabilities Act (ADA), which is typically accommodating of people in wheelchairs, it is fundamentally incorrect to create designs that inherently ignore specific populations of people.

Also, creating an appropriate living environment for people with dwarfism requires the participation of not just interior designers and the client but also professionals who specialize in other facets of the process. As occupational therapy students educated interior design students in the beginning of the design process by teaching them how to gather client-centered information, industrial design students contributed by showing interior design students how their ideas are put to actual use towards the end of the design process.

Not only was the project successful from the interdisciplinary standpoint but was also extremely productive within the particular teams of interior design students as well. Traditionally, group projects are not the norm for interior design studio projects, and when used those projects are usually of a short duration (no more than one week). This is in stark contrast to interior design projects in the professional world, where working on one's own almost never happens. Right away, students were asked to work in a manner that was new and uncomfortable for them, and none of the students had ever worked with another interior design student for nine consecutive weeks on one single project.

Industrial Design

The industrial design portion of the project took place after the completion of the occupational therapy evaluations and the establishment of several overall interior space plans. The highly developed research and evaluation skills of the OT students proved extremely valuable in assessing the clients' situations and areas of need, whereas the interior design student concepts provided a framework around which ideas could crystallize. Using the information provided by these two groups, the industrial design students were able to create products particularly useful to the clients and that would fit harmoniously within the interior spaces.

After reviewing the evaluations and interior design concepts, the industrial designers set about imagining themselves as the clients living in the proposed spaces. The students imagined a full day's schedule, from rising in the morning until lying down to sleep at night. As they went hour by hour throughout the day, they noted any situations where someone of short stature might encounter difficulties. All the students then discussed these difficulties, determined which ones were the most common and found possible ways to alleviate them. This process resulted in two separate concepts with which to proceed. Both enable those with dwarfism and averaged height persons to have increased vertical access to areas within their home.

The first concept is called the Kick Plate Riser, and it addresses the issue of access to standard height kitchen counters. People with dwarfism are placed at a disadvantage when kitchens are designed only for people of average size. Most are built with counter heights and depths that are often completely out of reach for those of shorter stature. Normally a stool is used to help with this problem, but constantly climbing and moving the stool from place to place is not only a nuisance but creates physical stress for those who often already experience hip and leg problems. The Kick Plate Riser integrates a retractable platform within the kick plate of a standard ADA cabinet that can create a continuous platform upon which to walk the length of the work area (Color Plate 25). Individual sections of riser could also be pulled out to facilitate persons of mixed height, such as our clients, working together.

At 8 to 8½ feet, the ceiling heights of most homes are often twice as tall as an individual with dwarfism. A variety of storage spaces, windows, and fixtures are often located in a room's upper half: generally out of reach of shorter individuals. These out-of-reach spaces lessen the overall utility of a home and significantly decrease its storage capacity. Typical ladders have rung spacing too great for those with dwarfism, creating a further barrier to accessing these higher spaces. The second concept, the Drop-Step Ladder addresses the issue of step/rung height for those with dwarfism or other difficulties climbing stairs and ladders. Reducing the rung height to 4 inches better enables a little person to climb, but the ladder also adjusts to an eight inch rung spacing in order to safely accommodate an average height person. This way, separate ladders for each individual do not need to be purchase and stored (Color Plates 24a and b).

Conclusion

"Design for Dwarfism" started out as a simple assignment for an interior design studio project. In the end, it forced students to question design, design education, and even civic responsibility. The experience was made much richer by working in collaboration with other professionals and/or students in related fields, working in collaboration within the class itself, and finally by having real clients.

All design should be responsive to the client's needs, whether those needs are physical, psychological, or aesthetic. Professionals and students need to be exposed to a variety of populations who need design, not just those that comprise the majority.

Source: American Occupational Therapy Association (AOTA). (2009, September). Living life to its fullest™ Podcasts. Retrieved on October 29, 2010, from http://www.aota.org/Consumers/consumers/Podcasts.aspx#12

Renovation of Historic Buildings

Although not frequent, some older adults live in historic homes or apartment buildings, and renovating the exterior of such buildings without affecting their integrity is an issue. However, homes or apartments can be renovated to meet the ADA, be inclusive, and still retain their historic integrity.

As a multifamily housing, a **brownstone** building built in 1897 in Dubuque, Iowa, was renovated into an inclusively designed building that combined private and community living with seven private residential units and a community kitchen. Prior to the renovation, the building was inaccessible, with several steps leading up to the porch and several small steps leading through the entrance and into the foyer. Because the preservation of the historic entrance was required by federal preservation standards, a creative design solution was needed (Preservation Iowa, 2010).

The design chosen was to pave a gradually inclined sidewalk along the side of the building that opened into an entrance with automatic door openers. When inside the building, an elevator gave access to all floors, including the basement. Creating a side entrance helped retain the historic character of the façade and alleviated the need for a special obtrusive ramp. The creation of the side entry was important for two reasons: It helped retain the historic character, and, from a human rights perspective, it alleviated the feeling of needing something "different" or "special" in the form of a big, obtrusive ramp. The side door was one of the compromises needed to make the project work (see Figure 5.1).

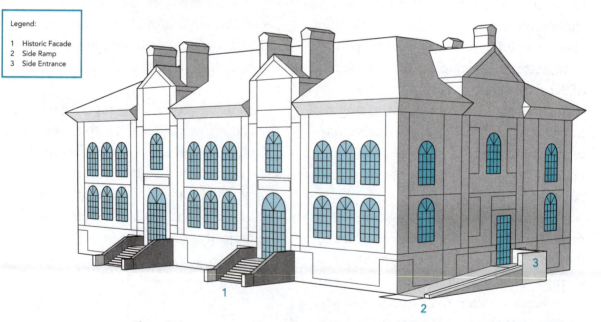

Legend:

1 Historic Facade
2 Side Ramp
3 Side Entrance

Figure 5.1

For the inclusive design renovation of this brownstone, a ramp was created on the side to be unobtrusive and preserve the historic façade. © Precision Graphics/based on a drawing by Linda L. Nussbaumer

When inside the building, there were other challenges to create accessibility. Four separate apartments made up the original building, but renovation design produced seven units and a community kitchen. For accessibility, hallways were widened for clearance and turning radius. Doorways were widened and doorstops removed. Where woodwork was replaced, it was custom made to replicate the original; this included staircase spindles and pocket doors (Preservation Iowa, 2010). Certainly, the renovation project preserved the integrity of the exterior and fostered independence and choice for those with disabilities.

An Inclusively Designed Home

Homes should reflect the owner's needs as well as those of their invited guests. In doing so, it creates "**visitability,**" which means that no one is excluded from entering because of barriers (e.g., steps) that are not accessible to wheelchairs or walkers (Concrete Change, 2008). If the home is inclusively designed, it includes family, friends, and other guests of all ages and abilities. To create visitability, the design begins by following the ADA accessibility guidelines and then applying inclusive design criteria that will create invisible accessibility. To have visitability, there are three essentials: a zero-step entrance at the front, back, and/or side of the house; all main floor doors (including bathrooms) have a minimum of 32 inches clear passage; and there is a minimum of a half bath (preferably a full bath) on the main level (Concrete Change, 2008). Additional features may be included in a visitability initiative, such as reinforcement of bathroom walls and accessible placement of electrical controls.

A home that is inclusive provides not only accessibility but also greater marketability for a number of reasons: It accommodates a wide variety of people, and it accommodates various impairments and assistive devices.

To meet inclusive design criteria, the house must be analyzed beginning on the pathway to the door and passing through all areas. The following suggestions for various areas of an inclusively designed home were developed from *Universal Design in Housing* (CUD, 2006), *Universal Design New York2* (2003), the Universal Design and Green Home survey checklist (Sandler, 2009), and *Universal Design Handbook* (2010).

PATHWAYS AND ENTRANCES

The pathway and entrance to the home must be welcoming and devoid of the obtrusive ramping. Guests, as well as the homeowner, must be welcomed with an easy-to-find, well-lit, and wide pathway. The following design features are suggested for the pathway and entrance:

- Lighting: Specify motion-detector-controlled lighting along the path to the entrance.

- Pathway: Provide a pathway with a minimum width of 3'0".
- Ramping: Avoid ramps, but if used, integrate them into the design. Gentle sloping is preferred to ramps.
- Sloping: Provide a gently sloped (1:20 maximum slope), obstacle-free path from public transportation, sidewalk, parking, or garage to a step-free front entrance.
- Landscaping: Include plants and shrubbery along the pathway to provide an aesthetically pleasing path to an entrance.
- Weather-protected entrance: Design with a porch, roof over stoop, awning, deep overhang, or other protective methods.
- Large house numbers: Make house numbers visible through size and material.
- Clear space: Design with a minimum 5'0" x 5'0" level clear space inside and outside the entrance.
- Shelf or bench: Provide a bench or shelf on which to set packages or articles at the entrance.
- Lighting: Provide sensor-controlled lighting at entrance.
- Doors: Specify doorways at 3'0" wide, an auto-powered door, and a peephole in the door at two levels (unless there is a sidelight or window).
- Hardware: Specify lever handles for all doors.
- Windows: Specify a full-length sidelight, window in the door, or windows close by for visibility.
- Threshold: Design with a stepless (zero-step) entrance or one half-inch maximum rise at entrance threshold (see Figure 5.2).
- Doorbell: Specify a lighted doorbell.
- Intercom: Specify an intercom with a portable telephone link and flashing light for an occupant to see.

LIVING AREAS

Open plans provide the most inclusive design. Fewer hallways and doorways not only provide better circulation for those with mobility impairments but also maximize sight lines. The following inclusive design features are suggested for living areas.

- Door openings: Design with clear door opening width (34 to 36 inches wide with 32 inches minimum).
- Thresholds: Design space with flush thresholds for all doorways.
- Floor space: Design with clear floor space (18 inches minimum) on pull (latch) side of door.
- Circulation: Provide a circulation path at 42 inches minimum width.
- Turning radius: Design with a 5'0" turning radius in all rooms.
- Vertical circulation stairs: Design for easy access between floors; stairs at appropriate width with space at bottom to install platform lift, if needed.
- Color contrast: Select material and colors to provide a color contrast between stair tread and riser to allow easy recognition of elevation change.

Figure 5.2

A stepless, or zero-step, entrance. Photo courtesy Linda L. Nussbaumer

- Lighting: Emphasize lighting at stairs to allow recognition of elevation change.
- Lighting controls: Provide a variety of light sources with adjustable controls.
- Handrails: Design stair handrails to extend horizontally beyond top and bottom risers.
- Vertical circulation elevator: Design with one set of stacked storage areas (i.e., closets in same location on all levels) that can become an elevator shaft later, or install a residential elevator with a minimum of 3'0" x 4'0" clear floor space.

KITCHENS

Kitchens have increasingly become the center of the home where families gather to visit, cook, study, and much more. A kitchen can be designed for a life span—usable by children, adults (short to tall), and people as they age as well as people with normal abilities and those with disabilities. The following is a list of features for an inclusively designed kitchen.

Circulation and Floor Plan

- Floor plan: Select a U or L shape for easy movement with an unobstructed work and traffic flow.
- Circulation: Provide circulation widths that are between 40 and 44 inches with a turning radius of 5'0" x 5'0" to 6'0" x 6'0".
- Clear floor space: Provide a minimum of 30" x 48" to maneuver at each work station.
- Visual barriers: Provide barriers to conceal kitchen essentials and mess with visual barriers, cabinet fronts, partial wall, or other methods.

- Sink faucet: Specify a single-lever faucet that mounts on the side of a low-profile sink.
- Cooktop faucet: Provide a pot filler at cooktop.

Flooring

- Flooring contrast: Specify flooring to provide a color contrast between floor surfaces and wall trim that allows easy recognition of the junction between these surfaces.
- Material: Hard nonslip flooring materials are water-resistant and easy to maintain.

Cabinetry Design

- Variable heights of base cabinets: Specify varied heights (28, 30, 34, 36, and 42 inches) of countertops, sinks, and cooktops for people who are tall, short (adult or children), sitting or standing; sinks and cooktops may be mechanically adjustable in 2-inch increments or electrically powered.
- Variable heights of wall cabinets and shelves: Specify varied-height wall cabinets and shelves within cabinets to make storage reachable.
- Base cabinets shelving: Specify full-extension, pull-out drawers and shelves, and racks in base cabinets to make it easier to reach all storage and maneuver large items in and out of cabinets.
- Corner cabinets: Specify a lazy Susan or other similar storage for corners.
- Roll-out carts: Specify a cart to store cookware under a cabinet or other feature, and provide additional work surface.
- Pull-out racks: Locate spice and towel pull-out racks strategically near appropriate work area.
- Pull-out work boards: Locate near oven, refrigerator, and microwave for ease in removal of food.
- Pull-down hardware: Provide pull-down, easy-to-use hardware to lower shelf contents stored in wall cabinets.
- Pantry storage: Specify full-height pantry storage with easy access pull-out and/or adjustable-height shelves to make storage reachable at all heights.
- Open storage: Specify open, visible, flexible storage available at the point of use.
- Glass doors: Specify glass doors to give greater visibility of content in upper cabinets.
- Hinges: Specify hinge swings that open to 170 degrees.
- Knee space: Provide knee space under sink, cooktop, and specific work surface areas. Cabinets with removable or slide-back hinged doors and removable sub-base will permit clear knee space or storage under cooktop, sink, kitchen island, and food prep area.

- Raised toe kick: Specify a toe kick of 9 inches in areas for wheelchair access.
- Hardware: Specify hardware that is easy to grasp and use (C- or D- shaped handles).
- Countertops: Specify durable, easy to clean and maintain, and heat-resistant countertops.
- Contrasting color: Specify contrasting color border treatment on countertops that makes for easier detection of the counters' edge and reduces likelihood of spills.
- Electrical outlets: Provide additional outlets to be set strategically under upper cabinets.

Appliances

The following provides examples of various options in appliances.

- Dishwasher: Raise the dishwasher by 8 to 10 inches above finished floor with top rack aligned parallel to countertop that makes it more convenient at the sitting position.
- Cooktop and oven
    - Controls: Select a cooktop or oven with front-mounted controls for easy reach and with easy-to-read print.
    - Burners: Stagger burners to eliminate the danger of reaching over hot burners and reduce the chance of burns or spills.
    - Hinges: Select an oven with side door hinges.
    - Oven racks: Place the oven so that its center or top-rack level is adjacent to the countertop.
- Microwave
    - Location: Place beneath the countertop.
    - Hinges: Select a microwave with side door hinges.
    - Controls: Select a microwave with front-mounted controls for easy reach.
- Refrigerators
    - Bottom freezer: May provide greater access to contents.
    - Opening: Specify doors that open 160 to 180 degrees.
    - Under-counter or drawer type: Install on raised platforms to allow for easier access.
    - Side-by-side: Specify full-extension, pull-out shelving to allow for easy reach of otherwise hard-to-get items.

Lighting and Electrical

- Glare-free lighting: Select lighting to illuminate work areas without glare.
- Electrical outlets: Locate outlets 18 inches above the finished floor.
- Light switches: Locate light switches 48 inches above the finished floor.

■ Lighting controls: Provide a variety of light sources with adjustable lighting controls on dimmer switches.

Figures 5.3a–c show an inclusively designed kitchen with conveniences. In Figure 5.3a, the sink is open for knees, but plumbing is not exposed. In Figure 5.3b, a switch allows the user to raise or lower the sink. In Figure 5.3c, doors open and can be pushed into cabinetry to easily use the cooktop. This allows the user to slide under and comfortably cook. The cooktop can also be designed to raise and lower as the sink does. Note the open shelving and glass doors on the upper cabinetry and varied height counters that provides access to people of varied heights.

Figure 5.3a–c

This inclusively designed kitchen provides (a) an opening for knees beneath a sink where plumbing is not exposed. The sink also features (b) a switch that raises and lowers the basin with its counter section so that users of various size and abilities can easily reach it. Under the counters, (c) doors can be opened and tucked away into cabinetry so users can easily slide their legs beneath and comfortably cook. Counters are also available that can be raised and lowered like the sink. This attractive kitchen also displays open shelving and glass doors on the upper cabinetry, varied height counters that provide access to people of varied heights, and a kick space at 9 inches. Photo courtesy GE

THE LAUNDRY AREA

The laundry area can also be challenging for people of different ages and abilities. It can be inclusively designed with washers and dryers that are easier to approach and reach, regardless of ability.

- Front-loading washers and dryers: Specify front-loading machines to reduce the need to bend, stoop, or lean over to reach clothes.
- Controls: Select machines with front controls for easy access.
- Pedestals: Specify pedestals installed 10 to 12 inches above the finished floor to operate machines in a seated position or a nonbent stand.
- Clear floor space: Provide a 36-inch-wide space across full width in front of washer and dryer that also extends 18 inches beyond right and left sides to provide easier access to appliances from a seated position. (Extended space can be part of knee space under counter tops and sinks.)
- Lighting: Provide a variety of light sources with adjustable controls.

Figure 5.4 shows a washer and dryer on a pedestal. At this height, the laundry is more accessible to various ages and abilities.

Figure 5.4

Washer and dryer placed on pedestal; this eliminates the need for users to bend and is accessible to those in wheelchairs. Ryan McVay/Getty Images

BEDROOMS

Though some guidelines state that only one bedroom and bathroom need to be accessible, to apply inclusive design and provide visitability, all rooms must be accessible. For bedrooms, the following are important in order to be inclusive.

- Turning radius: Provide 5-foot turning radius in key areas of the bedroom and next to closet or within walk-in closet.
- Clear floor space: Provide at least 36 inches on two sides of the bed.
- Doors: Specify 36-inch-wide swinging doors with lever handles and/or pocket doors.
- Closet: Provide walk-in or roll-in closets.
- Closet doors: Specify at least a 36-inch-wide sliding doors, where possible, that take up less space than bi-fold doors.
- Closet shelving: Provide adjustable shelving and clothing rods at varied heights and/or provide automatic coat lift for closets (walk in or wall).
- Lighting in bedroom: Specify saturated fluorescent and task lighting from various sources with adjustable controls.
- Lighting in closet: Specify fluorescent lighting with switch located just outside the closet doors.
- Lighting: Provide a variety of light sources with adjustable controls.
- Ceiling fan: Specify ceiling fan/light combination that is operated by remote control on a rocker style switch.
- Electrical outlets: Specify additional electrical outlets throughout the room and near the bed to accommodate medical or other equipment.
- Various connections: Locate telephone jacks, Internet, and/or other connections near the bed.
- Reinforced walls: Specify wall backing next to the bed and elsewhere for additional grab bar or medical device support.
- Reinforced ceiling: Specify reinforcement within ceiling to allow for future installation of lifts or devices with 600 pound capacity.

Figure 5.5 shows the automatic coat lift (UD Products, n/d) as it moves up or down to allow access to someone who has limited mobility.

BATHROOMS

Inclusive design features in bathroom design allow everyone to use the facilities (Mullick, 2010). Through research, two adjustable bathrooms—the moveable fixture bathroom and the moveable panels bathroom—were developed by The Center for Inclusive Design and Environmental Access along with the National Institute on Disability and Rehabilitation Research (NIDRR), U.S. Department of Education. The design provides independence for children and prolonged independence to the aging adult. "Unlike most current bathrooms, which are designed primarily for

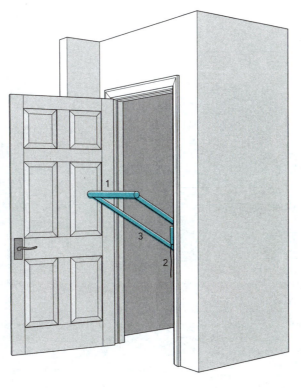

Legend:

1 Clothing rod
2 Cable hand control
3 Arm mechanism that raises and lowers

Note: Placement of mechanism set according to height needed to access clothing from a sitting position.

Figure 5.5

The automatic coat lift moves up or down to allow access to someone who has limited mobility.
© Precision Graphics/based on a drawing by Linda L. Nussbaumer

independent users, these bathrooms consider the needs of the human life cycle and address dependent use and care, provided alongside independent use of the bathroom" (Mullick, 2010, p. 30.5).

Ideas include height-adjustable toilets with foldaway arms, height-adjustable sinks, moveable shower panels, and more. However, until such fixtures are on the market, there are ways to provide access to various ages and abilities (e.g., pedestal sinks and zero-step showers.

Abir Mullick, a professor in the College of Architecture at Georgia Institute of Technology (2010), generated the adjustable fixture concept. Demonstrating his conceptual ideas, Figures 5.6a shows the fixtures at a level for a small child, whereas Figure 5.6b shows fixtures at a level for a taller individual. Figure 5.6c compares the height of each to indicate the variable heights. The zero-step unit also provides inclusive flexible features—push-button water controls with a remote control unit; hand-held shower head; a fixed shower head for tall individuals; and an adjustable shower seat. As shown in Figures 5-6a through c, adjustable bathroom fixtures may revolutionize bathroom design; however, until the idea becomes reality, there are ways to create accessible and adaptable spaces.

To begin, if there are several bathrooms in a home, all should be accessible and meet the following criteria.

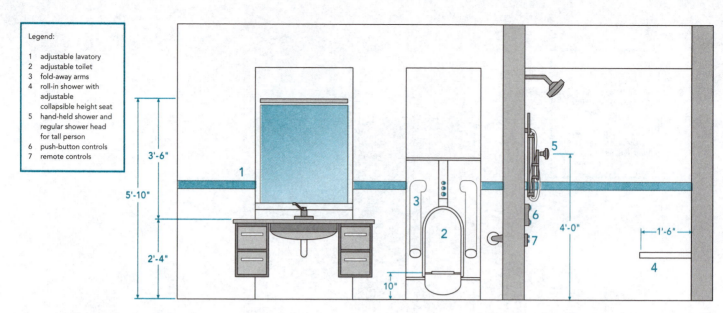

Figure 5.6a

Fixtures (vanity and toilet) in this bathroom adjust vertically and can accommodate people of different heights. In this example, the fixtures (lavatory, mirror, toilet, and foldaway arms) are at a lower level for a short person or child. The mirror moves with the lavatory unit. (Ideas generated from design by Abir Mullick.) © Precision Graphics

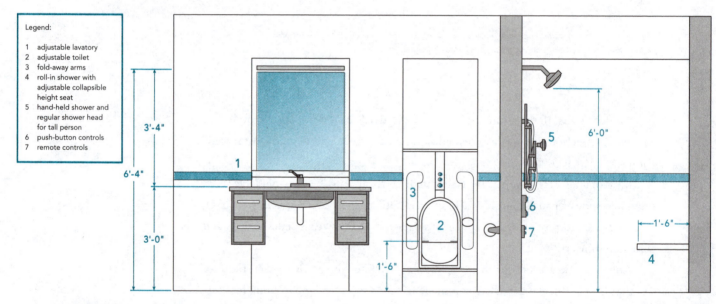

Figure 5.6b

This bathroom shows fixtures at their highest level for a tall individual. The height-adjustable toilet has several features that include adjustable toilet and arms; arms that can be folded away when not in use or lowered for support; and a bidet and dryer toilet bowl that also fold away into a cavity when not in use to provide greater clear floor space. (Ideas generated from design by Abir Mullick.) © Precision Graphics

Bathroom Basics

- Flooring: Specify slip resistant tile in–floor heat.
- Spatial layout: Consider the use and connection between fixtures to develop an accessible and adaptable floor plan.

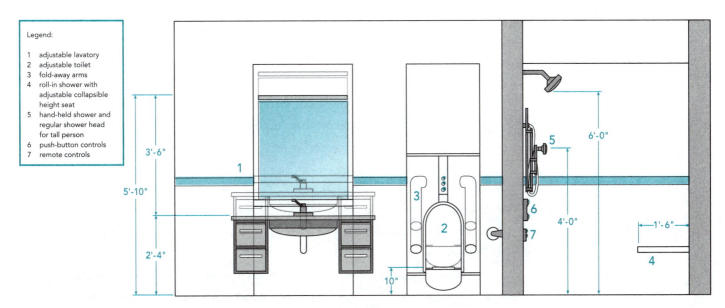

Figure 5.6c

This example shows the lowest height of a vanity, mirror, toilet, and arms with the highest possible level shaded. The movable fixtures in this bathroom provide easy access for the user. The sink with a built-in mirror, light, grab bars and storage moves horizontally along the handrail (close but away from toilet). The zero-step shower unit also provides inclusive features—hand-held shower head, push-button water controls with a remote control unit, and an adjustable seat. Additionally, there is a fixed shower head at a height convenient for a taller individual. (Ideas generated from design by Abir Mullick.) © Precision Graphics

- ■ Floor space: Provide minimum of 5'0" x 5'0" to 5'0" x 6'0" clear floor space.
- ■ Circulation routes: Plan for at least 40 inches to enter bathroom.
- ■ Reinforced walls: Install ¾–inch plywood and wood blocking for later grab bars' installation near the toilet, bathtub, shower, and sink.
- ■ Door openings: Provide a minimum of 32 inches clear opening; pocket preferred.
- ■ Fixtures: Specify self-cleaning or easy-to-maintain sink/faucet, showerhead, and toilet to allow for easy maintenance and independence.
- ■ Towel bars: Locate towel bars at varied heights.
- ■ Grab bars: Provide (or reinforce walls for future) grab bars in the toilet, shower, and tub areas.
- ■ Windows: Specify controls for windows, lighting, and fixtures that are easy to operate.
- ■ Vanity mirror: Locate mirror at height for seated person.

Bathroom Sink

- ■ Countertop sink: Place bowl close to the front edge for easy access.
- ■ Under sink: Design cabinetry under sink with removable doors or open space under sink for wheelchair access.
- ■ Wall-hung sink: Provides knee space for wheelchair access; includes counter space for grooming needs.

Cabinetry and Storage

■ Vanity cabinets: Design cabinetry with removable doors and adjustable shelves to provide open space or storage.

■ Lower cabinets: Design cabinetry with toe kick area at 9 to 12 inches high and sufficient space underneath for turning.

■ Storage: Provide at various heights with half or more located lower than 48 inches.

Toilet Area

■ Elongated: Provide toilet that is 16½ to 17½ inches long for easy access from a wheelchair.

■ Height: Provide toilet that is 17 to 19 inches from the floor for greater comfort.

■ Center of toilet: Locate toilet at least 18 inches from a wall, allowing grab bars to be within easy reach but far enough from the wall to permit access using a wheelchair.

■ Alcove or compartment location: Locate toilet by opening the space up for greater access.

■ Grab bars: Provide (or reinforce walls for future) grab bars in the toileting area.

Bathing and Shower Facilities

■ Shower unit: Provide one bathroom with a minimum 5'0" x 3'0" (5'0" x 4'0" preferred) no-step or low-step shower.

■ Bathtub: Provide a tub with nonslip bottom and built-in grab bars.

■ Shower controls: Locate controls near shower entry and 40 to 45 inches from finished floor to minimize stooping, bending, and reaching; locate additional controls within reach of shower seat or bench.

■ Bathtub controls: Provide lever-type controls that are offset near tub entry and locate controls to minimize stooping, bending, and reaching; provide a 2-foot-long platform at end of tub to permit easy entry or transfer, or to place toiletries.

■ Anti-scald fittings: Specify fittings that prevent injury due to high water temperature.

■ Showerhead: Provide fixed and detachable handheld showerheads with a 6-foot flexible hose on vertical slider bar.

■ Seat: Provide a fixed or stable seat or bench in the shower.

■ Reinforced wall: Provide support for future installation of grab bars in shower and/or bathtub. (Bathtub may be specified with built-in grab bars.)

Lighting and Electrical

■ Lighting: Provide a variety of light sources with adjustable controls.

■ Light switches: Provide backlit rocker-style light switches for night navigation.

Figure 5.7a and b

This bathroom was designed with (a) decorative grab bars and an accessible sink area. The shower is a zero-step design, and the tub (not shown) was installed to satisfy resale at a later date. This (b) shower unit features a zero-step design with fixed seating. © Corbis Premium RF/Alamy

- Switch location: Locate lighting controls within arm's reach while seated.
- Shielded light: Provide sufficient shielded light to prevent shadow at vanity while grooming.
- Electrical outlets: Provide outlets within reach at the point of use and easy to reach when seated.
- Sensor lighting: Provide movement sensor lighting for safety and energy efficiency.

Figure 5.7a and b show two bathrooms for individuals with physical limitations (e.g., multiple sclerosis [MS], Parkinson's disease, paralysis). These bathrooms were designed with features that provide accessibility and apply inclusive design criteria as well. For example, the entire sink area is open and accessible, and the large shower unit is designed to allow transfer from the wheelchair to a shower chair with ease. A side entry toilet is installed to provide ease of transfer from the wheelchair, and grab bars are installed around the toilet.

Housing for the Aging Population

Housing for the aging population should present the same characteristics as other inclusive homes. It should provide an attractive and inclusive design, offer invisible accessibility, accommodate various sizes and abilities, be highly marketable, and achieve all of the advantages of the inclusively designed house.

As the Baby Boomers age, their preferences in housing are different than previous generations. For example, Baby Boomers are consumers who enjoy conveniences and, as they age, want inclusive design homes—invisible accessibility with visitability. Also, according to Jeffrey P. Rosenfeld and Wid Chapman (2008), Baby Boomers are not apt to move (or not far) from their present location and will continue to enjoy dining out and socializing with friends. Baby Boomers are also involved in and will continue to pursue sports and hobbies during retirement. In fact, some Baby Boomers may not fully retire; they may either continue working in the same job or for the same company but in a different capacity, possibly from home (Rosenfeld & Chapman, 2008). For these reasons, whether they live in single- or multifamily housing, Baby Boomers need and expect housing to be as accommodating as their workplace has been. There are, however, some governmental requirements for residential housing.

FAIR HOUSING ACT (FHA)

Design and construction requirements for multifamily housing are governed under the **Fair Housing Act (FHA)**. The FHA states that in a multifamily housing complex that consists of four or more units with an elevator and built for first occupancy after March 13, 1991, all units within the complex must comply with FHA's seven design and construction requirements. These include:

- accessible entrance on an accessible route
- accessible public and common-use areas
- usable doors
- accessible route into and through the dwelling unit
- accessible light switches, electrical outlets, thermostats, and environmental controls
- reinforced walls in bathrooms
- usable kitchens and bathrooms (HUD, 2006, para. 11)

If the housing complex is without elevators, all ground floor units must comply with these same FHA requirements.

The FHA's design and construction requirements do not apply to detached single-family housing. However, if the home is funded by federal, state, or local dollars, accessibility may be required under other laws such as Section 504 of the 1973 Rehabilitation Act and Title II of the ADA. Clearly, compliance for the ADA is limited within residential housing; this means that few single-family homes are accessible, and those that are accessible are not inclusively designed. These homes would not have "visitability."

HOUSING OPTIONS

Whether accessible or not, older adults have various housing options and neighborhoods in which to live. These include multifamily housing, cohousing, congregate housing, **age-restricted or active adult communities**, continuing care retirement communities, and more. Even with the array of housing choices, many may prefer their present location—a multifamily complex or a single-family home. In some cases their residence may need to be retrofitted for "**aging in place.**"

Multifamily Housing

Multifamily housing complexes (e.g., apartments, condominiums, and so on) are considered independent living. Some complexes are designed specifically for senior living, whereas others are offered to various age groups. Apartments are rented, whereas condominiums are purchased. Floor plans generally offer studio, one-bedroom, and two-bedroom units. Some complexes may include a den or additional spaces within the unit. Accessible units are generally limited to the ADA requirement for accessibility. Figure 5.8a is an example of an accessible apartment unit in which the entry, kitchen, and bathroom are accessible. In the living room, the bookcase has open shelving that provides easy access to anyone regardless of height or ability (Figure 5.8b).

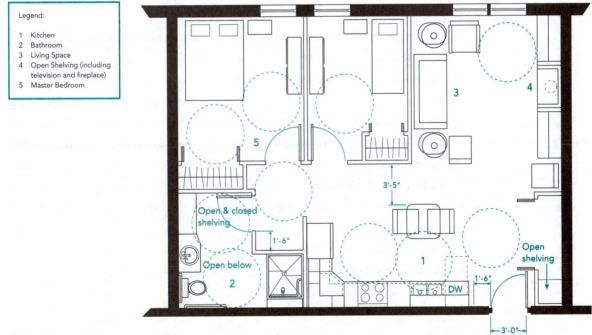

Legend:
1. Kitchen
2. Bathroom
3. Living Space
4. Open Shelving (including television and fireplace)
5. Master Bedroom

Figure 5.8a

An accessible unit has a kitchen, bathroom, accessible approaches at each door, and more. Circles throughout this plan indicate the 5-foot minimum turning radius that assures comfortable movement throughout the apartment from the door to the bath and bedrooms. (1) The kitchen has limited upper but open shelving, lazy Susan corner for easy access, front controls on the stove, open space under the sink, and a raised dishwasher. (2) The bathroom has a zero-step shower with grab bars and seat, grab bars by the toilet, open space below the sink, and open shelving for easy access to storage. (3) The living space provides ample room to turn. (4) Open shelving provides access to books and objects along with a remote control electric fireplace and television. (5) The master bedroom provides the greatest amount of room for turning and accessing the closet. At each room's entrance, a minimum of 1 foot, 6 inches provides the proper approach to open doors. © Precision Graphics/based on a drawing by Linda L. Nussbaumer

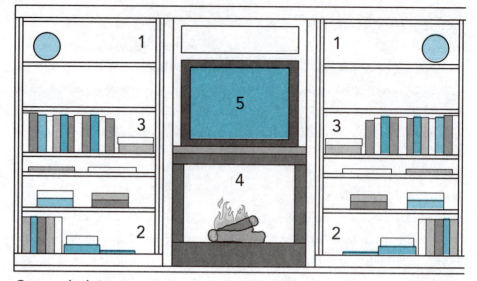

Legend:

1 Top shelves – difficult to reach
2 Bottom shelves – difficult to reach
3 Mid-level shelves – at arm's reach
4 Remote-control fireplace
5 Television

Open shelving

Figure 5.8b

The bookcase and shelving unit is designed with open shelving to make access easy and accessible. Open shelving provides access regardless of height—tall, short, or in a wheelchair. Because access to decorative items is generally not necessary, such items can be placed on (1) the top or (2) the bottom shelves. (3) Books and items used frequently can be placed at arm's reach. (4) A remote control fireplace and (5) television are easier to use for people of varied abilities. © Precision Graphics/based on a drawing by Linda L. Nussbaumer

According to HUD (2006), requirements apply to most public and private housing with limited exemptions. Exemptions may occur for owner-occupied buildings with a maximum of four units, single-family housing sold or rented when a broker is not used, and housing operated by organizations and private clubs with occupancy limited to members. On the other hand, if the multifamily housing with five or more units is federally assisted, there are no exemptions. In this case, 5 percent of the units or one unit at a minimum (whichever is greater) must meet stringent physical accessibility requirements. Two percent of the units or one unit at a minimum (which ever is greater) must accommodate persons with visual or hearing impairments.

When the ADA accessibility requirements must be met, inclusive design criteria could also be applied. However, few go beyond the ADA requirements.

Cohousing

Cohousing refers to a semi-communal neighborhood in which residents are actively involved in the design and operation of the community (AARP, 2010a; Cohousing, 2010). Cohousing began in Denmark and came to the United States in the early 1990s (Cohousing, 2010). In these communities, residents own their homes or condominiums, but they share facilities and other amenities (dining hall, pool, and more). It brings back the old-fashioned sense of neighborhood with front porches or congregating spaces, pedestrian streets, courtyards, social centers and more. Cohousing (2011) communities have been designed with six defining characteristics:

- Participatory process: People planning to live in the community participate in its design.
- Neighborhood design: The layout and orientation of buildings encourages a sense of community.
- Common facilities: Common facilities (e.g., dining hall, kitchen, and more) are used daily and are an integral part of the community but are supplemental to the private residences.
- Resident management: Residents manage their own communities and perform most of the work to maintain the property.
- Nonhierarchical structure and decision-making: Although leadership is expected, there is no one person with authority over others.
- No shared community economy: The community is not a source of income for members; however, on occasion, a cohousing community will pay a resident for a specific task (usually for a specific time or time-limited). For the most part, tasks within the community are considered a shared responsibility rather than conducted for pay.

Also, an advantage to the age-restricted community for the older adult is that cohousing residents often share the costs of health aides or an on-site healthcare provider (AARP, 2010a).

Accessibility is dependent upon individual needs; however, some cohousing communities have age restrictions. In this case, homes can be designed for aging in place (discussed later in this chapter).

Congregate Housing

Congregate housing provides each individual or family with a private bedroom or living quarters, and some with kitchens or kitchenettes to make light meals or snacks (Seniors-site, n/d). Residents share a dining room, recreational room, or other common facilities (AARP, 2010a). The advantages of congregate living may be the opportunity to rent or own and for residents to be together and participate in shared activities (Senior Resource, 2010).

An advantage of congregate housing is that it is a shared living environment that includes housing and service; for example, a professional staff such as social workers, counselors, nutritionists, and possibly others administer services and social activities. For the most part, residents are able to care for themselves, but the facility provides services such as housekeeping, speakers, entertainment, movies, transportation to shopping areas, and more (Senior-site, n/d).

Some congregate housing communities provide additional levels of care. These levels may include assisted living, skilled nursing, or Alzheimer's care (Senior Resource,

2010). In other words, these additional levels are similar to a long-term care facility and, perhaps, the resident would need to move to a different room or building to obtain these services.

With housing that is specific to the older adult related to medical needs, the ADA compliance is required; however, creating an inclusively designed space would provide equality to occupants.

Age-Restricted or Active-Adult Communities

An **age-restricted** or **active-adult community** can be like any other neighborhood or community with the exception that it limits occupancy to older adults (e.g., 55 and over) (Senior Resource, 2010). Within these communities, a mixture of housing types (single-family homes, townhouses, and apartments) are found and frequently connected by paths or sidewalks (AARP, 2010a).

Age-restricted or active-adult communities are retirement communities oriented toward an active lifestyle; therefore, amenities such as a clubhouse, tennis courts, a swimming pool, and a golf course are common within these communities (AARP, 2010a). This allows the active adult opportunities to play golf or tennis, exercise, swim, play cards, and enjoy other activities of an active lifestyle. Often these communities are found in resort areas or even in a university town, which can offer greater enrichment for the older adult (Senior Resource, 2010).

The ADA compliance is not required with exception of the shared facilities; therefore, each resident must design their own space to be accessible, if needed, as well as apply inclusive design criteria.

Continuing Care Retirement Community

The **continuing care retirement community (CCRC)** offers lifetime care in which the resident can buy-in or make an up-front annuity purchase along with monthly payments that cover amenities, services, and medical care (Senior Resource, 2010). It is a community that features independent-living apartments and homes. It may also offer meals and various recreational, social, and cultural activities. As a resident's health and abilities decline, the option to move into assisted living and nursing-level care is available (AARP, 2010a). Because the CCRC provides multiple levels of care, residents know in what community they may eventually move (Senior Resource, 2010b).

In the healthcare services facilities of the CCRC, the ADA accessible guidelines must be followed. Within each residence, compliance with ADA may or may not be required depending on the type of residence (home or apartment), but within the section of a facility where higher level care is required, such as an Alzheimer's unit, the ADA compliance is required. However, because providing an inclusive environment is not required, each residence or other aspects of the facility have the choice to apply inclusion and visitability.

Aging in Place

Aging in place is a concept in which individuals continue to live in their long-term homes and communities where they feel safe and comfortable and are able to maintain their independence for as long as possible, regardless of age, income level, or physical ability (AARP, 2010a). According to AARP (2010b), most residents prefer staying in their current homes and not entering a long-term care facility; however, being able to stay at home (or age in place) takes planning and, generally, a home modification.

Unfortunately, having to deal with a home modification is often the motive to move. According to Senior Resources (2010), the following are a few reasons given for moving:

- Deteriorating neighborhood and concern for safety
- Wishing to be near children (70 percent who are 65 and older live one hour from a child)
- Matching home's facilities to senior's facilities
- Avoiding stairs in a home
- Reducing to smaller home with lower maintenance costs
- Preferring a home that meets present needs (physical or otherwise)
- Needing cash because assets are tied up in the home
- Needing adequate transportation and unable to drive
- Retiring and looking for new lifestyle (para. 2)

Even though these are solid reasons to move, change can be difficult for the older adult. Having lived in one place for many years means that connections and friendships have been made and surroundings are familiar. Aging in place can reduce stress for the older adult.

Certainly in making home modifications, the ADA accessibility guidelines may be consulted for appropriate turning radius, clearances, openings, and more. However, home modifications that are inclusive go beyond and create a home-like environment.

Inclusively designed environments provide secure environments that are safe, ergonomic, and efficient. For example, zero-step entries and showers, nonslip floor covering, and grab bars reduce injuries due to falls. Lower cooktops with front controls reduce the need to reach and, thus, the risk of burns. As with the work environment, ergonomically designed work areas in the home eliminate physical stress. Additionally, homes designed for efficiency allow occupants to work stress-free in the kitchen and maneuver safely throughout the home. Case Study 5.2: "Aging in Place" describes a patio home that is designed for aging in place with some limitations.

RENOVATION OR NEW CONSTRUCTION

Most existing homes are designed for the average person. In fact, their designs do not consider various ages and abilities or changes that may occur within a lifetime (Mack,

As people age, their bodies change. Older adults have arthritic joints that make it difficult to walk up and down steps. Among other aging concerns, they have less mobility due to surgeries, as well as poor eyesight that makes it difficult to see the change in elevations. Of course, most people prefer to live in their homes as long as possible rather than moving to assisted living or nursing homes. Thus, for people to stay in their homes, these homes must be designed for "aging in place."

For many years, a Minnesota retired couple lived in a split-level—a home where they raised their two daughters. However, as they have aged, they found the split-level home more challenging. To reach every level, they climbed seven steps—from the entry or garage to the main level and from the main level to the bedrooms or lower level. Although they were comfortable in this home, they found it more difficult to go up and down steps continually and impossible for a family member with limited mobility to visit.

New Home/Same Independent Lifestyle
When a patio home came on the market, they saw its advantages and decided it was time to move. This home was on one level with a zero-step front entrance and lever handle on the front door that would provide the couple and their visitors with a comfortable, accessible entrance into the home (see Case Study Figure 5.2a). The open foyer also provided space to turn a wheelchair with ease.

The home exhibited other features that made it appealing to age in place. The open floor plan provided easy access throughout the living space—from the foyer to the living and dining area. All doors were 36 inches wide, and when doors are open, a person using a wheelchair could easily enter the bedrooms or bathrooms. Case Study Figure 5.2.b shows

Case Study Figure 5.2a

A zero-step entrance is one where entrance is gained without the need for steps. This provides inclusivity and visitability to family or friends whether able-bodied or wheelchair-bound. Photo courtesy Linda L. Nussbaumer

the floor plan and indicates features that provide easier access to someone with limited mobility.

However, there are some features that are not accessible. To enter from the garage, there was a one-step entry. This could be ramped but would take up space needed for vehicles. If not ramped, the owner would need to use the main entrance rather than the garage entrance. Although the front entrance provides the needed access, this could be difficult in the winter when ice or snow was on the walkway.

When inside the back entrance, a laundry area is on the left. Although located on the main level with a turn radius, its location by the back door could be difficult as other family members enter. The kitchen layout is open, but using the sink, stove, or counter spaces would be difficult for someone in a wheelchair. All counters are 36 inches high, no kick space for the feet was provided, and sink and cooktop access would be from the side of the chair.

The sunroom is located off the dining room, and within the spatial layout, the sunroom is located on the southeast corner of the home. Thus, the sunroom would often be a sun-filled space and provide natural light to read, particularly for someone with poor eyesight. However, the slides on sliding door threshold would create difficult access for someone in a wheelchair. This could be resolved by replacing the existing sliding door with a zero-step threshold door.

Another area of concern is in the master bath. Although a 36-inch opening to the bathroom is provided and a seat is provided in the shower unit, access for someone in a wheelchair would be difficult. Access to the sink is from the side, no grab bars are installed, and the shower has a one-step entrance. Many door openings lack maneuvering clearances on the latch side for a frontal approach; they are less than 18 inches, nonexistent, or obstructed by closet doors or vanities, and clothing. Areas of concern are circled on the floor plan (see Case Study Figure 5.2b).

Renovations or Simple Changes

To make this plan accessible, various changes could be made (see Case Study Figure 5.2c). It would begin with a ramp in the garage for access to the back door. Office walls could be moved so that the laundry area could be refigured to remove obstructions. To make the back entry more accessible, the utility area could be resized to keep the back door open, and also the closet could be changed to hooks and shelves.

The kitchen could be redesigned for accessibility. Sink and cooktop areas could be moveable and open below for wheelchair legs. The microwave and ovens with side-hinged doors could be located at eye level with counter or boards to provide as a landing area.

Walls may be moved to provide the appropriate approach to bedrooms. The master bath closet could have open shelving and the shower unit could have a zero-step threshold. The master bedroom closet could be reconfigured for wheelchair access. The guest bathroom vanity could be replaced by a pedestal or

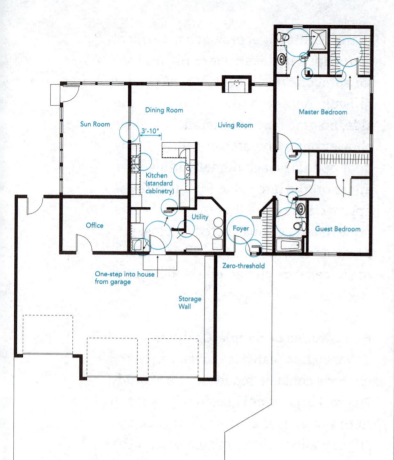

Case Study Figure 5.2b

Floor plan for an existing patio home, where there is no need for a staircase. Everything is on one floor—living area, private areas, laundry, and utilities. However, not all features provide an inclusive environment, such as the bathrooms, closet, laundry, kitchen, and back entry. © Precision Graphics/based on a drawing by Crystal Creek Builders

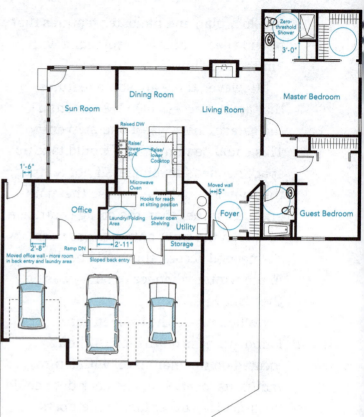

Case Study Figure 5.2c

The floor plan for the patio home was revised to become more inclusive for aging in place. Changes include accessible approaches to each room and the back entry, greater space in the back entry and laundry area, accessible kitchen, zero-step to sunroom, a zero-step shower, and accessible walk-in closet. © Precision Graphics/based on a drawing by Linda L. Nussbaumer

wall hung sink to provide the appropriate approach at the door.

Although not all features were accessible in the original plan, basic changes could be made to allow the couple to live in the home for a longer period of time without a renovation of the space. They could add a ramp in the garage, replace the sliding door with a zero-step threshold, replace the stove with front-controls, change

the sink front cabinet, change the bathroom sink to provide needed space, and remove closet doors.

However, this couple felt that if they had major physical or health problems, they would choose to move into an assisted living or nursing home. For now, this patio home would allow them to age in place much longer than their previous home, and they were enjoying living on one level.

2006). Particularly, for older adults, the ability to maneuver through and maintain their existing homes may become difficult. When older adults decide they would like to age in place, they must decide whether to build new or renovate. Many feel that building new would not be cost effective; however, this may not be true.

A study summarized by InformeDesign (2008, June 25) compared the cost of new construction to a renovation to implement the ADA and be inclusive to facilitate aging in place. This study revealed that it is more feasible to build new than renovate. This means that building new will provide a better living environment for the older adult. It also means that building to accommodate changes through a lifespan is more economical over time. See Study Sketch 5.1: "Aging in Place Housing Options" for more details.

Sustainable Design and Inclusive Design

In designing, it is easy to compartmentalize various aspects of sustainability and ADA compliance. However, it is possible to combine all features of sustainable and inclusive design into one encompassing design, acknowledging ADA accessibility guidelines as well as specifying renewable and nontoxic products.

One example is the Utah House (USU, 2010) at Utah State University Extension's sustainable building demonstration and education center. This house promotes sustainability, energy and water efficiency, and healthy indoor environments as well as being inclusive.

APPLYING SUSTAINABILITY

The Utah House preserves natural resources for future generations in the following ways:

- Efficient use of resources (energy, water, materials, land)
- Minimization of waste
- Conservation of the natural environment
- Creation of a healthy built environment, all parts of sustainable design.

The design also includes various energy-saving features, such as south-facing windows to maximize heat gain, daylight rooms to reduce the need for electric lights, **photovoltaic (PV)** panels on the roof, and Energy Star® appliances to reduce energy and water usage. Water conservation design features were included, such as a front-loading washer to conserve one-third the energy and water. Healthy building materials, interior finishes, and design strategies were also applied, such as low VOC paints, carbon monoxide detectors, whole-house ventilation, and more.

STUDY SKETCH 5.1: Aging in Place Housing Options

As older adults age and find it difficult to maneuver through and maintain their existing home, they must decide whether to build new or renovate. InformeDesign (2008, June 25) summarizes a "case study that compared new construction and renovation costs" to implement the ADA and universal design guidelines that facilitate aging in place.

Method

The study site was a home owned by an elderly person who wanted to age in place. The home consisted of a living room, dining room, kitchen, bathroom, two bedrooms, an unfinished basement, attic, and enclosed porch. Researchers analyzed the floor plan (e.g., entryways, circulation patterns) to uncover any accessibility problems for someone with mobility limitations.

Costs were estimated to renovate the existing home so it would comply with the ADA and be inclusive as well. Costs were also estimated for building a new home of similar size and characteristics. Cost of renovating and building new were compared.

Findings

The existing floor plan did not allow for easy access; therefore, to make the home accessible required several modifications (e.g., adding an exterior ramp to the porch entrance, installing nonslip flooring, enlarging the bathroom and hallway, removing a hall linen closet). Renovation costs were estimated between $50,000 and $66,000. The large cost could be impossible for an older adult to afford and make relocation necessary.

The estimated cost for constructing a similar home without applying the ADA or being inclusive was $99,142. The estimated cost for constructing a similar home by applying the ADA or being inclusive was $102,842. This difference is $3,700. However, renovation costs were almost one-half the cost of new construction.

Criteria

From these findings the following criteria were recommended:
- Build new because it is more cost-effective to apply the ADA accessibility guidelines and inclusive design than renovate an existing home.
- Integrate the ADA accessibility guidelines and inclusive design into new construction to create useable environments for everyone.
- Design houses with flexibility and adaptability to accommodate all ages.
- Educate contractors and the public on the importance of building homes to accommodate all ages.

Implications

These criteria are important to accommodate all ages and abilities in order to eliminate the necessity of renovating an existing home as the occupants age and abilities change.

Source: InformeDesign. (2008, June 25). "Aging in Place Housing Options." Retrieved on July 12, 2010, from http://www.informedesign.umn.edu/Rs_detail.aspx?rsId=3074

APPLYING INCLUSIVE DESIGN

Inclusive design features considered a wide array of users (e.g., people of all ages, sizes, and abilities). Barrier-free entries, wide doorways, and lever handles are just a few of the accessible features. To create inclusive design, the following were also included:

- Living space (living room, kitchen, laundry, bedroom, and bathroom) on one level (see Figure 5.9)
- Separate work areas in kitchen
- Multilevel seating areas in kitchen
- Knee space under the sink
- Stove with top level burners
- Side-by-side refrigerator
- Microwave below counter for easy access
- Main bedroom with emergency access to outside
- Spacious closets
- Smoke detector and visual strobe for those with hearing impairments
- Zero-step main entry
- 36-inch-wide doorway
- Lever handles

The Utah House combines a great resource for the use of sustainable practices with inclusive design features into one environment (e.g., front-load washer on a pedestal conserves water and is easy for most people to use).

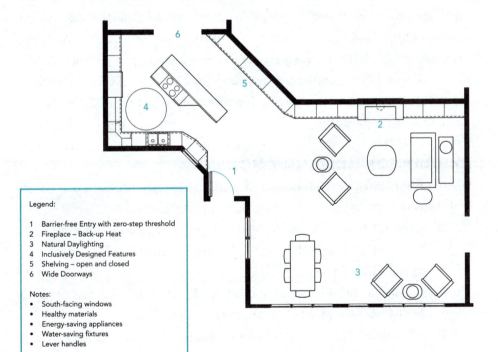

Legend:

1   Barrier-free Entry with zero-step threshold
2   Fireplace – Back-up Heat
3   Natural Daylighting
4   Inclusively Designed Features
5   Shelving – open and closed
6   Wide Doorways

Notes:
- South-facing windows
- Healthy materials
- Energy-saving appliances
- Water-saving fixtures
- Lever handles

Figure 5.9

The Utah House combines sustainability with inclusive design features. All living spaces are on one level, and this plan shows the living, dining, and kitchen areas in which easy and accessible movement is provided. © Precision Graphics/based on a drawing by Linda L. Nussbaumer

Affordable Housing

Affordable housing represents a dwelling that is safe and an adequate size for a family. This type of housing is offered for rent or purchase with the cost of utilities limited to no more than 30 percent of the occupant's income (AARP, 2010a). Housing may be created using pre-fabrication, Habitat for Humanity housing, or funding from public housing.

PREFABRICATED (THE PREFAB) HOUSE

Prefabricated (the prefab) house is a type of house that is constructed from easy-to-assemble building parts and is manufactured off-site, such as built in a factory (About.com, 2010). Buyers are offered a limited number of floor plans, and limited options and upgrades are allowed. Changes could include accessibility as a requirement but this may depend on the manufacturer. Some prefab manufacturers, such as FabCab manufacturers, design affordable housing for all abilities, thus providing an inclusive environment. This begins at the front door with a seamless, gradual entry with integrated landscaped pathway. All doorframes are wider and sliding doors are included where needed. The greatest difference is applied in the bathroom and kitchen where appliances are situated to modify use by a range of abilities. Some features include walk-in showers, easy on/off faucets, drawer dishwashers and refrigerators, and antimicrobial glazed tile and grippy cork mosaic floor to prevent illness or falls. FabCab designs focus on invisible accessibility (FabCab, 2011; Mansueto Ventures, 2010). Figure 5.10a shows an accessible, inclusive kitchen, and Figure 5.10b shows a vanity accessible to all abilities.

HABITAT FOR HUMANITY HOUSING

Habitat for Humanity (HH) housing is an affordable type of housing that is built to three specific guiding principles—simple, decent, and affordable.

- Simple: HH houses are modestly sized, large enough for the homeowner's family's needs, and small enough to keep construction and maintenance costs at a minimum.
- Decent: HH houses use quality, locally available building materials and are designed to reflect the local climate and culture.
- Affordable: HH houses use labor provided by volunteers and partner families, efficient building materials; modest house sizes and no-profit loans make it affordable for low-income families to purchase an HH house (HH, 2010).

HH requires applicants to meet specific qualifications such as citizenship, steady income, good credit, and more. Applicants are also required to invest sweat-equity hours in the building of their home, make a down payment and mortgage payments,

Figure 5.10a

FabCab Housing provides some features (e.g., knee space at the sink, a countertop microwave, and pull hardware) of an accessible, inclusive kitchen. FabCab Design © 2010, Dale Lang

Figure 5.10b

FabCab Housing provides a vanity accessible to limited physical ability with knee space for a wheelchair and easy to reach drawers with pull hardware. FabCab Design © 2010, Dale Lang

as well as attend homeowner education classes (HH, 2011). Even with these strict requirements, HH is committed to building homes for people in need such as those with disabilities. When feasible, HH houses apply basic accessible design features, such as a zero-step entrance and wide passage doors and hallways. However, "houses built in partnership with families with disabilities include additional accessibility features" (HH, 2010, para. 4).

PUBLIC HOUSING

Often people with disabilities have lower incomes and limited access to appropriate housing. In particular, such housing is much scarcer in the rural areas. InformeDesign (2008, November 5) summarized a study that examined barriers to access to affordable and accessible housing. The West Virginia Housing Action Network conducted a study of consumers and providers of public housing. The Consumer Housing Forum included 27 subjects with disabilities. The Housing Providers Summit included 14 subjects who were professionals from various organizations such as **Housing and Urban Development (HUD)**, housing authorities, the West Virginia Department Fund, real estate, banks, and other housing providers. Both groups discussed the barriers related to obtaining low-income, accessible housing in rural areas.

Some of the major findings for consumers relate to excessive costs, waitlists, location and access to services, and discrimination against those with disabilities noted through housing design. Providers perceived cost to be higher for accessible housing, concerns with government regulations, limited incomes of those with disabilities, concerns for cultures and the environment, and limited knowledge and understanding of those with disabilities.

Cultural Sensitivity

Cultural sensitivity means considering the needs of others. Tasoulla Hadjiyanni, Ph.D and Assistant Professor at the University of Minnesota, (2003, January) states that designers must realize that immigrants have left their homeland for a better life, but the immigrants also need to retain a connection to that culture. It is important, therefore, for designers to acknowledge and respond to what makes one culture different from another and thereby provide residences that support cultural identity.

Hadjiyanni (2003, January) suggests the following procedure:
1. Consider differences.
2. Understand the perspective of a cultural group.
3. Develop the programmatic guidelines.
4. Act as agents of change.

To acknowledge and identify cultural differences, designers can ask the following questions: How different are we from each other, and how long will these differences last? Answers to these questions will help determine if a design response is cultural or western (Hadjiyanni, 2003, January, p. 2).

To understand the perspective of a culture, designers cannot assume to know and understand another culture. They must search for answers to questions that they may encounter by conducting interviews among a cultural group. Questions to ask may include: Which elements of your culture do you value and wish to retain and pass along to your children? How do your cultural practices interact with American cultural practices? By answering these questions through interviews, "designers can begin to identify the logic inherent in a culture and the practices that must be supported through housing design" (p. 3).

The research gathered about a culture and its cultural perspectives can help determine the traditions and activities that must be supported in housing design. The research may also determine the characteristics of spaces, room adjacencies, number of occupants as well as types of storage, furniture, and other considerations related to cultural choices.

Becoming an agent of change will help other designers and communities understand and appreciate cultural differences. Designers can raise awareness regarding problems that immigrants and cultural minority groups face. "They can also help celebrate the richness in our lives that results from such cross-cultural encounters" (p.4).

Critical regionalism is a type of cultural sensitivity. In this case, it relates to avoiding sameness and applies ideas and concepts of the region. A position paper summarized by InformeDesign (2006, July 17) developed criteria for applying cultural regionalism. This includes avoidance of cultural sameness; however, it must also represent the culture as a whole. See Study Sketch 5.2: "Impact of Critical Regionalism" for details related to findings and criteria developed from those findings.

Housing Outside the United States

Often in the United States, it has been assumed that other cultures have similar preferences. Though many parts of the world have become westernized or are influenced by Western cultures, other cultures still hold to their traditions.

A GLOBAL VIEW: JAPAN

Understanding another culture (e.g., Japanese, Korean, or others) is very important in design; however, research about other cultures may be difficult because of the language barrier. InformeDesign (2006, June 22) summarized a review of literature that presents research conducted on the environment and aging in Japan. The criteria found in this summary remind designers to analyze the research on design for aging cross-cultures

STUDY SKETCH 5.2: Impact of Critical Regionalism

Critical regionalism can be an advantage or a disadvantage. It avoids sameness by preserving local feeling, but sometimes encounters opposition from those outside the community (i.e., design consultants, planners) and then destroys what it seeks to preserve. InformeDesign (2006, July 17) summarized a position paper that analyzes Luis Barragan's work on the architectural concept of critical regionalism and its impact on cultural identity, modernity, and local custom.

Findings

The analysis determined findings on critical regionalism as follows:

- Deliberately uses geographical and cultural conditions.
- Avoids cultural sameness.
- Frequently uses romanticized and even primitive ideas of a place.
- Ignores current socio-political, economic, and aesthetic makeup of a place.
- Often uses and reduces a single, fashionable national style when it is intended to represent a whole set of unique national styles.
- Represents actual conditions of a particular place.
- Makes people comfortable in their environment by reflecting current cultural conditions.
- Should not be based on one architect's style.

Criteria

Criteria were identified and reported the following:

- Avoid applying cultural sameness.
- Emphasize regional features unique to a particular place.
- Know each region is different and requires a unique style to reflect local values and identity.
- Avoid creating a faux setting that merely acknowledges a sentimental nostalgia of a region rather than its current energy.
- Adapt architecture to local environment and surroundings to acknowledge the local culture.

Implications

Applying critical regionalism is best after conducting a thorough research to develop a firm knowledge of the culture.

Source: InformeDesign. (2006, July 17). "Impact of critical regionalism." Retrieved on July 12, 2010, from http://www.informedesign.umn.edu/Rs_detail. aspx?rsId=1502

and investigate a culture's approach to intergenerational housing as well as assistive devices. It is also important to understand the various unique design elements of a culture. In Japan, for example, the older adult considers bathing areas as therapeutic spaces and that the inclusion of nature is a therapeutic element. Thus, research aids in the understanding of a client's culture because preferences or traditions may be very important to the individual.

A GLOBAL VIEW: THAILAND

In some cultures, children and family members care for the older adult. This tradition is changing, however, because of modernization, urbanization, Western cultural influence and other factors. Therefore, understanding the needs of pre-retirees in countries such as Thailand will help in the design of future housing. InformeDesign (2009, August 4) summarized a study that analyzed the acceptance of nontraditional housing options for older adults in Thailand as well as their attitudes toward housing.

Results from the study indicated that inclusively designed single-family homes were a preferred option. This indicates that inclusively designed homes are preferred among older adults in countries such as Thailand and not just in the United States. Thus, inclusive design is a worldwide or universal concept. For further details see Study Sketch 5.5: "Preferred Housing among Older Adults in Thailand."

Summary

The home is where a person should feel comfortable and safe, and for that reason, it should be adaptable to various aspects of a person's life. Unfortunately, this is not always the case. Through this chapter, emphasis has been placed on not only creating accessible housing but also, and most importantly, inclusive housing. It begins by considering quality versus quantity and being able to modify the home for the occupant and visitors.

Housing for the older adult may be in single- or multifamily housing, or it may be in retirement communities or congregate housing. However, many older adults and Baby Boomers are most apt to prefer their long-term homes and age in place. Therefore, inclusive design should be considered for all aspects of the home (e.g., pathway, entrances, living areas, kitchen, bathrooms, and more). Housing can also integrate sustainable practices along with inclusive design. This would include selecting products and materials that are sustainable, energy efficient, conserve water, nontoxic, and inclusive.

Lastly, in designing affordable housing or housing for another culture, a great deal of effort must be taken to budget, plan, and research. Affordable housing (e.g., prefab, Habitat for Humanity homes, public housing) may not be designed for accessibility; however, with carefully planning and budgeting it is possible. Additionally, designers must also be sensitive to various cultures. People from other cultures may have special needs, and designers must be aware and understand them as well as design an inclusive space. Thus, everyone, regardless of their income or culture, should have the opportunity to live in inclusively designed environments.

Inclusive Design Projects

EXPERIENTIAL PROJECT

1. How can an historic residential building be re-created to be inclusive?

Historic buildings are difficult to design to meet the ADA requirements and even more challenging to design for inclusivity. However, it is possible to provide access without affecting an historic façade.

Locate an historic residence in your community. If possible, tour the building; then determine ways the building can become accessible and inclusive. In a written analysis, explain ways to renovate an historic building and still preserve its historic integrity. Include ideation sketches in the analysis for inclusive design techniques for the building and its interior.

APPLICATIONS PROJECTS

1. How can homes respond positively to the aging eye and hearing limitations?

Often residences are designed for the average individual but not for accessibility or inclusivity; however, inclusivity relates to many limitations—physical, mental, visual, and hearing limitations. In this exercise, the focus is on visual and hearing limitations. Review issues of the aging eye and hearing limitations; then list ways to create a supportive environment for the older adult with both limitations.

2. How can homes be transformed for visitability and aging-in-place?

Many residential floor plans neither provide visitability nor an aging-in-place design. This exercise helps students understand issues with residential plans and considers ways to create inclusive plans.

Select a floor plan from one of the following websites: http://www.coolhouse-plans.com/ or http://www.houseplans.com. Print the plan, and analyze it as follows:

1. List the inclusive features found.
2. List areas that are not inclusive.
3. State how the noninclusive areas will be addressed.
4. Sketch a revised plan to create an entirely inclusive design.

CHAPTER 6

Commercial Design: An Overview

"Design shapes the way we live. So it ought to serve everyone."

—*Eva Maddox*

OBJECTIVES

- **Describe the connection between the design process and commercial environments**
- **Understand how a post-occupancy evaluation can determine ways to change or improve existing and future projects**
- **Discuss the integration of inclusive design related to different aspects of a building**
- **Discuss how VOCs on one building affect another**
- **Discuss the importance of indoor air quality in the environment**
- **Understand the difference between quality and quantity of light**
- **Discuss how lighting and acoustics can affect productivity**
- **Describe the challenges with historic buildings related to accessibility and inclusive design**

KEY TERMS

- accessibility specialist
- assisted listening system (ALS)
- automated teller machine (ATM)
- Braille
- daylighting
- heating ventilation and air conditioning (HVAC)
- indoor air quality (IAQ)
- Landmarks Preservation Commission (LPC)
- occupational therapist
- polyvinyl chloride (PVC)
- post-occupancy evaluation (POE)
- quality lighting
- quantity of light
- reverberations
- text telephone (TTY)
- transgenerational design
- typology (type)
- volatile organic compounds (VOCs)
- wayfinding

ommercial design categories include office, hospitality, healthcare, retail, institutional, recreation, transportation, and outside environments. Within each category there are many **typologies** (or types). For example, the hospitality category includes various types of lodging as well as food and beverage facilities. All commercial design types must comply with the ADA, but not all apply inclusive design criteria.

Because the design process is important to commercial design, this chapter begins by reconnecting inclusive design to the design process. In particular, the designer must begin by considering and asking questions related to the entire space, outside and inside as well as specific aspects of the interior environments. This reconnection of inclusivity to the design process will prepare the designer for a closer look at how the inclusive design process works in the various design types.

Environmental issues and renovation of historic buildings affect all design types and may even compromise the application of inclusive design. However, by law, commercial environments must apply the ADA in new construction and for major renovation projects. This means that almost every place of business and every public building must be accessible to individuals with physical, cognitive, visual, and hearing impairments. Although all commercial environments have the same accessibility requirements, each design type may have different issues. The challenge is to create inclusive environments regardless of type.

The Design Process and Commercial Environments

Designers must comply with the ADA, but they also should strive to create inclusive environments. To determine ways in which inclusive design is integrated into the various stages of the design process, consider the following:

- Programming Phase
  - Develop the design statement; use who, what, and where.
  - Collect data, such as facts and evidence to apply inclusive design criteria and respond to user needs.
  - Analyze the data that include applying the ADA and inclusivity.
  - Write the program that includes inclusive design needs.
- Schematic (or Conceptual) Development Phase
  - Develop conceptual sketches that show inclusivity.
  - Create preliminary layouts that are accessible and adaptable.
  - Select the most suitable plan that fulfills program needs.
  - Select appropriate products and materials that provide a secure environment: healthy, safe, and environmentally friendly.

- Design Development Phase
  - Develop the final drawings—floor plans, furniture plans, elevations, and more—that fully apply inclusive design criteria.
  - Develop schedules, such as finish, doors, and more.
- Contract Document Phase
  - Specify products and materials that are appropriate for good **indoor air quality (IAQ)**.
  - Develop construction documents that show adaptability.
- Contract Administration Phase
  - Construct or install products and materials in an environmentally safe manner.
  - Supervise the project and keep the inclusive design criteria in mind during inspections.
  - Conduct a walk-through and examine for the application of inclusive design criteria.
  - Conduct a **post-occupancy evaluation (POE)** that includes questions addressing inclusive design criteria—responsive to user needs as well as accessible, adaptable, and secure environments.

Regardless of design type, an inclusively designed space is achieved when it is well researched and planned at every phase of the design process.

THE IMPORTANCE OF THE POST-OCCUPANCY EVALUATION (POE)

After a project is completed, evaluating the entire project is important. This can be accomplished using the POE, a site visit and project review conducted from the designer's and the client's point of view. As discussed in Chapter 3, the purpose of a POE is to determine the success of a project—the solutions, the process, and client satisfaction. POEs are conducted by several methods (Piotrowski, 2007). Questionnaires may be a uniformly applied standardized form, customized for the individual client, or a combination of standard questions with customized questions for the client. The sample post-occupancy evaluation provided in this chapter shows a POE that includes an overall and individual evaluation.

Specialists

An **accessibility specialist** is someone who determines if the built environment is compliant with the ADA. In some states, such as Texas, accessibility specialists are registered with the state. The specialist's purpose is to promote and facilitate consistency in the application of accessibility in the physical environment (TRASA, 2010).

Sample Post Occupancy Evaluation

Project: _____

Date: _____

Area or Department: _____

Purpose of evaluation: Assist your company and the design firm in evaluating the design and planning of the office and your work area. Your answers will be anonymous.

Rate the following items using the scale provided:

1. Very satisfied | Satisfied | Neutral | Dissatisfied | Very Dissatisfied | N/A
      5   4   3   2   1   0

   Rating _____

Overall setting:

1. Overall amount of space allocated _____

2. Shape of the work space _____

3. Adequate guest seating _____

4. Density of people _____

5. Location of workstation _____

6. Quality of lighting _____

7. Quality of temperature control _____

8. Overall color scheme _____

9. Overall image (brand, color, atmosphere) _____

10. Overall environment (comfort) _____

11. Overall noise level in the workplace _____

12. Space layout and furniture meets functional work requirements _____

13. Amount of storage _____

14. Ease of circulation _____

15. Flexibility for change, growth, and reconfiguration _____

16. Number of meeting spaces for private conferencing _____

17. Adequate furniture for private conferencing _____

18. Location of private conferencing spaces _____

19. Number of meeting spaces for team sessions _____

20. Location of spaces for team sessions _____

21. Adequate furniture for team sessions _____

22. Visibility to coworkers _____

23. Departmental and team proximities and adjacencies _____

24. Overall comfort _____

25.   Overall rating of the new office environment _____

Personal work station or office space:

1. Location of individual workstation on floor _____
2. Work space allowance for office or work station _____
3. Workstation or furniture arrangement _____
4. Guest seating is adequate _____
5. Desktop space for paper work is adequate _____
6. Desktop space for equipment needs is adequate _____
7. Location and adjustability of computer area _____
8. Function of workstation or furniture _____
9. Adequate storage for materials and equipment when not in use _____
10.   Adequate file drawer space _____
11.   Adequate nonfile drawers for supplies in your office _____
12.   Adequate shelving for reference materials for your office _____
13.   Accommodations for security of work area and documents _____
14.   Workstation or furniture style _____
15.   Furniture color _____
16.   Adjustability of desk chair to provide comfort _____
17.   Lighting levels in your work area are comfortable _____
18.   Adequate task lighting _____
19.   Glare-free computer screen _____
20.   Convenient printer location _____
21.   Convenient copy machine location _____
22.   Workstation or office designed to provide visual privacy _____
23.   Adequate acoustical privacy _____
24.   Suitable workstation or office area _____
25.   Adequate space for team sessions _____
26.   Opportunity to personalize workstation _____
27.   Aesthetically pleasing workstation or office area _____
28.   Overall satisfaction with new workstation or office _____

Provide additional comments here:

An example of questions used on a post-occupancy evaluation form adapted from various sources: 1) Becker, F. (1990). *The Total Workplace.* New York: Wiley; 2) Coleman, C. (2002). *Interior design handbook of professional practice.* New York: McGraw-Hill; 3) Piotrowski, C. M. (2007). *Professional practice for interior designers.* New York: Wiley.

The accessibility specialist works on compliance of the ADA in the built environment whereas an **occupational therapist** (OT) helps the individual perform daily activities within the built environment. According to the AOTA (2010), the OT generally provides services as follows:

- Customized treatment programs to improve one's ability to perform daily activities
- Comprehensive home and job site evaluations with adaptation recommendations
- Performance skills assessment and treatment
- Adaptive equipment recommendations and usage training
- Guidance to family members and caregivers (para. 2)

The American Occupational Therapy Association, Inc. (AOTA) website, http://www.aota.org/Consumers.aspx, provides information for the consumer about returning to work as well as work-related injuries. Click the Professional category on the left. Then, click the Fact Sheets link to find information about the role of the OT. Then, click an area of interest, such as productive aging; rehabilitation, disability, and participation; or work and industry (AOTA, 2010). Other information found on the website assists not only the professional (i.e., evaluation sheets) but also helps the consumer understand the OT's role in rehabilitation, returning to work, and more.

As noted in Chapter 2, an accessibility specialist as well as an OT should be included in the beginning of the design process so appropriate measures can be taken to assist all people regardless of ability. A team approach that includes an accessibility specialist and an OT will ensure accessibility as well as ways to provide inclusive environments.

Integration of Inclusive Design

Danise Levine (2003), the assistant director at the Center for Inclusive Design and Environmental Access at the University of Buffalo, developed ideas and a checklist to comply with the ADA and apply inclusive design as well. Her ideas can be integrated throughout the design process. The following includes questions related to each area.

OUTSIDE TO INSIDE

To implement inclusivity throughout the design process, it must also move from outside in, beginning from the time guests or clients exit their automobiles in a parking lot or approach a building from the street. Easy access to an entrance is key. (See Figure 6.1.)

Questions that Address Outside to Inside

- Is there priority parking close to the entrance for different users (e.g., senior citizens, pregnant women)?
- Is the parking lot safe and secure?
- Is the parking lot illuminated?
- Are all pathways illuminated?
- Are there optional pathways to access the entrance?
- Are all pathways easily accessible?
- Are all pathways free of obstacles?
- Is the pathway easy to maneuver (even nonreflective)?
- Is the passenger loading zone illuminated?
- Is the passenger loading zone accessible to all?
- Is a protective covering provided over the passenger loading zone?
- Is an accessible entrance separate or the same for everyone?
- Is there good signage that indicates the entrance?
- Does the door automatically sense that someone is arriving?
- Is the door easy for anyone to open if a sensor is not used?

CIRCULATION

When inside the building, accessibility is required by law. However, some interior environments may still be difficult to maneuver. Therefore it is important to create circulation that is inclusive and meets everyone's needs.

Figure 6.1

A good example of easy access is shown in Figure 6.1, where anyone, regardless of ability, can move from a parking lot to the sidewalk and toward the entrance easily. © Shutterstock

Questions that Address Circulation

- Is there plenty of clear floor space in the entrance or lobby?
- Is enough space allowed for a group of people to meet without blocking the entrance or affecting circulation?
- Is the welcome, information, registration desk, or other similar area easy to locate?
- Does an elevator or ramp connect every level?
- Are all paths of travel illuminated and easily located?
- Is the elevator lobby close to the entrance or an important entrance function?
- Is there plenty of clear floor space to make a 180-degree turn in the elevator lobby for a large group, wheelchairs, strollers, or to pull luggage?
- Are call buttons at the appropriate level and easy to locate?
- If elevators are not appropriate, is there an escalator, a moving walkway, or a method of moving large numbers people quickly?
- Is there a voice-activated announcement or color-coding provided when there are changes in elevation, movement, or a similar change?
- Are transitional spaces such as hallway or corridor illuminated?
- Are transitional spaces devoid of obstacles?
- Are transitional spaces wide enough to accommodate a group of people?
- Is the space easy to circulate with appropriate signage, markers, and other wayfinding devices?

ENTERING AND EXITING

Many people have difficulty entering a building whether or not they are in a wheelchair. Some may have loss of dexterity in their hands; some may use walkers; some may have temporary immobility and use a walker, cane, or crutches; and some may have visual limitations and find it difficult to locate a handle. For these reasons, commercial environments must be easily accessed. (See Figures 6.2 and 6.3.)

Questions that Address Entering and Exiting

- Is the entrance door on a sensor?
- If not, is it easy to maneuver through the door with packages, strollers, small children, arthritic hands, canes, crutches, or wheelchairs?
- Is the pathway clear at the entrance?
- Is the entrance also an emergency egress?
- Is the escape route safe, easy to locate, and well marked?
- Are exit signs illuminated at the floor level?
- Are there visual and audible signaling systems?
- Is a place of refuge provided for emergency use?
- Is there a two-way emergency communication system in remote areas?

FINISHES

All surface finishes (walls, ceiling, floors) must be finished to meet fire and building codes as well as comply with the ADA. However, inclusive design goes beyond just meeting and complying with a standard.

Questions that Address Finishes

- Are all walking surfaces stable and firm?
- Are all walking surfaces smooth and level?
- Do all hard or resilient floor coverings have nonslip finishes?
- If floor covering changes are needed, are they within a half inch?
- Are colors easy on the eyes?
- Are materials nonreflective?

ENTRY, LOBBY, RECEPTION AREAS, AND AMENITIES

Entrances generally have lobbies or reception areas close by. If waiting is necessary, amenities such as fountains, telephones, waste receptacles, and restrooms should be provided. (See Figures 6.4a and b.)

Figure 6.2

Braille signage accommodates those with poor vision. Here the sign is written in both the English language and in Braille. © Stephan John/iStockphoto

Figure 6.3

Retail stores are required to keep corridors free for exiting. However, within the stack of merchandise and to display as much merchandise as possible, racks hang close together. In this example, it would be difficult to move between racks without bumping into clothing, and it would be impossible for someone in a wheelchair or using crutches to navigate this section of clothing display. Photo courtesy Linda L. Nussbaumer

Figures 6.4a and b

Waiting areas must be inviting and comfortable for the user. Figure 6.4a is inviting because of its openness and materiality. The path of travel is clear, which provides easy access to anyone. Materials are nonreflective, and colors are neutral—both are comfortable to the eyes. Figure 6.4b is also very open but less inviting for a couple of reasons. Although open, the height is overwhelming and, therefore, not inviting to the occupant. Some materials are reflective, as found on the finish of the shiny black tile. Reflective light can cause eye irritation and fatigue. Additionally, the two-story windows increase the amount of light, thus causing a reflection. © Shutterstock (a); © Nikada/iStockphoto (b)

Questions that Address Entry Areas

- Are all entry doors automated and on grade?
- Is there seating for people who must wait?
- Is seating conveniently located to amenities, such as fountains, telephones, waste receptacles, and restrooms?
- Are amenities at adjustable or alternative heights?
- Do fixtures and grab bars accommodate various needs?
- Is a directory and **wayfinding** information provided that includes visual, tactile, and audible forms?

SEATING

Seating is fixed for some commercial environments whereas other seating is moveable. However, to reach rooms (auditoriums, classrooms, conference rooms) or areas (lobbies, reception areas, stadium-seating areas, ballrooms, pre-function rooms), some people may have difficulty or not be provided the same access. (See Figure 6.5.)

Questions Related to Seating

- If not at the entrance, is there directional signage to guide people to their destinations?
- Is there an area for large groups when they enter a lobby, for example?

- Is there space for people with varied abilities but not limited to one area?
- Are amenities easy to locate and accessible to everyone?
- Is there space for wheelchairs with fixed seating, and are there optional places for a wheelchair?

WORKSTATIONS

Workstations are found in most commercial buildings. Workstations must be accessible and adaptable for present and future employees.

Questions that Address Workstations

- Do all workstations have accessible circulation through the building layout?
- Is the workstation adjustable for changing needs?
- Is there extra space for future accommodations?
- Is there an option to sit or stand at the workstation?

EXHIBIT SPACES

Museums or exhibit spaces in public buildings are frequent destinations for travelers and educational groups. With varying abilities, these spaces must be accessible but also designed with everyone in mind.

Figure 6.5

Furniture selected for waiting areas should accommodate a variety of occupants. This example provides individual armchairs and a sofa as well. This furniture can accommodate individuals with less strength and who may use their arms to lift themselves from the chair. Various-sized chairs provide options for those of varying sizes and abilities. © Fai Wong/iStock

Questions that Address Exhibit Spaces

- Is information in major exhibition spaces provided in alternative languages?
- Is seating located throughout the exhibition space?
- Is the path through the exhibition space accessible?
- Is descriptive information located at accessible sight lines for all displays?
- Is alternative media such as audio-visual presentations and interactive devices at accessible reach with operable controls provided?

VARIOUS TYPES OF OTHER ROOMS (SLEEPING, CLASSROOMS, AND MORE)

Although there are a variety of room types, locating and accessing these spaces have similar concerns for inclusive design.

Questions that Address Various Concerns

- Does signage have tactile characters, well proportioned and easy-to-read fonts, good contrast, and **Braille**?
- Is signage mounted at the required height?
- Is the room numbering system logical so that it is easy to find rooms?
- Is there an audio signage for key destinations?
- Are rooms fully accessible or adaptable for various needs?

OUTDOOR SPACES

Some commercial designs provide outdoor spaces for natural beauty as well as restorative purposes. These spaces as well as outdoor recreational spaces (playgrounds, playing fields, tennis courts) must also be designed for all to use.

Questions that Address Outdoor Spaces

- Is there an accessible path of travel to and through the outdoor space?
- Is seating available that will accommodate a variety of sizes and abilities?
- Is there an area that provides protection from sun and rain?

PRODUCTS AND SERVICES

Products and services are provided in many different types of commercial environments, from registration in a hotel lobby to products in a retail space. All products and services should be accessible to everyone, whether they are reaching for the products or signing a check at the cashier's counter.

Questions that Address Products and Services

- Can the product be reached by anyone regardless of ability or stature?
- Are there varied counter heights and widths to accommodate varied sizes and mobility?

- Is privacy between users provided for everyone regardless of counter height?
- Are aisles unobstructed?
- Is there plenty of clear floor space for a wheelchair to maneuver through aisles without obstructing others?
- Are there no protruding objects from walls or in aisles that reduce the clear floor space, turning radius, and general circulation?
- Is signage at a level for anyone to see?
- Are products adequately illuminated?

LIGHTING AND ACOUSTICS

Illuminating a space properly and providing appropriate acoustical levels is essential in interior environments and, especially, for an inclusive environment.

Questions that Address Lighting and Acoustics

- Is adequate natural light flowing into the space?
- Is the occupant able to control natural lighting with shades, blinds, or other means?
- Are external shading, light shelves, tinted glass, baffles, or other methods provided to minimize direct or reflected glare?
- Are artificial light controls within reach and operable from a wheelchair or with a closed fist or open hand?
- Does the artificial lighting support task performance?
- Is adequate artificial lighting provided for security and safety?
- Are higher illumination levels provided for key features such as signs, stair treads, landmarks, and more?
- Are **reverberations** (echoes) controlled to provide the best sound level for the activity?
- Is background noise controlled to allow conversation but also support concentration?

THERMAL COMFORT

Physical comfort is important to the well being of occupants and, particularly, job satisfaction and productivity. It also helps in creating an inclusively designed space.

Questions that Address Thermal Comfort

- Are all controls within reach and operable from a wheelchair or with a closed fist or open hand?
- Are spaces heated and cooled effectively?
- Are controls available for occupants to adjust to individual needs?

VARIOUS SYSTEMS

Security systems, emergency alarms, public address systems, telecommunications systems, and more are required; however, for inclusive design, additional methods of communication or alarms can provide greater security.

Questions that Address Various Types of Systems

- Are emergency communications devices placed in strategic locations?
- Is access to the building monitored directly or through video?
- Is there two-way emergency communications in all remote areas?
- Is there a system to direct users toward safe routes during an evacuation?
- Along with the **assisted listening system (ALS)**, is there an equivalent public information announcement system through audible and visual modes?
- Is current information available through wireless web access?
- Is the public telephone hearing-aid compatible with volume control and **text telephone (TTY)** access?
- Is the public telephone mounted within reach with clear floor space?
- Are TTYs or electrical outlets and shelves provided at all public telephone locations?
- Is the telephone system hearing-aid and TTY compatible?
- Are **automatic teller machines (ATM)** and public Internet access points within required reach, provided with clear floor space, have operable controls and alternative input and output methods?
- Is it possible to use multiple payment methods?
- Are ATMs adaptable to different statures, sensory abilities, and languages?

RESPONSIVE, ADAPTABLE, ACCESSIBLE, AND SECURE

These questions address not only the ADA but also inclusive design needs that are responsive, adaptable, accessible, and secure. Additionally, these questions and more can be asked during various phases of the design process so that the design is truly inclusive. Other concerns arise beyond these questions, such as environmental concerns and renovations of historic buildings.

Specific Areas of Concern

Lighting and acoustics are particularly important to create a secure environment (related to health, safety, and welfare). Lighting is especially important, not only for a secure environment but also in the interest of being adaptable and responsive to individual needs. When properly designed, a building's acoustics provide comfort to the user.

LIGHTING

Both the quality and quantity of light affect an environment and the well being of its occupants. Quality lighting produces not only an aesthetically pleasing environment, but it also provides comfort and safety. Quantity of light is the measurable amount of light used within the space and includes both artificial and natural lighting for visual comfort and security.

Achieving Quality Lighting

Quality lighting helps users function comfortably, feel safe, and reside in an aesthetically pleasing environment; therefore, to achieve quality lighting, designers must apply design theory, human factors, and conservation principles. Quality lighting also includes layered lighting (natural and multiple artificial sources), which means the use of natural light through daylighting as well as various sources of artificial light to provide quality lighting.

It is also important to consider the color rendition and temperature of a light source to create quality lighting. The **color rendering index (CRI)** number ranges from 0 to 100 and corresponds to the way an object appears under a light source. "The higher the CRI number, the better the color rendering ability of the lamp" (Winchip, 2011, p. 30). For example, an incandescent lamp has a CRI number of approximately 95 compared to the common 4-foot fluorescent lamps, which are 62 (see Table 6.1). This means that lamps with a CRI of 80 or more are closer to natural light and create a more comfortable and pleasing environment.

Color temperature indicates the degree of red or blue found in natural and artificial light sources and is measured in **kelvins (K)**. If the number of kelvins is lower, the color of a light source appears warmer with a tone of red. On the other hand, if the number is higher, the color of the light source appears cooler with a tone of blue. Thus, "measured in kelvins, the warm color from a candle is approximately 2,000K whereas the cool daylight is 5,000K. Also measured in kelvins, lamps range from 3,000K to 4,100K" (Nussbaumer, 2009a).

TABLE 6.1 Color Rendering Index (CRI)

LAMP	CRI INDEX
Incandescent	95
Premium cool white compact fluorescent light (CFL)	88
Premium 4-foot fluorescent	85
Premium warm white CFL	84
Common warm white CFL	80
Common 4-foot fluorescent lamp	62
Common high-pressure sodium	22

Source: Color Rendering (2007).

Daylighting is an important addition to enhance quality lighting. It can provide a connection to the outdoors and increase an individual's general well being. For people who work indoors, the benefits of daylighting include better health, which results in reduced absenteeism, increased productivity, and financial savings. Studies also show that daylighting decreases the frequency of headaches, eyestrain, and seasonal affective disorder (SAD) (Edwards & Torcellini, 2002).

There are, of course, some negative aspects of daylighting. If not controlled, it can cause glare, fading, and higher interior temperatures when not needed. The amount of daylight must be controlled, and materials must be chosen that eliminate glare.

Applying Best Practices for Quality of Lighting

Technically, the quantity of artificial light in a space is achieved by calculating lumen or point-by-point; however, calculating the quantity of light will not be discussed in this book. For more information, refer to *Fundamentals of Lighting* (2011) and *Designing a Quality Lighting Environment* (2005) by Susan Winchip. In this book, artificial and natural lighting will be discussed as they relate to creating an inclusive environment—adaptable and secure.

Artificial lighting should be carefully chosen to create a comfortable, healthy environment. Lighting might come from a variety of sources, mountings, and directions with the ability to control light levels. These include:

- Lamps (or light sources): Used in luminaries include incandescent, fluorescent, and high-intensity discharge (HID), and come in a variety of sizes, shapes, and materials.
- Luminairies (fixtures): May be surface mounted, recessed, suspended, track, structural, portable, or furniture integrated.

The direction of light may be direct, indirect, semi-direct, semi-indirect, or diffused (Winchip, 2008; 2011).

Determining the appropriate lamp, luminaire, and direction of light depends on the purpose of the lighting. The purpose could be to create ambient (general), task, and/or accent lighting. A combination of these should be used to create a layered composition.

For quality lighting, glare must be eliminated. To do so, ambient (general) lighting should provide indirect light using both daylight and energy-efficient fluorescent lamps. For task lighting, it is important to direct light toward the task or activity (paper and computer tasks). By using diffusers where needed, the light will not cause glare.

Another important aspect of quality lighting is that the specific space and human activity must be kept in mind. Examples of specific areas include a kitchen, office, fitness room, and so on; human activities include preparing meals, reading, dining, and more. Interior elements (e.g., materials, colors, texture, and furniture) and the architectural elements (e.g., shape, details, and more) also affect the quality of light.

For example, shiny materials may reflect light whereas textured materials may absorb light. Careful consideration must be taken when selecting and layering lighting for a specific area as well as responding to occupants (Winchip, 2011).

Lighting Affects Human Health

Lighting also affects human health and behavior both positively and negatively. For example, poor lighting can cause eyestrain, headaches, premature aging, and other conditions; flickering lights may trigger seizures for individuals with epilepsy. Lighting may also affect human emotions. Sunshine may generate cheerful feelings whereas gloomy conditions can generate "feelings of depression and sadness" (Winchip, 2005, p. 324–5).

Lighting affects worker productivity and more. According to the National Lighting Bureau (NLB, 2010), lighting can enhance work environments, increase productivity, improve security, and facilitate maintenance. This was the case when the San Diego Federal Building and Courthouse was renovated. In fact, the $1.3 million investment paid for itself in less than eight months with significant improvements in productivity, safety, security, and energy efficiency (see Figure 6.6).

Several indoor environmental quality (IEQ) factors (i.e., noise, lighting, temperature, and air quality) impact human health. This is indicated through the InformeDesign (2010, July 7a) research summary, "Comparing Environmental Research in Office and Health Care Environments." A couple of examples include daylighting and fluorescent lamps: access to daylight may improve health; and a fluorescent lamp with magnetic ballast negatively affects human health, but the negative affects are reduced with digital ballasts. See Study Sketch 6.1: "Comparing Environmental Research in Office and Health Care Environments" for further details.

Lighting affects behavior as well as human health both positively and negatively. Daylight brightens an environment and direct sunlight is a source of vitamin D; however too much daylight can cause glare that causes squinting. Poor lighting can cause eyestrain, headaches, premature aging (wrinkles from squinting), skin cancer, and other conditions. Flickering lights upset individuals with autism or may trigger seizures for individuals with epilepsy.

Lighting can also affect human emotions. For example, sunshine may generate cheerful feelings whereas gloomy conditions (rainy or cloudy) can generate a depressed or sad feeling. Artificial lighting can also create similar perceptions (Winchip, 2005; 2011). Lighting affects everyone differently, and thus, to create a comfortable inclusive space, a layered composition is best (various sources, such as artificial and natural, mountings, directions) with controls to brighten or dim as needed.

ACOUSTICS

Noise in any interior environment can be disruptive; therefore, sound-absorbing materials can be applied to control noise. These materials may be applied to or installed on interior floors, walls, ceilings, and furniture. Selection of sound-absorbing materials for commercial spaces is especially important because of the greater number and movement of people (Nussbaumer, 2009a). Acoustics must be carefully considered in its design and when creating an inclusive environment.

The noise reduction coefficient (NRC) for materials provides sound absorption amounts. For example, concrete or terrazzo is .02; wood is .03; carpeting on concrete is .45; and carpeting with pad is .70 (NRCs, 1998; Nussbaumer, 2009a). In areas where sound must be absorbed to provide comfort for the occupants, the higher NRC is needed.

When hard surfaces are selected for a space, methods of absorbing sound must be determined. New innovative ideas have emerged to absorb sound in spaces where there are many hard surfaces. One example is SoundScapes® Acoustical Canopies and Shapes by Armstrong®. These ceiling and wall treatments absorb sound and reduce background noise, thus allowing occupants to converse and work. The product acts

Figure 6.6

The new courthouse in San Diego connected the existing federal building (at the left and off the picture frame) to the new building through plazas, gardens, a water feature, and pedestrian paths. The design incorporated daylighting throughout the entire building. press@richardmeier.com

as a sponge for reverberant noise and absorbs sound waves on both front and back surfaces. Figure 6.7a shows a large open space whereas Figure 6.7b shows an open conferencing area with ceiling clouds designed to absorb sound.

Various Concerns in Commercial Design

Several specific concerns for commercial environments relate to environmental concerns and the renovation of historic buildings. Both must be addressed to create an inclusive environment.

ENVIRONMENTAL CONCERNS

Environmental concerns must be addressed to have inclusive and secure environments. Particularly, the quality of indoor air (IAQ) affects the health as well as the productivity of those who use the environment on a daily basis. Problems caused by poor **indoor air quality (IAQ)** can be attributed to modern technology, synthetic materials and fibers, newer cheaper products (i.e., plastic, chemical by-products), and the energy crisis of the 1970s that led to the tightening of buildings (Nussbaumer, 2009a; 2009b). Therefore, interior products and materials must be carefully selected to provide spaces that are inclusive of everyone.

RENOVATIONS OF HISTORIC BUILDINGS

Another challenge is the renovation of historic buildings. Often it is difficult to meet and comply with the ADA and next to impossible to apply inclusive design concepts. However, some commercial business owners work hard to design accessible environments, but run into regulatory barriers.

Challenges with Historic Building Restoration and Accessibility

An example of a building restoration challenge occurred in New York City. The owner of a restaurant located in a landmark building had attempted to meet the ADA accessibility guidelines and completed the paperwork to install an exterior stairwell handrail, but the **Landmarks Preservation Commission (LPC)** rejected the request. The LPC states they did not reject the request, however, and when a business wants to put accessibility features in place, the LPC would never turn down a barrier-free access. The LPC's job is to "figure out a way to solve a problem without detracting from the historic building or diminishing its significance" (Beane, 2010, March 4, para. 4).

Misunderstandings occur when renovating and altering the exterior of an existing structure, such as landmark or historic buildings. The law considers an extensive renovation as the equivalent of new construction. This means that the entire structure must be made accessible unless the owner proves that compliance would cause an undue economic burden. Between the extensive renovation and its costs, many buildings are still not accessible.

In "Preservation versus Accessibility," Horace Havemeyer III (2009, October 13) describes several common problems with accessibility into an historic building. Using crutches, he stepped down and, then up four steps to gain entrance. When inside, he learned that there was an elevator, but it did not stop on the main floor. Handing one crutch to his wife, he tackled the stairs with his left hand on the railing and his right arm on the crutch. When on the second level, if he needed to use a bathroom, he needed to maneuver himself down two flights. Unfortunately, in preserving an historic building, accessibility is often ignored or may not be possible. It is difficult to provide accessibility at a front entrance of an historic site because, if on the National

a

b

Figure 6.7a and b

The ceiling clouds absorb sound and allow conversation and work to take place in both (a) large open space and (b) smaller space that also requires sound-absorbing materials. Each has used an appropriately shaped canopy for the needs its space requires. Armstrong Ceiling and Wall

Register of Historic Sites, it cannot be changed—only preserved. An example of one is described in Case Study 6.1, "Vizcaya Museum and Gardens."

Making Historic Renovation Successful and Accessible

There have been successful renovations in which the exterior was preserved and accessibility gained. Wesleyan University in Middletown, Connecticut, was founded in 1831 and has many historic buildings. The university needed a performing arts center in the middle of campus; however, there were several challenges. The layout of the new building was to provide an accessible path through the site and into the building. While still maintaining the integrity of the historic building, principal entrances (front and rear) into the historic building had to be kept and include a modern main campus walk. The Institute of Human Centered Design's (2010) website described the inclusive design features included in the project:

- Flexible use throughout the entire renovation
- Inclusively designed worship platform
- Seamless path of travel from the new building to both historic buildings
- Flexible lighting that can adapt to a wide array of functions
- Good acoustical conditions including isolation of **heating ventilation and air conditioning (HVAC)** noise

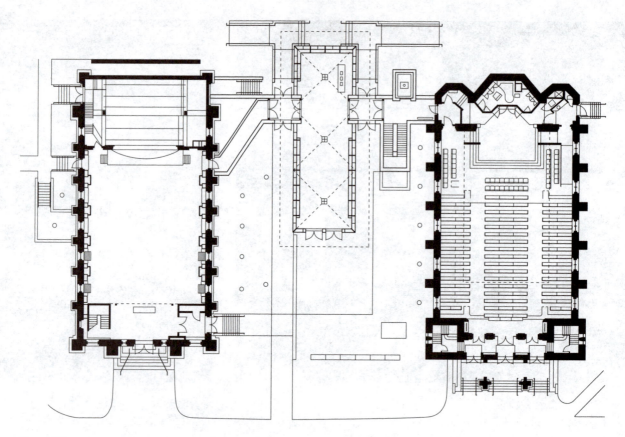

Figure 6.8a

This floor plan shows the new modern building in the center that provides access to two pre-existing buildings at Wesleyan University in Middletown, Connecticut. The new design also preserves the integrity of the historic buildings. © Precision Graphics

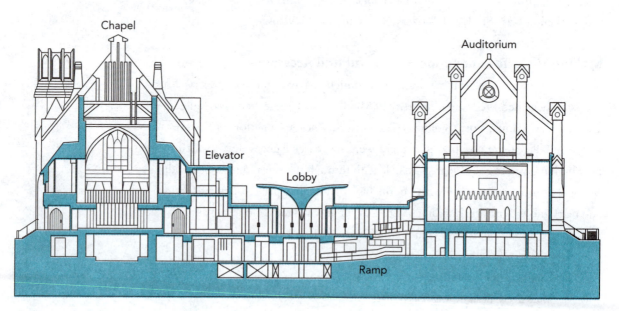

Figure 6.8b

The cross section shows two historic buildings with the modern entrance between. (Placement is viewed from the opposite side of the floor plan in Figure 6.8b.) The chapel is on the left and the auditorium on the right. An elevator near the chapel provides access to the chapel's balcony. © Precision Graphics

The map on the campus website provides information for those with mobility limitations—valuable information to know before visiting the campus. Also described are environmentally sustainable features:

- The existing historic buildings were renovated; Memorial Chapel for a variety of uses and the 92 Theater into a state-of-the-art theater—an adaptive reuse project.
- The glass pavilion is sited between existing north and south buildings. It is designed with roof overhangs to minimize heat gain and preserve transparency, thus eliminating the need for shading.

The intent of this project was to create seamless physical access to two historic buildings. The floor plan and section in Figures 6.8a and b show how the modern building in the center connects the historic buildings on either side. Because these historic buildings are not at the same level, ramping was required to enter the theater or auditorium from the central building. The glass lobby provided an entrance that does not distract from the historic buildings (see Figure 6.8c). To continue the inclusive environment, a ramp was included to access the altar area and an elevator was installed near the chapel to provide access to the balcony (see Figure 6.8d).

Historic buildings are often found in the heart of the city or even on university campuses. Some were hotels, apartment buildings, school buildings, or commercial

Figure 6.8c

The new, modern lobby feeds guests to either historic building through covered walkways. © 2003 Anton Grassl/architect: Robert Olson + Associates LLC

Figure 6.8d

The chapel interior renovation included a ramp to the altar, flexible lighting that offers a wide array of functions, and quality acoustics that feature isolation of HVAC noise. © 2007 Anton Grassl/architect: Robert Olson + Associates LLC

buildings. The challenge in renovating such buildings is to preserve history—the exterior in particular—and still be accessible and apply inclusive design. The problem will continue on into the future, but each situation must be dealt with individually and may be dependent on its intended use.

Making Auditorium Seating Accessible and Inclusive

Many public assembly buildings (e.g., opera houses, theaters, movie theaters, and more) present a challenge to accessibility. If the building is an historic site with steps at its entrance, access for wheelchairs is frequently not available. Fortunately, at most historic sites, visitors are directed by signage to the accessible entrance. If the building provides access at the main entrance, it will also have an accessible lobby. The greatest challenge occurs with auditorium seating. Many theaters limit seating for wheelchairs.

The Mitzi E. Newhouse Theater in the Lincoln Center for Performing Arts offers four accessible seating spaces and two companion seats located in row H (the last row). These seats are located in the sections on either side of the center orchestra section. The theater's capacity is 334—a ratio of 4/334 or 1.1 percent. As Baby Boomers age, this may be satisfactory. Because seating is in the round, these are excellent seats (see Figure 6.9a).

On the other hand, the Vivian Beaumont Theater in the Lincoln Center for Performing Arts in New York City offers four accessible seating spaces and four companion seats located in row O (see Figure 6.9b). Each pair (wheelchair and companion) is located in four different sections with the exception of the center section. The theater's seating capacity is 752—a ratio of 4/752 or .05 percent. In comparison to the Newhouse Theater, the percentage is low. Additionally, because row G is considered the best theater seats, this places those with limited mobility twice as far back in the theater.

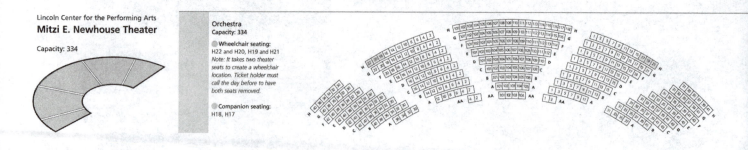

Lincoln Center for the Performing Arts
Mitzi E. Newhouse Theater

Capacity: 334

Orchestra
Capacity: 334

● Wheelchair seating:
H22 and H20, H19 and H21
Note: It takes two theater seats to create a wheelchair location. Ticket holder must call the day before to have both seats removed.

● Companion seating:
H18, H17

Figure 6.9a

The Mitzi E. Newhouse Theater in the Lincoln Center for Performing Arts offers four accessible seating areas and two companion seats located in row H (the last row). These seats are located in the sections on either side of the center orchestra section. © Lincoln Center for the Performing Arts, Inc.

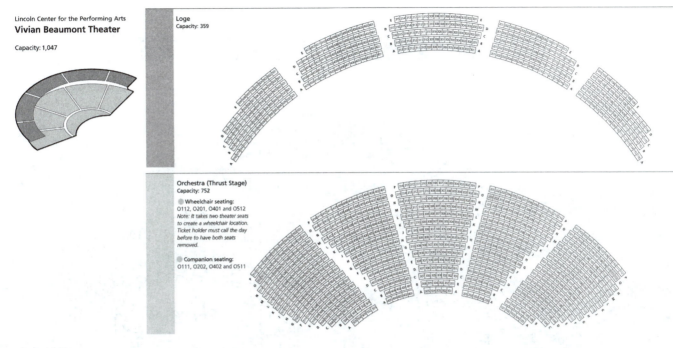

Figure 6.9b

The Vivian Beaumont Theater in the Lincoln Center for Performing Arts in New York City offers four accessible seating areas and four companion seats located in row O. © Lincoln Center for the Performing Arts, Inc.

As a comparison, the historic Orpheum Theater in Minneapolis, Minnesota, offers four accessible seating areas on the lower level and six on the upper level with an equal number of companion seats. Accessible seating is located on a flat, level area with padded armchairs that may be removed when a wheelchair is required. This theater provides not only a higher number of accessible seating but also options for additional seating. (See Figures 6.9c and d.)

In Boston, the Huntington Theater Company's Virginia Wimberly Theatre provides sidewalk-level access and an accessible box office. Wheelchair access is located at both orchestra (lower) and mezzanine (upper) levels, and the theater offers six accessible seating areas on the lower level and eight on the upper level (see Figure 6.9e). This theater also provides assistive listening devices and a sign language interpreter.

Supplementary large-type and Braille house programs are distributed at some of Lincoln Center's performances. Similar to the Wimberly Theatre, assistive listening devices are available or sign language can be arranged. Through the center's Department of Programs and Services for People with Disabilities (PSPD), staff is trained to be aware and sensitive to those with disabilities.

From this information, theaters provide accessible auditorium seating with limitations. The number of wheelchair seating is limited; the choice of location is also limited; in historic theaters without elevators, accessible seating is not available; and some provide hearing and visual assistive devices whereas others don't. Clearly, an effort is made to provide access to people, but not all theaters are inclusive to people of varying abilities.

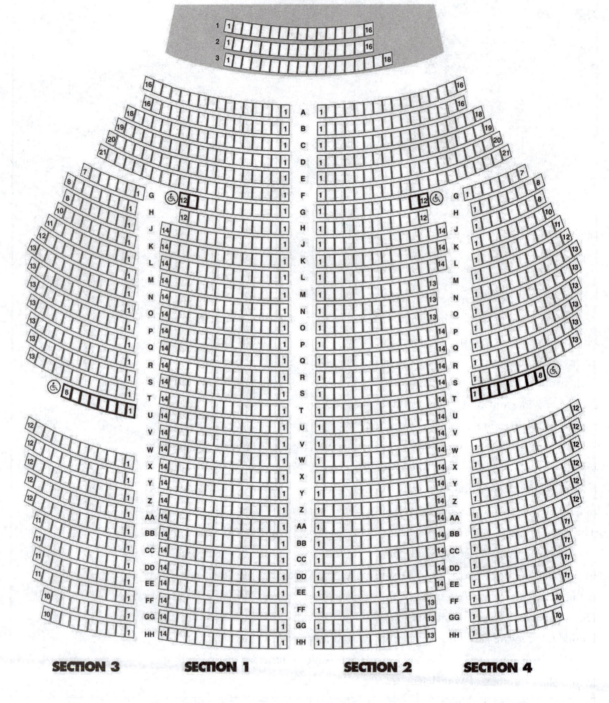

Figure 6.9c

The historic Orpheum Theater in Minneapolis, Minnesota, offers four accessible seating areas on the lower level and six on the upper level with an equal number of companion seats. Courtesy of Hennepin Theater Trust

Figure 6.9d

The Orpheum Theater in Minneapolis, Minnesota, provides two levels of seating. As an historic building and interior, renovations must comply with the National Historic Register; however, accessible seating is available on both levels. Courtesy of Hennepin Theater Trust

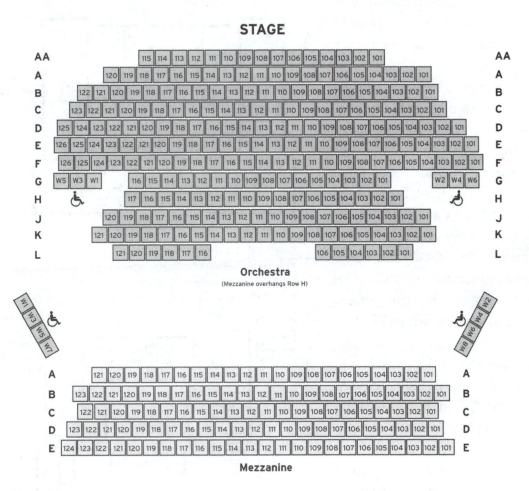

Figure 6.9e

In Boston, the Huntington Theater Company's Virginia Wimberly Theatre provides a greater number of choices for accessible seating than most theaters. huntingtontheatre.org

In 1916, Vizcaya was built as the industrialist James Deering's Miami winter home on the Atlantic Ocean. An agricultural industrialist, Deering had visited European villas and appreciated the beauty; therefore, his home was built in the style of Italian Renaissance and Baroque villas along with elaborate formal gardens, also designed in the European style. Today Vizcaya is an historic museum, which contains its original furniture and furnishings and provides a wonderful history lesson for all who visit.

At the entrance and throughout the property, access is through sets of steps. Six steps are found at the main entrance (see Case Study Figure 6.1a) and another four steps continue beyond this entrance to the entrance hall on the left or clients room on the right (see Case Study Figure 6.1b). Although an elevator exists in the home, the public can use only the staircase to access the second and third levels (see Case Study Figure 6.1c). The gardens also are laden with steps, which limit areas those in a wheelchair can access.

The museum and gardens can be accessed only through the side archway, as seen in Figure CS 6.1d, the accessibility plan. When in this area, wooden ramps are found that allow entrance into the main level (see Figure CS 6.1e). As can be seen on the accessibility plan, however, the wheelchair symbol indicates areas where a wheelchair can enter.

Case Study Figure 6.1a

To enter the Vizcaya Museum and Gardens in Miami-Dade County, Florida, the visitor must ascend a set of stairs. Photo courtesy Linda L. Nussbaumer

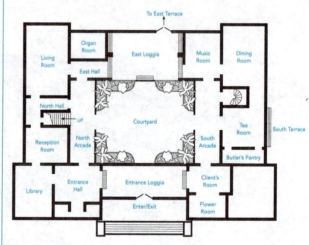

Case Study Figure 6.1b

To access Vizcaya, visitors must ascend not only steps at the entrance but within the main entrance and loggia on the ground floor.
© Precision Graphics

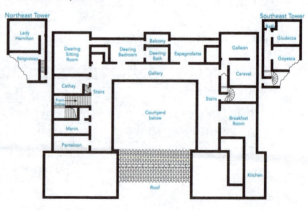

Case Study Figure 6.1c

Access to the second and third levels at Viscaya is only via a staircase.
© Precision Graphics

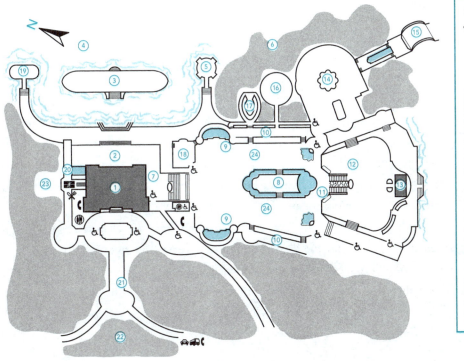

Legend:

✕🍴🏬	Cafe & Shop
🚻	Restrooms
☎	Public Telephone
🚗🚗	Parking
♿	Wheelchair Access

1 Main House
2 East Terrace
3 Stone Barge
4 Biscayne Bay
5 Tea House
6 Mangrove Shore
7 South Terrace
8 Center Island
9 Semi-Circular Pools
10 Statuary Walks
11 Water Stairway and Grottos
12 Mound
13 Casino
14 Fountain Garden
15 Peacock Bridge
16 Maze Garden
17 Theater Garden
18 Secret Garden
19 Yacht Landing
20 Swimming Pool
21 Ticket Booth
22 Rockland Hammock (Native Forest)
23 David A. Klein Orchidarium
24 Parterres

Case Study Figure 6.1d

The accessibility plan indicates entrances and areas for wheelchair access. © Precision Graphics

Prior to a visit, viewing an historic site's website often provides information regarding accessibility. For Vizcaya Museum's website (http://www.vizcaya-museum.org), information is provided regarding accessibility for wheelchair access and those with hearing or sight impairments. The mansion's floor plans (see Case Study Figures 6.1b and c) as well as an accessible plan can be downloaded from the website. For those who are deaf or hard of hearing, sign language interpreters are available to accompany a guided tour; however, a minimum of five working days advance notice is needed. Guidebooks are also available in Braille and large print and can be purchased at the ticket booth.

As with many historic sites, the integrity of Vizcaya's façade and the interior must be preserved; therefore, accessibility

Case Study Figure 6.1e

A wooded ramp behind the main entrance provides access into the ground floor of the museum. Photo courtesy Linda L. Nussbaumer

is hidden from public view. Not only are such sites somewhat inaccessible, but they also do not meet the criteria for inclusive design.

Source: Miami-Dade County (2006). Vizcaya Museum and Gardens. Retrieved on February 1, 2011, from http://www.vizcayamuseum.org

Summary

Commercial environments must apply the ADA, which means that virtually every place of business and every public building must be accessible to individuals with physical, cognitive, visual, and hearing limitations. Providing inclusion is not always a priority; therefore, this chapter begins by connecting inclusive design to the design process and includes questions to ask that are not only about meeting the ADA but also apply inclusive design to various aspects of a design. Two special areas of concern (lighting and acoustics) affect human health and are, therefore, important in creating a secure environment.

Two other important concerns related to commercial as well as residential design are environmental issues and the renovation of historic buildings. In both cases, there are two areas of concern. For environmental issues, using green materials may not necessarily be nontoxic to the environment. For renovation of historic buildings, the challenge is to keep the historic integrity and provide access to those with mobility limitations.

Inclusive Design Projects

EXPERIENTIAL PROJECTS

1. What are ways to connect the design process and commercial environments with inclusivity?

The design process is a systematic method of solving a design problem; however, the process is also cyclical, and it is important to understand the connection between the design process and commercial environments. In written format, complete the following.

1. Describe the connection between the design process and commercial environments.
2. Describe where and how inclusive features will be integrated into the design process.

2. How can commercial environments be inclusive?

Commercial environments must be accessible to everyone and must begin in the parking lot (when applicable). The question the designer must ask is, "Are these environments inclusive?" Locate a commercial space, and examine its integration of inclusive design criteria (responsive, adaptable, accessible, and secure) related to different aspects of the building in each of the following areas.

1. Outside to inside
2. Circulation

3. Entering and exiting

4. Finishes

5. Lobby or reception area

6. Seating

7. Workstations

8. Products and services

9. Lighting and acoustics

In written format, answer the following question for each area: "Is the design responsive, adaptable, accessible, and secure?"

APPLICATION PROJECT

1. Is the historic building accessible or inclusive?

Historic buildings are seldom accessible and, therefore, not inclusive; however, they can be renovated to be both accessible and inclusive. Locate an historic building (e.g., courthouse, library, church, or another historic commercial building). When looking at the building, consider:

1. Is it accessible or inclusive?

2. If the building is accessible or inclusive
   a. Describe how it is accessible.
   b. If it is not inclusive, describe how it can become inclusive.

3. If the building is not accessible or inclusive
   a. Describe the challenges to make the building accessible.
   b. Describe ways to create accessibility and inclusivity as well.

Office Design

"I try to give people a different way of looking at their surroundings. That's art to me."

—*Maya Lin*

OBJECTIVES

- Understand how technology is changing office design
- Determine various electronic communication methods used in offices today
- Describe the various generations and how they can work together successfully
- Discuss how diverse cultures can affect the workplace environment
- Describe an inclusive office as it relates to ergonomics and proxemics
- Describe a comfortable office environment in physical, functional, and psychological categories
- Compare the similar responsibilities of facility managers and interior designers
- Compare the home to the corporate office relative to inclusive design

KEY TERMS

- anthropometric
- Baby Boomers
- GenXers
- hot-desking
- hoteling
- Millennials
- productivity
- proxemics
- Traditionalists
- virtual office

Offices are affected by the ADA for two main reasons. Offices are generally open to the public and, therefore, legally must be accessible to the public. Also, according to ADA Reasonable Accommodations guidelines, offices must be accessible to their employees. To be considered inclusively designed, an office must be accessible and inclusive. Additionally, the fully inclusive office of the twenty-first century must be accommodating in terms of technology and diversity. Moreover, they must be responsive, adaptable, accessible, and secure places to work. Employees must be comfortable both physically and psychologically to be productive.

Offices of the Twenty-First Century

Our world and today's offices are rapidly changing. Among those changes are advances in technology, diversity of workers, concerns for **productivity** and job satisfaction, and health concerns related to physical activity and indoor air quality. Many of these changes have enhanced the opportunities to apply inclusive design as well as ergonomics and sustainable design.

TECHNOLOGY

The driving force behind many of today's changes is technology. In the last several years, advancements in technology have greatly affected the workplace from office machines to office design. Rather than communicating face to face or by phone, information is shared through the computer or other electronic devices (e.g., BlackBerry, iPhone, iPad, and others). Methods of communication occur through various means—email, texting, video conferencing, and so on. Each method provides various types of access (inclusive) and sustainable practices.

Electronic Communications

The web gives access to information needed to learn about any number of topics. Most computers make access to information fairly easy for the majority of people, providing them with instant Internet portals to research in the library, visit a firm to learn about their work, shop for products and materials in an office supply store, and much more. This saves time and energy as well as provides access to all.

Email provides opportunities to communicate with an individual or group anywhere in the world, and this communication can take place using a computer or various types of handheld electronic devices (e.g., BlackBerry, iPhone, iPad). These various communication tools (computer or phone) may provide inclusive access and allow the majority opportunities to communicate with others at a distance.

For those with hearing limitations, email via computer or videophone as well as texting through cellphones are excellent means of communication. For those with visual limitations, inclusive access many be included or add-ons for some computers (as noted in Chapter 4). Additionally, those with mobility difficulties may find communicating from a distance to be safer and more hassle-free than having to move from one place to another. These various methods of communication provide reasonable accommodations within an office.

Video Conferencing

Video conferencing provides excellent means of communicating with a group of people at a distance. The combination of video and audio is an excellent alternative for those with hearing or visual limitations. For some conferencing methods, documents are shared; however, for those with visual limitations, documents may be more difficult because Braille is not included. These individuals will need to rely entirely on the audio portion. However, future technological advances may provide the ability to translate text to Braille.

Virtual Office

The **virtual office** is either an office of the future that senses the occupant's arrival or an office that is not found in one physical location but rather is in a virtual location and accessed through the computer.

The office of the future is one that responds instantly to the occupant's arrival by adjusting the temperature, lighting, and airflow to the preferred settings. It unlocks sealed personal information folders on the computer; it announces one's entrance through overhead lights, alerts coworkers, signals through an exterior electronic message board when the occupant is ready for visitors, the day's agenda, and anything else that needs to be announced (Levitch, 2003; Nussbaumer, 2009).

Companies may conduct their business fully or in part through the computer, and employees who are hired by one or more companies work remotely and use information and communication technologies to conduct business. This "virtual office is characterized by the use of teleworkers, telecenters, mobile workers, **hot-desking**, and **hoteling**, and promotes the use of virtual teams" (CBS Interactive, 2010, para. 1). Because a virtual office is cost effective and efficient, it can increase an organization's flexibility and, at the same time, reduce the cost of maintaining the traditional office. Everything needed to conduct business through the virtual office is in a briefcase or car, i.e., cellphone, laptop computer, fax, printer, etc. Thus, work can be done anywhere at anytime (Nussbaumer, 2009; Piotrowski & Rogers, 2007).

Virtual meetings may take place by phone conference calls or video conferences using products such as Skype. Particularly important in video conferencing is when participants can see each other. This conferencing method provides inclusion of those who may have mobility, visual, and hearing limitations.

Visual problems may occur if someone is wearing a color or pattern that causes visual discomfort to other viewers. Review of color interactions (e.g., afterimage, vibrating boundaries, simultaneous contrast) may assist in selecting the right colors and/or patterns to wear.

Other issues relate to fast movements, which may also be difficult to see, and gestures must be carefully planned so they are not misunderstood.

Technology and Sustainable Practices

Video conferencing and the virtual office may be inclusive of those who have difficulty traveling, but it is also sustainable and a practical method of doing business. In many instances, traveling is not necessary, thus saving fuel costs. Information is exchanged electronically, without paper, thus saving an important resource.

Benching

The workbench has been reinvented and applied to office design. "It's not 'one-size-fits-all.' Rather, it is creating the right bench solution" (Steelcase; 2010, May). The bench solution, which started in Europe, addresses the way business is now being conducted—preference for collaboration and networking over closed-off cubicles; the need to reduce real-estate costs; and ability to adapt spaces as business changes.

The challenge of using the bench concept is to configure workstations so that they are inclusive—in particular, responsive, adjustable, and adaptable. Figure 7.1a uses the bench concept without adjustability whereas Figures 7.1b and c use the bench concept with a height-adjustable computer bench.

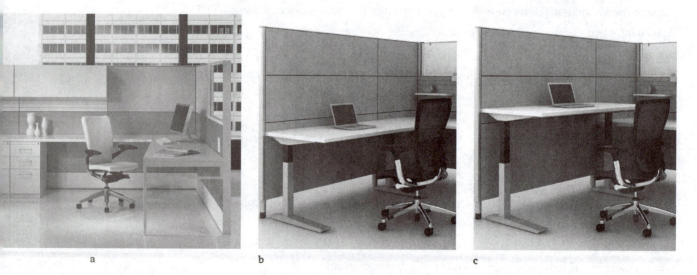

a   b   c

Figure 7.1a–c

The bench concept can be configured in various ways, as illustrated by these two examples that support individual work in an open space. One configuration (a) supports work that is routine, but without adjustability, whereas the other (b and c) provides greater flexibility with a bench that adjusts to various heights from sitting to standing. Courtesy of Haworth

Inclusive Design is for Everyone

More-Than-Accessible Entrances

In Color Plate 1, this door is easy to open for most people, but for this young man using a wheelchair, the door is difficult to open. He draws attention trying to open it. *© Image Source/Superstock*

However, in Color Plate 2, automatic doors slide open from either direction upon a person's approach whether they are in a wheelchair, are using a cane or crutches, walking, or have visual or other limitations. *© Juice Images/Alamy*

Designing beyond ADA compliance creates spaces that are not just accessible but easy to use and enjoy. Such spaces become inclusive for everyone. Creating these types of spaces takes a great deal of thought and planning.

INCLUSIVE DESIGN:

    1. draws no attention to a disability

    2. is easy for everyone to use

    3. excludes no one

Color Plate 1

Color Plate 2

Color Plate 3

Color Plate 4

Building Access

Wheelchair access into a public building is required by the ADA; however, there are times when access is not possible (Color Plate 3). *© Roman Milert/istockphoto*

A person using a wheelchair or lacking mobility does not have access from one level to another by stairs. The solution is an elevator, wheelchair lift, or ramp. In this case, a ramp is impossible because the slope is too great.

As designers, situations where access is difficult must be examined carefully to develop an appropriate accessible solution.

Exterior ramps are often installed to provide access. Although this solution can often provide a less-than-glamorous entrance, they do meet the minimum standards for ADA compliance.

The integrity of this exterior has been compromised, and it separates those with a disability (Color Plate 4). *© AlphaCare Supply LLC*

The ramp design draws attention to one with a disability. It says, "This is the only place you can enter if you are disabled or have limited mobility; you are excluded from using the stairs."

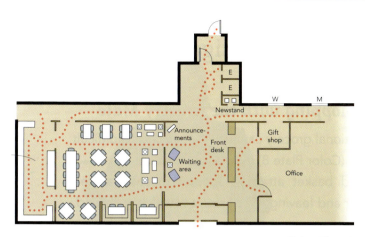

Color Plate 5

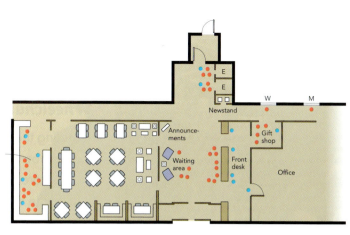

Color Plate 6

Behavior Mapping

Interior designers hand sketch behavioral maps to note where important areas are located and where movement takes place. In this example of a hotel lobby (Color Plate 5), the basic layout is provided with waiting area, reception area, restrooms, office, gift shop, and dining and lounge. Furniture is sketched, and small dots represent where the designer observed people moving through space. © *Precision Graphics/based on a drawing by Linda L. Nussbaumer*

In Color Plate 6, color dots represent where people congregate for the longest period of time. Blue dots represent employees while red dots represent where guests check in at the register, visit, use computers, select food from a buffet, or wait. © *Precision Graphics/based on a drawing by Linda L. Nussbaumer*

An important part of data collection is observing the environment to be designed. Here, the designer is making observations: movement and congestion (Color Plate 7). *Photo courtesy Linda L. Nussbaumer*

These sketches only touch the surface of research; providing a design that is inclusive for everyone into a building and its spaces takes a great deal more study throughout the entire process.

For more examples of research methods, turn to "Case Study 3.1, The Importance of the Programming Phase," in Chapter 3: Integrating Inclusive Design into the Design Process.

Color Plate 7

Inclusive Residential Design (continued)

Color Plate 24a

Color Plate 24b

eliminates the need to use stairs, is important for both now and in the future. The (a) first level accommodates daily living, sleeping, and hygiene. The (b) second level focuses on studying and working. *Illustrations rendered by Rachel Bolella, Priscila Coronel, Mary Dore, and Mayra Guerra*

The industrial design students designed a ladder that accommodates users of various heights (Colors Plate 24a and b). The ladder in (a) the first illustration appears to have fewer rungs but with a simple adjustment, (b) rungs spread to create additional steps for a person of shorter stature. *Illustration rendered by professor Matt Johnson, Kean University*

With research, the industrial design students developed a platform that pulls out to be used (Color Plate 25). This accommodates people of shorter heights, and is especially helpful for those with dwarfism. *Illustration rendered by professor Matt Johnson, Kean University*

Color Plate 25

Inclusive Commercial Design

Playgrounds for All Abilities

Playgrounds should be designed to not only meet but exceed ADA requirements for playgrounds. This would give access to all children regardless of their ability.

The swing for a wheelchair can be a part of a swing-set for all types of swings, which allows children of all abilities to play together. © *Stock Connection Distribution/Alamy*

Rough and smooth textures help students learn by touch. Children can also explore various shapes and explore the nine different interactive panels (Color Plate 27). *Photo courtesy of Landscape Structures Inc.*

Color Plate 26

Photo courtesy of Landscape Structures Inc.

Color Plate 27

Inclusive Commercial Design

Moving Beyond Universal Healthcare

Children with visual limitations deserve the same opportunities as children with good eyesight. Within the Julie McAndrews Mork Building at the Anchor Center for Blind Children in Denver, Colorado, this is a reality.

The facility is uniquely designed for teaching very young children who have visual limitations.

For more on the Anchor Center's design, turn to Case Study 8.2: "Designing for Children with Visual Impairments" in chapter 8.

Color Plate 31 The Grand Hallway directs children to classrooms. As children navigate the hallway, the sound from shoes and canes indicates a floor covering change and alerts children that they are nearing the first, second, or third classroom pod. Photo courtesy Anchor Center for Blind Children

Color Plate 32 The Light Walk stimulates natural light by illuminating the way for children who can see some light. Photo courtesy Anchor Center for Blind Children

Color Plate 31

Color Plate 32

Color Plate 33 A child touches a flower in the Sensory Garden—a garden that features a variety of elements to stimulate the senses and help children learn about the world around them. Photo courtesy Anchor Center for Blind Children

Embracing all senses, the building itself is a teaching tool. The facility includes:

- carefully planned stimuli, including textures, lights, and sounds
- The Sensory Garden
- The Braille Trail
- The Cane Walk Lane

It is also designed with a large, open Grand Hallway that provides a sense of security as children maneuver down it. Additionally, the building's wayfinding methods help children locate classrooms and give them confidence in their ability to navigate through the facility and out into the world.

Inclusive Commercial Design

Flexibility in Hospitality

The design for an inclusive restaurant must be flexible. There must be adequate clearance for all to maneuver comfortably on foot or by wheelchair. That means unobstructed circulation, lifts or elevators at all levels, and movable and removable seating.

Color Plate 34 This restaurant floor plan (a) illustrates fairly good circulation. At the entrance, circulation and space provided is sufficient. Wheelchairs can comfortably access the meeting rooms, but easy access is limited to the entrance side. Within the main dining area, (W) wheelchairs can comfortably access some but not all tables.

© Precision Graphics/based on a drawing by Linda L. Nussbaumer

Color Plate 35 Compared to the floor plan in Color Plate 34, the dining area of this restaurant floor plan (b) limits space for (W) wheelchairs to fewer locations to allow wait staff and other guests to easily navigate the space. *© Precision Graphics/based on a drawing by Linda L. Nussbaumer*

Color Plate 34

Color Plate 35

Color Plate 36

Several features must be in place to create inclusion within a food and beverage facility:

- Adequate maneuvering clearances provided at the entrance
- Adequate maneuvering clearances and space provided for service lines to prevent congestion and accommodate groups of people
- Unobstructed, easily maneuverable circulation allowed between tables
- Lifts or elevators provided to connect all levels
- Movable and removable seating provided to offer the greatest flexibility
- A comfortable eating environment provided for all guests
- Circulation paths installed with nonslip flooring

Color Plate 36 This restaurant appears to be accessible with good clear space; however, a wheelchair at a table may challenge movement for the wait staff. *Photo courtesy Hyatt Hotels*

Inclusive Design for Religious Facilities

Churches have yet to be required to make their entire facilities accessible, particularly for historic buildings or those that may have a difficult time raising funds for an elevator.

However, even where portions of a church are made accessible, they may not pass as inclusive with access through all entrances and for all activities.

For more on how to meet this challenge, turn to Case Study 9.1, "Comparison of One Town's Religious Facilities," in Chapter 9: "Hospitality, Retail, and Other Commercial Design."

Color Plate 37 When approaching the entrance to the Lutheran church, there is a choice between two steps or a concrete sloped ramp. *Photo courtesy Linda L. Nussbaumer*

Color Plate 38 Moveable seating within the sanctuary provides optional access to a person in a wheelchair. *Photo courtesy Linda L. Nussbaumer*

Color Plate 39 Entrance ramp to the Methodist church provides the only accessible entrance for persons with limited mobility or who use a wheelchair. *Photo courtesy Linda L. Nussbaumer*

Color Plate 37

Color Plate 38

Color Plate 39

DIVERSITY IN THE OFFICE ENVIRONMENT

Electronic communication (e.g., email, texting) is important but cannot entirely replace in-person discussions within the office setting. Video conferencing as well as communicating in person brings a diversity of workers together. Offices today and in the future will also include various generations as well as cultures; in an inclusively designed office, generations and cultures will work together harmoniously.

Generational Diversity

The term *generation gap* comes to mind when thinking of various generations. The *gap* here refers to the difference between the eras in which the different generations grew up and the differences between the experiences they encountered. To work successfully side by side with various generations, it is important to understand these differences to create harmony in the workplace.

Lynn C. Lancaster, a faculty member at the University of Minnesota's Carlson School of Management, and David Stillman, graduate of the University of Wisconsin-Madison and a roving reporter for CBS are partners in a consulting firm and authors of *When Generations Collide: Who They are, Why They Clash, and How to Solve the Generational Puzzle at Work*. In their book, Lancaster and Stillman (2002) categorize a century of generations by their dates of birth. Current generations are described as:

- **Traditionalists** (Vets or Matures): 1945 and before
- **Baby boomers**: 1946–1964
- **GenXers** (Generation X): 1965–1980
- **Millennials** (Generation Y or Gen-Y): 1981–present

Traditionalists This generation grew up during one of two wars or the depression. Traditionalists are conservative, hard workers, patriotic, loyal, respectful of their leaders, and follow the chain of command in the workplace.

Baby boomers Baby boomers grew up during times of tragedy (e.g., the Vietnam conflict; the Kent State massacre; and John Kennedy, Bobby Kennedy, and Martin Luther King assassinations). The hippies, a subculture of the Traditionalists and Baby boomers, found escape in drugs and free love and a political voice through protest. Differing from the Traditionalists, Baby Boomers have had access to many products and experiences through the television, which brought advertisements, protests, the civil rights movement, hippie behavior, and more to the forefront. They are consumption driven, educated, competitive, idealistic, goal oriented, and optimistic, but they challenge authority.

GenXers Growing up with greater access to numerous electronics, GenXers were exposed through the media to the indictment of certain role models, violence on television, and faces of missing children on milk cartons. Often, both parents worked, which made GenXers resourceful and independent. They are also skeptical and have less respect for authority.

Millennials Millennials grew up with technology and the media blurring lines between fantasy and reality. Technology (cellphones, laptops, and more) was in their pockets and backpacks. However, they were realistic about the challenges of life and concerned about violent outbreaks at schools, illegal drug activity, and gangs. Thus, personal safety was an important workplace issue. Overall, they were realistic, technologically savvy, optimistic, used to challenges, practical, connected, and good collaborators.

With such different backgrounds, it may seem that these generations would have difficulty working together; however, using each generation's characteristics, "Generational Mixes: Can Their Difference Bring Them Together?" combines generations together and presents ideas for smooth working relationships. To have an inclusive environment that is designed for all, various generations must be able to work together harmoniously.

In redesigning an office, employees of various generations may perceive changes differently, especially if the change affects the way they work. InformeDesign research summary (2010, September 15) "Generational Differences in Response to an Office Redesign" summarized a study that compared office workers' perceptions and attitudes of an office redesign. One aspect of the redesign changed the cubicle size within an open office environment. Because of the open and collaborative change, Millennials perceived the change more positively than GenXers and Baby Boomers. This reinforces differences in these generations.

Generational Mixes: Can Their Differences Bring Them Together?

Bringing Together Traditionalists and Baby Boomers
- Let staff know that there will be a discussion of a particular topic.
- Meet to discuss and develop ideas in a creative "brainstorming" session.
- Bring to the management for their approval.

Bringing Together Traditionalists and GenXers
- Let staff know that there will be a discussion of a particular topic.
- Allow time for each person to develop ideas.
- Then, bring everyone together to share and develop ideas by allowing everyone's ideas to be brought forward.
- Bring a variety of prioritized ideas to management.

Bringing Together Traditionalists and Millennials

- Let staff know that there will be a discussion of a particular topic.
- In the meeting, begin by allowing management to discuss past experiences (mentoring).
- Then, be open to input from everyone.
- Collaborate in the development of ideas.
- Include management in the collaborative discussion.
- Make a decision with everyone at the table.

Bringing Together Baby Boomers and GenXers

- Let staff know that there will be a discussion of a particular topic.
- Work separately to begin developing ideas.
- Meet to discuss and develop ideas in a brainstorming session.
- Include management (as participants, not leaders) in brainstorming session.
- Make a decision with everyone at the table.

Bringing Together Baby Boomers and Millennials

- Let staff know that there will be a discussion of a particular topic.
- Work separately to begin developing ideas.
- In the meeting, collaborate in the development of ideas.
- Include management (as participants, not leaders) in the collaborative discussion.
- Make a decision with everyone at the table.

Bringing Together GenXers and Millennials

- Let staff know that there will be a discussion of a particular topic.
- Meet to discuss and develop ideas in a collaborative session.
- Include management (as participants, not leaders) in the collaborative discussion.
- Make a decision with everyone at the table.

Bringing Together Traditionalists, Baby Boomers, and GenXers

- Let staff know that there will be a discussion of a particular topic.
- Allow time for the GenXers to work separately and develop ideas.
- Meet and work together to share ideas in a brainstorming session.
- Share with management.

Bringing Together Traditionalists, Baby Boomers, GenXers, and Millennials

- Let staff know that there will be a discussion of a particular topic.
- Working separately, develop ideas.
- In the meeting, begin by allowing management to discuss past experiences (mentoring).
- Include management (as participants, not leaders) in the collaborative discussion.
- Make a decision with everyone at the table.

Bringing Together Baby Boomers, GenXers, and Millennials

- Let staff know that there will be a discussion of a particular topic.
- Working separately, develop ideas.
- Include management (as participants, not leaders) in the collaborative discussion.
- Make a decision with everyone at the table.

Cultural Diversity

In the past, the majority of office personnel were Caucasian and African-American with Christian-based faith. However, today, office personnel are diverse with people from all parts of the world (e.g., the Middle East, Asia, Russia) with varied religious beliefs. All are or will be part of the business world.

Within the context of an office that is inclusive, respect must be given to those who may dress according to their culture or observe religious customs that affect their need for privacy or space design. As with various generations, all cultures should learn about one another to have a smooth working relationship. For example, understanding the differences between Caucasian American and Asian cultures or Middle Eastern traditions is important whether these differences are slight or very obvious.

It is most important to develop respect between and among cultures. This can be accomplished by having sessions in the office to share information about each other's cultures. If, however, this becomes uncomfortable, reading material with the opportunity to ask questions would be appropriate. Lanie Denslow's (2006) *World Wise: What to Know Before You Go* is an excellent source that provides greater detail of various cultures and their manner of doing business. Although its focus is for Americans who work in other countries, information about the people and their customs provides insight and aids in the ability to work with non-Americans in the United States.

According to Herman Miller (2010a), work styles and cultures in China, Russia, or India still use the hierarchical or top-down approach—a style that has been most comfortable for the Traditionalists. However, some cultures are making changes and creating more collaborative spaces. Regardless, all office personnel should be sensitive to and respectful of other cultures and their traditions. In this way, the office environment will truly be inclusive.

Gender Differences

Men and women often differ in ways they communicate, perceive situations, handle feelings, and more. Because most offices employ both genders, their preferences can affect the office environment. The InformeDesign research summary (2009, September 28) "Private Office Environment Preferences Vary between Genders" examines gender differences in personalization and satisfaction in the private offices of university educators in Turkey. The 170 subjects (99 male and 71 female between ages 22 and 66 years old) were full-time engineering and architecture faculty at Gazi University in Ankara, Turkey. All subjects in the research study worked in private offices. Results revealed that gender differences in preference for personalization and satisfaction within the offices may not vary as greatly as one would expect; however, understanding and respecting difference is important for a smooth-working office. Further details can be found in Study Sketch 7.1: "Private Office Environment Preferences Vary between Genders."

Figure 7.2

Agreement and respect among various generations, genders, and possibly cultures is part of an inclusive environment. Courtesy of Haworth

Clearly, differences will continue to exist between generations, cultures, and genders; however, working together and being respectful of and responsive to one another will produce a harmonious and inclusive environment. Figure 7.2 represents that diversity and harmony.

Inclusive Design in the Office Environment

Office design has changed greatly since the ADA passage. In fact, many offices not only comply with the ADA as required, but also may apply inclusive design criteria.

For offices to be inclusive, designers must respond to everyone's needs, create accessible and adaptable environments using ergonomics and human factors, and create secure environments considering the health, safety, and welfare of all who use the space. In particular, when applying **ergonomics** and **proxemics**, aspects of inclusion are practiced.

ERGONOMICS

Ergonomics is the study of "the relationship between human beings and their functions within their environment—the way bodies work efficiently in space" (Nussbaumer, 2009, p. 128). Ergonomics applies **anthropometric** data so that people can comfortably and efficiently perform a task whether standing, sitting, or walking. Information from ergonomic studies is used to design furniture, computers, workstations, automobiles, and more.

Private Office Environment Preferences Vary Between Genders

Because private office environments have no restrictions on personal items displayed, they offer greater opportunities to study gender personalization differences. Thus, this study examined gender differences in personalization and satisfaction in the private offices of university educators in Turkey.

Method

The 170 subjects (99 male and 71 female between ages 22 and 66 years old) were full-time engineering and architecture faculty at Gazi University in Ankara, Turkey. All subjects in research study worked in private offices.

Findings

Results determined that female subjects were more likely to personalize and make changes to their offices than male subjects.

- Female subjects displayed personal items more often; however, the type of items may vary with age and profession.
- Male subjects were unlikely to rearrange their temporary layout or make changes.
- Title and profession (designer/engineer) rather than gender was important in making permanent changes to the office.
- Profession rather than gender or academic title affected preferences for desk placement.

Criteria

The following criteria should be considered when designing private offices:

- Gender differences in preferences may not vary significantly for personalization and satisfaction.
- Male employees may be less attached to their personal office space than female employees.
- Female employees may see their office as a home-like and comfortable environment but may be willing to make changes to the office layout.

Implications

From this study, it was recognized that preferences for personalization and satisfaction with private office did not vary greatly between genders; however, male employees are less attached to their personal office environment than female employees.

Source: InformeDesign. (2009, September 28) "Private office environment preferences vary between genders.' http://www.informedesign.umn.edu/Rs_detail.aspx?rsId=3359

To create inclusively designed environments, each individual's physical stature must be considered for the task to be performed. Thus, applying individual and furniture measurements to the selection of furniture leads to a comfortable and efficient design. However, planning for adjustability is important as tasks vary (e.g., working on the computer, reading, or completing paper work). The "Ergonomic Evaluation Checklist" provides a checklist to evaluate ergonomics to design furniture for individuals in an office situation.

PROXEMICS

Proxemics studies "the relationship between humans in a particular culture and their use and perceptions of space" (Nussbaumer, 2009, p. 130). In particular, it defines the relationship between humans within a space. Often the manner in which a space is arranged can encourage or discourage human interaction; therefore, designers must carefully consider the activities and purpose of the space as well as the people who will use it.

The comfort level each person has with another relates to the various spatial zones of proxemics—intimate, personal, social, and public. The comfort level in each of these zones varies from person to person and, often, the culture in which they were raised. Therefore, when designing spaces to be inclusive and meeting the responsive criteria, designers must also consider and respond to individual needs within the built environment. While collecting data during the programming phase, important questions related to proxemics must be developed to address each person's need for privacy and/or interaction and cultural differences. In this way, an inclusively designed environment can be created. Figure 7.3 provides a graphical representation of proxemics and the spatial zones.

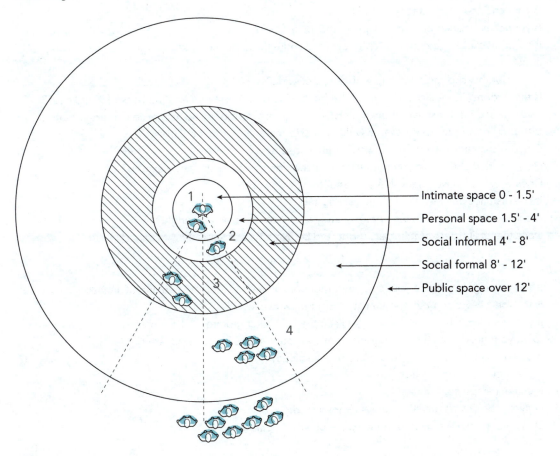

Intimate space 0 - 1.5'
Personal space 1.5' - 4'
Social informal 4' - 8'
Social formal 8' - 12'
Public space over 12'

Figure 7.3

The four distance zones of proxemics are concerned with distance between people: spatial zones of proxemics—(1) intimate, (2) personal, (3) social, and (4) public—that extend from the individual in the center. © Precision Graphics/based on a drawing by Dean Isham

Ergonomic Evaluation Checklist

A checklist to evaluate ergonomics aids in the appropriate furniture design for individuals in an office situation:

Desk/Workstation

1. Do you have enough room on your work surface for all your computer accessories?
2. Is your desk surface deep enough to provide at least 18 inches between your eyes and the computer screen?
3. Are your most frequently accessed items (e.g., phone and manuals) easy to reach?
4. If your desk has a fixed height, is the keyboard tray adjustable?
5. Have you removed all under-desk obstructions?
6. Do you have a document holder to hold paper for prolonged computer inputting?
7. Do your arms rest upon or contact any sharp or square edges on your work surfaces?
8. If a large percentage of your time involves using a phone, do you use a phone headset?
9. Is your source light out of your line of sight?

Chair

1. Is your chair height adjustable?
2. Is your chair back adjustable up and down?
3. Is your chair back contoured to support the lower back?
4. Is your backrest large enough to support your entire back, but not interfere with the use of your arms?
5. Is your lumbar support a minimum of 12 inches wide?
6. Is there room (2 to 4 inches) between the front edge of the seat pan and the back of your knees?
7. If your feet do not rest flat on the floor when your chair is properly adjusted, do you use a footrest?
8. Is the top of your footrest covered with a nonskid material to reduce slippage?
9. Do your chair arms interfere with you getting close to your work?
10. Do your chair arms allow you to sit with your shoulders relaxed and not elevated?
11. Does your chair have removable armrests?
12. Is the distance between your armrests adjustable?
13. Are your knees bent, forming approximately a 90-degree or greater angle?
14. Does the chair have a stable base supported by five legs with casters?

Monitor

1. Is the viewing distance to your computer monitor somewhere between 18 and 30 inches?
2. Is the top of your computer screen at or just below eye level?
3. If you wear bifocals or trifocals, can you see the computer monitor without having to tilt your head back to read the screen or view other items in your work area?
4. Is your computer monitor free of glare or reflections?
5. Is the monitor screen clean?
6. Is character size easy to read?
7. Do you have blinds on the windows near your computer?
8. Do you use a glare screen to reduce glare on your monitor?

Keyboard

1. With your chair adjusted properly, is your work surface at approximately elbow level?
2. Are your shoulders relaxed and not elevated when you work at your work surface?

3. Is the height of your keyboard low enough so your arms are relaxed at your side?
4. When you address your work surface to type or write, is there approximately a 90-degree angle between your forearms and upper arms, and are your elbows close to your body?
5. When you address your work surface to type are your wrists in line with your forearms and not bent upward, downward, or side to side?
6. Do you have a wrist rest to support your wrists in a straight and neutral position?

Mouse, Trackball, or Other Input Device
1. Is your mouse, trackball, or other input device (e.g., touchpad) located directly in your immediate reach zone?
2. Is your mouse or trackball positioned next to your keyboard?
3. Is your mouse or trackball placed together with your keyboard on an adjustable work surface or tray?
4. Is your mouse work surface stable?
5. Is the mouse or trackball at the same level as your keyboard?

Work Habits
1. Do you take short and frequent breaks every 20 to 30 minutes?
2. Do you frequently change body positions while working?
3. Do you provide your eyes with vision breaks every half hour?
4. Are you free from experiencing any pain or discomfort while working?

Sources: Center for Disease Control and Prevention (CDC). (2000b). "Ergonomic checklist." Retrieved on November 2, 2007, from www.cdc.gov/od/ohs/Ergonomics/compergo.htm; and Nussbaumer L. L. (2009). *Evidence-based design from interior designers.* New York: Fairchild Books.

A COMFORTABLE OFFICE ENVIRONMENT

In an inclusively designed work environment, employees are comfortable doing their jobs. Employees who are comfortable are also productive and profitable to their employer. For example, an employee may incur discomfort due to poor ergonomics causing an injury such as repetitive stress injury. The discomfort causes pain and either slows down the work or the employee must take time off to rest or have surgery. This negatively affects productivity. Thus, employees' comfort predicts operational efficiency, retention, well-being, and worker health—all of which affect the bottom line (Herman Miller, 2008).

A survey among 500 office workers conducted by Herman Miller (2008) found that "having an office that is comfortable to work in as the most highly valued workstation attribute" among all workers (para. 12). Comfort was also found to be important in determining job satisfaction. In the Herman Miller study (2007), 27 attributes of the workstation were rated. Seven of the 27 workstations attributes that workers highly valued were as follows:

- An office that is comfortable to work in
- A sufficient amount of work surface area (desks, tables, file tops) in my office
- The option to place a computer in the most suitable location
- The capability to keep all of my important work within arms' reach

- The capability to contain sounds within my office
- The capability to keep out distracting noises from outside my office
- The capability to provide visual privacy

Comfort is difficult to measure because it is subjective and changeable. In other words, comfort for one person may be different for another and can also change from one minute to the next. Thus, comfort affects people's physical, functional, and psychological comfort (Herman Miller, 2007).

Physical Comfort

Physical comfort relates to physiological needs such as ergonomics. By connecting data between the human body's measurements and the tasks it performs, ergonomics aids in creating an environment that provides comfort and facilitates efficiency.

Physical comfort also relates to temperature, lighting, and noise within the environment. Standards have been defined that address physical comfort related to temperature, lighting, acoustics, and ergonomics. Unfortunately, standards often satisfy the majority, which leaves about 20 percent who will still be uncomfortable and dissatisfied. For example, one temperature, the same sound level, or one light level cannot satisfy everyone equally (Herman Miller, 2008).

Thus, Cornell University's Human Factors and Ergonomics Laboratory conducted a study to better understand the effect of temperature on efficiency. The federal government recommends 68 degrees to conserve energy; therefore, workers were tested for productivity at 68 degrees and for comparison at 77 degrees. The study found that at 68 degrees "workers performed monotonous keyboarding tasks 54 percent of the time with a 5 percent error rate. When the temperature was raised to a toasty 77 degrees, keyboarders worked 100 percent of the time with a 10 percent error rate" (Herman Miller, 2008, p. 3). This means that although lowering the temperature may be a sustainable practice, it negatively impacts productivity.

Results from this study suggest that providing individuals with the ability to adjust temperature to their personal preference, the firm may still maintain an overall lower temperature in the space. "Many workers would be more comfortable if they could adjust the heat or turn on a task light, for example. But very few buildings or workstations enable occupants to control lighting, temperature, ventilation rates, or noise conditions" (Herman Miller, 2008, p. 3). Such technology is available to allow for these adjustments, but many firms have not been sold on the idea that personal comfort is important to productivity. And yet, "having some control over the workspace can improve comfort and the ability to get work done and reduce stress. This in turn can lead to greater productivity and better health" (p. 3). The concept of providing individuals the ability to control light levels is reinforced in the InformeDesign research summary (2004, May 28), Study Sketch 7.2: "Lighting Preferences in the Office Environment."

STUDY SKETCH 7.2: Lighting Preferences in the Office Environment

An experiment was performed to determine lighting preferences in a mock-up office space that used both conventional and user-controlled lighting systems. Its purpose was to determine if the preferred lighting conditions would affect users' comfort level and their ability to perform tasks more efficiently, interactively, and creatively (InformeDesign, 2004, May 28).

Method

The research method used was an experiment using a "mock-up" space with six workstations, open-plan, and no windows. Subjects were randomly assigned in one of two areas. In the experimental group, subjects (47 in LC group) were in control of dimmable lighting. In the control group, subjects (47 in NC group) were unable to control the dimmable lighting until the end of the day.

During the experiment, each group would complete a day of office tasks in the same room. At the end of the day, the NC group also completed a questionnaire that asked, "what they would change in the lighting system" (para. 5). Each morning and afternoon, subjects were given a variety of computer-based tasks and visual performance tests. Then, at various times of the day, computer questionnaires were given regarding their satisfaction with the lighting.

Findings

This experiment found that as glare on computer monitors increased, subjects preferred to have the desktop light levels increased. At the end of the day when the control group (NC) was able to control their light levels, subjects who experienced lighting levels closest to their preference rated the lighting quality, as well as satisfaction with the overall space, higher.

Implications

The experiment indicated that occupants prefer to control lighting levels at the workstations. Unfortunately, daylighting was not part of this experiment and could have affected the results.

Source: InformeDesign. (2004, May 28). "Lighting preferences in the office environment." Retrieved on July 20, 2010, from http://www.informedesign.org/Rs_detail.aspx?rsId=1672

Functional Comfort

Functional comfort and physical comfort are linked to productivity. Specifically, functional comfort relates to the user's needs and the job's demands. Functional needs include flexibility and privacy. For example, an office that frequently conducts team meetings for creative endeavors will need space close to the workstations for informal meetings. On the other hand, an office where privacy is needed for frequent and confidential client meetings, space must be enclosed. In either case, if these are not provided when needed, productivity, job satisfaction, and stress level will be affected. Thus, "functional comfort enables workers to interact effectively with their environment" (Herman Miller, 2008, p. 6). Clearly, designing spaces that meet specific functional needs of the firm's personnel creates an inclusively designed environment.

Psychological Comfort

Psychological aspects of design relate to an individual's ability to control elements of the job, create one's own territory and set boundaries, and connect with nature or beauty.

Controlling elements of the job relates to job satisfaction and psychological comfort. Examples might include the ability to control light, temperature, or noise levels.

Creating one's own territory provides a means of self-expression within a space and contributes to psychological comfort. Territories are created when the occupant is able to control visual, auditory, or physical interruptions and to personalize the space. This ability to create one's own territory allows workers to express status, personality, and emotions; control their workspace, and even manage stress. According to research by Meredith Wells, PhD, "the ability to personalize is so innate and adaptive that approximately 70 to 90 percent of employees do it, even in the face of organizational displeasure" (Herman Miller, 2008, p. 5).

Although hard to measure, the beauty element of the work environment does affect psychological comfort. This may be in the architectural beauty, artwork on the walls, a natural element, and other means. Although not all spaces can provide exposure to natural light, it is an important contributor to psychological comfort and can affect one's mood. Certainly, "psychological comfort addresses the human need for control over the job and the workspace, and ideally, the ability to work in a space that provides visual interest or natural elements" (Herman Miller, 2008, p.6).

The office layout in Figure 7.4 shows ways to accommodate a variety of positions (e.g., administrators, managers, teams, and more). It provides space for various functioning groups as well. As described by Steelcase (2010, May), a functioning group includes residents, project teams, functional teams, and nomads. This office layout includes residents (daily functions such as administration, operations, and customer service), project teams, functional teams, and nomads (hoteling) as well as a conference or training room. In the main section of the building, those who tend to work separately or need private space are located at the perimeter, and those who work in teams are found at the center. The functional team that works more consistently as a team is located in a separate space. Nomads (those who are in the office only on occasion) take spaces in the lunch area; for private meetings, they may use the enclosed small or team meeting area. The kitchen and lunch area provides space for informal discussion with the majority of the staff. However, most importantly, spaces within and throughout the plan were designed with circulation that is wide and allows easy movement throughout the entire plan—evidence of inclusive design.

An office environment affects people's physical, functional, and psychological comfort. In an inclusively designed office environment, employees are comfortable in all of these aspects. Thus, an employee who is comfortable will be productive and, ultimately, profitable to the firm. (See the examples in Color Plates 28–30 in the color pages of this book.)

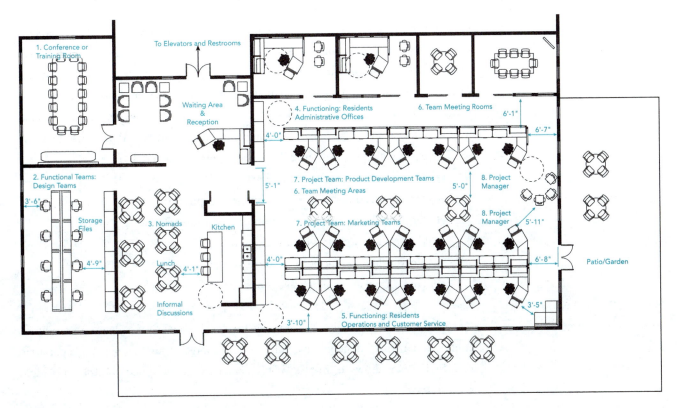

Figure 7.4

Floor plan with a variety of working relationships and configurations: (1) Conferencing and training, (2) functional teams (collaborative), (3) nomads (informal work and discussion area), (4) functional residents (administrative closed offices), (5) functional residents (operation, and customer service in open offices), (6) team meeting rooms or areas (closed and open spaces), (7) project teams and (8) managers (individual workstations in open office space). Individual workstations allow for privacy or close contact; however, several spaces are not large enough or open for wheelchair access. © Precision Graphics/based on a drawing by Linda L. Nussbaumer

EMPLOYEE PRODUCTIVITY AND SATISFACTION AFFECT THE BOTTOM LINE

Office expenses are affected by employee productivity and satisfaction as well as the expenses related to physical systems—structural, electrical, flooring, wall, workstations, seating, and circulation. However, the bulk of the total office system investment is not in these physical systems; rather, it is the salaries of employees. In fact, salaries make up "84 percent of the cost per square foot of a commercial building. The other expenses being rent, maintenance, and energy" (Herman Miller, 2008, p. 3). Clearly, employee needs and satisfaction with the job as well as the ability to work comfortably is essential to the bottom line.

SEATING DESIGNED TO FIT EACH INDIVIDUAL

Hoteling, hot desking, or other mobile office methods are common, and chairs must be adjustable for each individual using the office. However, in some offices, each person has their own desk or workstation and office chair. In this case and to be ergonomically correct, chairs may be ordered to fit individual needs. Although most office chairs are designed for adjustability, some chair manufacturers design chairs for each individual. For example, when customized, Sitmatic guarantees a fit for each individual. For a custom-fit chair by Sitmatic, their personnel measure each individual to determine the appropriate size chair along with adjustable elements. Measurements include the lower leg height, elbow height, eye height, upper leg height, lumbar height, thigh breadth, elbow-elbow distance, and dominant eye. Along with the measurements, Sitmatic provides questions to help personalize a task chair:

- Do you like a chair with armrests?
- Do you need corrective lenses while computing?
- Do you like a chair that locks in one position after being adjusted?
- Do you like a chair with a rocking motion?
- Do you like a chair both lockable and rocking?
- Do you use an adjustable keyboard tray?

Sitmatic chairs can also be designed for special needs, such as for an amputee, an individual with a degenerative tailbone, and a large individual needing a bariatric size. Figure 7.5 shows examples of two chairs, each designed for the individual regardless of size.

Figure 7.5

Sitmatic Chairs are designed to accommodate the individual's comfort and health, regardless of their size.
Courtesy of Sitmatic

LIGHTING

Lighting is an important element in an office environment. For an inclusively designed office, a secure environment relates to the visual, physical, and psychological comfort of the office worker.

The quality of light affects the health of office workers. As an example, poor overhead lights, glare from windows, or other light sources can cause visual discomfort that affects the health—physical and psychological. With computers being an important part of the office environment, video display terminals (VDTs) have been know to cause visual discomfort as well as other health issues such as muscle strain (physical) and stress (psychological). An InformeDesign research summary (2003, June 4), "Computers are Causing Health Problems," reports on the link between health issues and computer VDTs, and provides criteria that can reduce or alleviate health issues from VDTs (see Study Sketch 7.3: "Computers are Causing Health Problems").

Another aspect of lighting that can provide an inclusively designed environment would allow an employee to have personal dimming control. An experiment summarized on InformeDesign (2010, August 18) investigated providing personal dimming controls to employees in a private office setting. The experiment of personal dimming control provided employees with the ability to adjust lighting levels as well as conserve energy. This meets inclusive design criteria—it responds to the individual; it's adaptable to the individual; and it is secure for the individual.

Facilities Management

Facility management is a multidisciplinary profession that ensures the built environment functions well by integrating people, place, process, and technology (IFMA). Facility managers' responsibilities vary and depend on the facilities and the industry in which they work. The facility may be a sports complex, a hospital, hotel, or a retail establishment. Often, the facility managers are in charge of selection and maintenance of interior finishes and furnishings; they may also make choices related to aesthetics, cost, ergonomics, and they might facilitate work of others. They must also have a basic knowledge of the business operation to improve the space (e.g., work flow, circulation) to increase productivity. They must consider all aspects of access for people with disabilities (the ADA), and should apply inclusive design (Advameg, 2010).

With the increase of virtual offices, facilities management may also change. Although a physical office environment will exist, the managers may take on a different appearance because of changing technologies, attitudes, workforce demographics, and globalization (McLennan, 2007).

STUDY SKETCH 7.3: Computers are Causing Health Problems

As the number of computer users has increased, so have health issues. The concern is that video display terminal (VDT) users are experiencing vision problems, musculoskeletal disorders, and radiation effects on pregnancy. This InformeDesign (2003, June 4) summary is a review of ergonomic literature and reports that health issues have been linked to computers.

Findings

Findings from the review indicate that extended computer use causes several physical problems to vision and the musculoskeletal system. VDT use may cause computer vision syndrome (CVS), an eye and vision problem that relates to close work on a computer. Using a computer keyboard, mouse, or other peripherals may cause musculoskeletal disorders (MSD) such as repetitive strain injury (RSI) and carpal tunnel syndrome (CTS). RSI disability claims have increased, and CTS has been linked to more absenteeism than other injuries. Positively, studies have not linked VDT use to spontaneous abortion, early delivery, or reduced birth weight. Most important, some companies have implemented ergonomic programs that have reduced RSI claims.

Criteria

The report suggests that an ergonomics program be implemented to reflect the worksite. For an ergonomic program to work, there must be commitment and willingness of management to identify and develop solutions for problem tasks, training and educating employees as well as providing medical management as needed. To reduce health problems, the following are important criteria:

- Know current legislation addressing ergonomics.
- Reduce glare from both natural and electric lighting on computer screens.
- Provide the ability to increase font size on the screen.
- Specify chair with optimal adjustability.
- Provide adjustable keyboards that allow wrist to be straight and at elbow height.
- Place mouse for wrist to float and arms at a 90-degree angle.
- Increase the distance between the VDT and worker to reduce radiation exposure.
- Provide training and education about user behavior.
- Allow for frequent breaks to stretch or exercise and rest eyes.
- Become educated on ergonomics in the workplace.

Implications

This review has brought important data to the forefront. Ultimately, if the previously mentioned criteria are followed, health issues related to VDT use will be reduced or alleviated.

Source: InformeDesign. (2003, June 4) "Computers are causing health problems." Retrieved on July 20, 2010, from http://www.informedesign.org/Rs_detail.aspx?rsId=1335

Space Planning

In corporate offices, facility managers or interior designers will deal with space planning as changes take place. Their redesign of spaces must comply with the ADA and the ADA Accessible Guidelines (ADAAG) as well as apply inclusive design. In applying inclusive design, their work will follow the four underlying inclusive design criteria discussed in chapter 2: responsive; adaptable; accessible; and secure.

An important part of space planning is circulation. Circulation must allow movement for all people—able-bodied as well as those with mobility challenges and visual limitations or hearing limitations. But most important, it must not draw attention to one or the other. Rather, information and movement should be comfortable and convenient for all.

Home Office

Because of the changes in many corporate offices, employees may subcontract hours and conduct business from home offices. The home office is usually equipped in a manner similar to the corporate office—ergonomically correct workstations and chairs; appropriate technology such as phones, Internet connection, servers, fax machines, printers, and more; sufficient storage; and the ability to move freely within the office layout. As the virtual office, hoteling, or **hot-desking** continue to increase, so will the need to work from a home office—an inclusively designed office.

Summary

All elements of the office environment change over time; some changes occur more often and more rapidly than others. Technologies have made the greatest strides and seem to be accelerating. Keeping up to date with technological advances is a challenge for office design. Another challenge presents itself with a mix of generations and cultures working together. Although diverse, working together brings greater appreciation.

Because employees' salaries make up the greatest expense, having a physically and psychologically comfortable place to work brings job satisfaction and increased productivity. Therefore, creating a comfortable office environment in the home or corporate setting is essential, which can be accomplished with inclusively designed spatial layout and circulation, ergonomically designed workstations and chairs, good indoor air quality through appropriate material selection, appropriate lighting, and good acoustics.

Whether it is the facility manager or the interior designer, designing and planning the space, complying with the ADA and its accessible guidelines, and applying inclusive design is a necessity in today's office environments.

Inclusive Design Projects

EXPERIENTIAL PROJECTS

1. How can various generations work together successfully?

Describe the various generations and how they can work together successfully.

1. Generations (Traditionalists, Baby Boomers, Generation Xers, and Millennials)
2. Groups (nomads, functioning, collaborative, and residents)

2. How can the comfortable office be the most productive workplace?

A productive office is a comfortable office in each of these categories—physical, functional, psychological. Describe how an office would be designed to be comfortable in these three categories. Sketch aspects of the office to explain the ideas.

APPLICATION PROJECT

1. How do you design an inclusive office environment?

Design an office space that includes variability in the following areas:

1. Generations and cultures
2. One employee with a physical limitation
3. One employee with a hearing limitation
4. One employee with a visual limitation

The space must also be inclusively designed.

CHAPTER 8

Healthcare and Institutional Design

"Always design a thing by considering it in its next larger context—a chair in a room, a room in a house, a house in an environment, an environment in a city plan."

—*Eliel Saarinen*

OBJECTIVES

▸ Discuss challenges faced when designing inclusively for healthcare facilities such as hospitals, medical offices, long-term care, nursing homes, and assisted living

▸ Discuss challenges faced when designing inclusively for institutional facilities such as educational venues, child care facilities, playgrounds, and so on

KEY TERMS

- ❭ active adult communities
- ❭ Alzheimer's disease
- ❭ Autism
- ❭ bariatric(s)
- ❭ cerebral palsy
- ❭ concurrent design
- ❭ congregate housing
- ❭ continuing care retirement community
- ❭ dementia/Alzheimer's Care
- ❭ epilepsy
- ❭ high speech intelligibility
- ❭ Huntington's disease
- ❭ multiple sclerosis
- ❭ neurological disorders
- ❭ Parkinson's disease
- ❭ reverberation
- ❭ restorative
- ❭ transgenerational

ost healthcare design and institutional categories (e.g., government, libraries, education, and so on) must comply with the ADA. However, there are exceptions: Childcare facilities located in a residence or managed by a church or religious organization, as long as the church itself operates the childcare program, are not required to comply with the ADA. Even when meeting the ADA is not required, following these guidelines is recommended in order to create inclusively designed environments for everyone.

Healthcare

There are many types of healthcare facilities (hospitals, medical offices, nursing homes, assisted living, and so on), and most are a blend of design categories such as office, hospitality, residential, and retail design. For example, the nursing home includes dining facilities, assembly spaces, resident rooms, physical therapy, and office spaces.

The primary focus for healthcare facilities is delivering efficient and quality care (Cama, 2006), and to do so, facilities must be accessible and easy to maneuver in. For example, hospitals and all public areas must be accessible and meet the ADAAG; they must have a minimum of 10 percent accessible patient rooms and toilets, and within these rooms, a five-foot diameter turning radius for wheelchairs is required (Piotrowski & Rogers, 2007). However, this constitutes accessibility only to rooms and spaces, but not inclusive design.

HOSPITALS

As new ideas and products are developed, patient rooms in newly constructed or renovated hospitals are making great improvements. The most significant change is the single-patient room, which provides all patients with privacy, safety, and accessibility.

The Benefits of Single-Patient Rooms

The InformeDesign research summary, "Considering Single-Patient Rooms in Hospitals" (2009, January 8) summarizes a review of literature that examines the benefits and concerns of implementing single-patient rooms (i.e., single bed, single bathroom). Rooms are separated into zones for the patient, staff, and family with some overlap, and the benefit of a single patient versus two in the room is that the patient and family have greater privacy (see Figure 8.1). In particular, it allows for increased communication among patient, family, and hospital staff. Additionally, the single bathroom not only provides privacy for the patient but also reduces spread of infection. Certainly, hospitals that are designed with all single-patient rooms promote inclusion—designing equally for all. For further details see Study Sketch 8.1: "Considering Single-Patient Rooms in Hospitals."

Making Patient Rooms Look Less Institutional

In the past, support for the patient meant moving equipment carts (e.g., intravenous stand) in and out of the room and plugging them into the outlets with cords dangling from the wall. Patient rooms in new hospitals are now designed to use a headwall system (see Figure 8.2). These systems eliminate the institutional look and increase a more home-like atmosphere. They are also ergonomically placed to minimize the need for caregivers to bend and reach (Hill-Rom, 2010a). Meeting inclusive design criteria, a headwall system is responsive, adaptable, accessible, and secure.

Accommodating those Who are Size-Challenged

Obesity trends among adults are high. In fact, one-third of adults in the United States are obese with 32.2 percent among men and 35.5 percent among women (Flegal, Carroll, Ogden, & Curtin, 2010, January 13). **Bariatrics** refers to the branch of medicine concerned with the treatment of obesity. The term is also used to describe products (Bariatric furniture or seating) for the obese (Merriam-Webster, 2011).

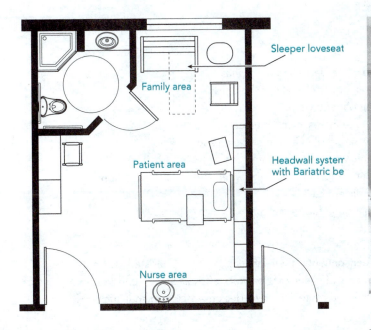

Sleeper loveseat

Family area

Patient area

Headwall system with Bariatric be

Nurse area

Figure 8.1

This patient's room is separated into zones for family, patient, and nurse. Note also the headwall system and bariatric bed. © Precision Graphics / based on a drawing by Linda L. Nussbaumer

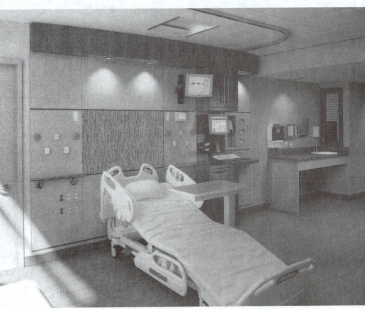

Figure 8.2

The Hill-Rom® Elements™ System covers the structure and flexible cabling for gas and electrical services. Rather than rolling carts in and out of a patient room, services are easily accessible in the headwall system. This saves time, money, and the hassle of coordinating multiple services. A computer/chart area may also be installed at the bedside, which saves time and steps to record information as well as enhances patient care. The design also changes an institutional atmosphere into a comfortable one. © 2011 Hill-Rom Services, Inc. Reprinted with permission—all rights reserved

STUDY SKETCH 8.1: Considering Single-Patient Rooms in Hospitals

During the last half of the twentieth century, hospitals featured two-, three-, and even four-bed patient rooms, which are now insufficient for patient safety and privacy. This InformeDesign research summary (2009, January 8) summarizes a review of literature that examines the benefits and concerns regarding single-patient hospital rooms (i.e., single bed, single bathroom).

Findings

In the research, single-patient rooms in which patients are not transferred after surgery are considered safer for the following reasons:

- Decreases transfer of germs because rooms are easier to clean and disinfect
- Improves patient care by eliminating transfer of patient from one area of hospital to another (e.g., intensive care, step-down, post-surgery)
- Improves efficiency of hospital staff
- Respects patient privacy
- Reduces noise level
- Improves sleep, mood, and pain tolerance
- Allows greater family support

There are also disadvantages associated with single-patient rooms:

- Increases walking and time required by staff to care for patient
- Isolates patient from others if help is needed
- Increases construction costs

Criteria

Based on findings, the following criteria are identified when designing a hospital:

- Design using single-patient rooms for patients' privacy, safety, and dignity.
- Compare cost of single-patient rooms to multipatient rooms.
- Design single-patient rooms with a family area to increase communication.
- Include private bathrooms that decrease the spread of infection and increase privacy.
- Provide double rooms as an option for patients who prefer a roommate.
- Design hospitals with easy access to patient and support areas with wireless nurses' workstations and accessible, organized supply rooms for efficient care.
- Realize that single-patient rooms may be required in future designs.

Implications

Single-patient rooms increase communication between patients, their families, and hospital staff. A single bathroom provides privacy and reduces spread of infection. Efficiency of hospital staff must also be considered. Thus, hospitals designed with all single-patient rooms promote inclusive design—a design that includes everyone.

Source: InformeDesign. (2009, January 8). "Considering Single-Patient Rooms in Hospitals." Retrieved on August 4, 2010, from http://www.informedesign.org/Rs_detail.aspx?rsId=3207

Furniture manufacturer KI realized the need for seating for size-challenged individuals, so they selected Paul James and Dan Cramer to design a line of furniture that everyone could use. They began by conducting extensive research that included watching how size-challenged individuals selected their seating and how they sat. The researchers found that individuals who were larger avoided large-sized seating because of the stigma (i.e., a large piece for a large person). More often, they sat sideways and used the arms to raise them from the chair. Thus, the wide chair was not necessarily the solution; however, the chair must be both structurally sound and aesthetically pleasing. Their solution was organic and adaptable to all shapes and sizes and provided seating for anyone—inclusive (Wiens, 2010, April). Figures 8.3a–d shows various ways the Arissa® seating can be used.

Of course, some furniture is specifically designed for the size-challenged in a healthcare setting. This furniture must not only be wider but also structurally sound, as noted earlier. Figure 8.4 shows a Bariatric Recliner for the patient who is larger (Hill-Rom, 2010b). This Hill-Rom® Art of Care® Manual Bariatric Recliner was designed to accommodate patients and visitors up to 660 pounds. It is also designed for comfort and functionality with an independent footrest, a back-assisted lift, and a 30-inch-wide seating surface.

a   b   c   d

Figure 8.3a–d

KI's Arissa seating's design and style appeals to a wide range of people of all shapes and sizes. It supports up to 750 pounds and yet its design does not appear oversized. This inclusive design provides universal appeal. Courtesy KI Arissa

Applying Sustainable and Inclusive Design in Hospitals

Sustainability in hospital design seems contradictory because hospitals are large complex facilities that operate 24/7 and have heavy energy loads. On the other hand, a sustainable environment is a healthy environment that uses nontoxic products. Recently, the architecture firm Anshen+Allen studied a full-scale mock-up of a hospital room. The Martin C. Pedersen (2009, September 16) study applied various sustainable features. To name a few, the study used renewable materials with low VOCs, PVC-free, FSC-certified wood and polyurethane furniture, recycled polyester upholstery, energy-efficient lighting, antimicrobial silicone upholstery, and so on.

Along with these features, the infrastructure includes energy- and water-efficient features to reduce energy consumption. Additionally, hospital design can also include other sustainable features such as daylighting and atrium spaces. These areas provide a sense of peace and calm that comes from the natural environment and promotes healing. In the patient rooms, beds at an angle and facing the window support healing (Tisch; 2001, March). Clearly, hospitals can apply sustainable practices that promote healing and provide a healthy, inclusively designed environment for everyone.

Figure 8.4

The Hill-Rom® Art of Care® Manual Bariatric Recliner provides room for the larger patient.

Considering the Caregiver

Noted previously, ergonomics and appropriate spaces are important for the staff—the caregivers. But work also takes place outside the patient's room. Work areas should provide flexibility to sit or stand at a computer. Adjustability of monitor screens and keyboards provide ergonomic needs for staff of varied heights. The space must also be illuminated to provide adequate light and without reflective glare (Wiens; 2009, March).

Although hospital design must comply with the ADA, there still are opportunities to create an inclusive environment. This may be by designing single-patient rooms that provide privacy to everyone, selecting seating for all shapes and sizes, creating a sustainable, healthy environment, and providing ergonomically designed work areas for hospital staff.

LONG-TERM CARE FACILITIES

Long-term care facilities provide housing and care for the elderly or those in need of healthcare services. Some are long-term living arrangements such as nursing homes/long-term care, and **dementia/Alzheimer's care**, assisted living residences, independent residential living, **congregate housing**, **continuing care retirement communities**, and **active adult communities**. Others are outpatient care such as adult day care and geriatric outpatient clinics (Kliment, 2004).

All long-term care facilities must be accessible but are not required to be entirely inclusive (responsive or adaptable, in particular). Using the questions presented in Chapter 5 may help create inclusive environments for long-term care facilities. In particular, the following are important areas:

- Outside to inside
- Circulation
- Entering and exiting
- Wayfinding
- Seating
- Lighting and acoustics
- Thermal comfort
- Information systems

Designing Nursing Homes for a Positive Effect on Residents

Nursing homes (often called long-term care facilities) house residents that can no longer care for themselves and, thus, need assistance 24/7. Many nursing homes have been known for negative effects on residents and poor quality of life (Kane, 2001). The reason is that in the 1970s, nursing homes were designed as institutions (hospitals), and people were placed in nursing homes due to concerns based on incontinence or memory loss. It was assumed that these facilities would be healthcare settings, but these concerns are not healthcare problems (i.e., people with dementia are healthy but you may find them walking up and down the corridors all day). Many people are placed in these settings because families find them difficult to handle, not due to health issues; they were moved from a comfortable home to an institution. Fortunately, many facilities have changed, and in some cases, these facilities have developed more residential settings with landscape, interior design, and residential detailing to de-institutionalize and humanize the environment (USC Architecture, 2008). Certainly changes have taken place to create a more positive environment.

Previewed in chapter 2, the Eden Alternative® philosophy advocates the creation of positive living environments to improve quality of life of long-term care for residents. The guiding principle of Eden Alternative® abandons the institution model and adopts the human habitat model where children, pets, and plants are an important part of daily life (Nussbaumer & Rowland, 2007; Thomas, 2002).

The Eden Alternative® philosophy states that it eliminates the plagues of loneliness, helplessness, and boredom in many ways. One is that residents may enjoy the companionship of humans and animals. For example, in these homes, there is an array of activities with interaction between residents and children, dogs and cats can visit residents' rooms, and birds sing (Nussbaumer & Rowland, 2007; Thomas, 1996). "Residents may choose to be involved in activities such as gardening, cooking, woodworking, reading, playing cards, and taking classes" (Nussbaumer & Rowland, 2007, p. 17). Residents may not only choose the activity but also at what time they want to participate. Being able to make decisions, residents "continue to grow as human beings and be respected as contributing members of society" (Nussbaumer & Rowland, 2007, p. 17).

Another process that reduces the feelings of helplessness is one in which residents and staff are able to contribute to how the home operates; however, having residents and staff as partners in a facility is very difficult for many administrators to understand. And yet, Eden Alternative® facilities successfully operate as a community with staff members functioning as facilitators as well as caregivers. Staff members develop close ties to residents and know not only their medications but also their backgrounds and interests. The staff and residents work as a team to make decisions for the community. For the staff, the home is no longer the workplace; it is a home. For the residents, it becomes an intimate, personal place; it becomes their home (Nussbaumer & Rowland, 2007; Salter, 2002; Thomas 1996).

Eden Alternative® homes are close-knit communities or neighborhoods (Nussbaumer & Rowland, 2007; Salter, 2002). The facility's structure is frequently divided into several connected buildings. Each building may be designed in the residential style where eight to ten residents reside. Spaces within the building are divided as a home with a kitchen, a dining room, a living room, bedrooms, bathrooms, and a laundry room. The kitchen is in a residential style with small dining room to accommodate the smaller number of residents. The living space is small and intimate, and nursing stations are absent. If desired by the residents, space is allowed for animals and/or birds (Nussbaumer & Rowland, 2007; Thomas, 2002). As with residential design, the color palette for interior finish materials is not limited. "With this type of structure and design, the neighborhood functions as a residence and creates a home-like atmosphere" (Nussbaumer & Rowland, 2007, p. 18). A student project described in Case Study 8.1, "Living Environments for the Elderly," applies the Eden Alternative® and inclusive design.

Neurological Disorder Patients Can Benefit from Inclusive Design

Neurological disorders (e.g., **Autism, cerebral palsy, multiple sclerosis, epilepsy, Alzheimer's disease** and related **dementia, Huntington's disease, Parkinson's disease**, and so on) affect one billion people worldwide (Medical News, 2010). Individuals with neurological disorders have various symptoms that sometimes progress or worsen over time. Symptoms may be the slow loss of coordination and balance or ability to speak clearly. Symptoms may begin with a mild and intermittent twitching or numbness in an arm or leg. They may have tremors, rigid muscles, slowed motion, loss of automatic movements (swinging the arms, blinking) or unconscious actions, and in time, they may have symptoms of dementia (Medical-Look, 2010).

Using the inclusive design criteria as a guide, products can be designed to enable individuals with a neurological disorder to complete various tasks. Using these products will not restore the individual's capabilities (e.g., strength, coordination, etc.), but it *will* widen the range of tasks the individual can perform. To explain further, the idea is to redefine the problem, change the environment, and select *different* products to enhance the individual's quality of life. Some examples would be to consistently specify lever handles, locate duplex outlets just above knee height, provide automatic motion-activated soap dispensers, and so on (Joines, 2009). The key is to specify products that are easy to use, require little pressure or strength to operate, are at heights that are reachable in a sitting position, and so on. With this in mind, products and environments will be responsive, adaptable, accessible, and secure for the user.

Positive Environments for Those with Alzheimer's and Related Dementia

Of the neurological diseases, Alzheimer's disease has received greater attention, particularly as baby boomers age. According to Margaret P. Calkins (2009), in the 1970s, M. Powell Lawton, Ph.D. (senior research scientist and director emeritus of the Polisher Research Institute of Philadelphia Geriatric Center) studied the role of the built environment on behavior and emotions (e.g., expressions of anxiety, agitation, wandering, or other challenging behaviors) of individuals with Alzheimer's disease and related dementia. More recently, healthcare providers and designers recognize the importance

With an increasing number of older people in the United States, there is a greater need for long-term care. In the past, many older people had one choice when they no longer were able to care for themselves—a nursing home. Many older people fear entering a nursing home where, in many cases, people exist rather than live (Kayser-Jones, 2002; Nussbaumer & Rowland, 2007). Today, there are alternatives such as assisted living; however, many assisted living facilities still feel more like nursing homes and separate the elderly from other ages and activities (Nussbaumer & Rowland, 2007).

In 1991, Dr. William Thomas created the Eden Alternative® to provide living environments rather than institutions for the aging population. These principles incorporate a variety of ages and activities within a facility to give the elderly meaning to their lives. Eden Alternative® (2009) Principles are found on page 49:

Project Objectives

In a university senior level studio, students converted a former middle school into a living environment for all ages. The project addressed the issue of creating a living environment. The objectives included the following:

- To create a living environment using the Eden Alternative® principles and universal design principles.
- To collaborate with other disciplines—gerontology and landscape design.
- To work separately on elements of the project as well as work as a team to complete the entire project.
- To develop the program requirements.

Program Requirements

Students created a timeline in which they worked through the phases of the design process (program development, schematic development, design development, and contract development) as it applied to their project. They included the time that was spent learning from the gerontology students and discussing ideas for their project with landscape design students.

An important part of the program development phase is research. The research process included various activities. Students researched design literature for evidence on and to develop an understanding of elderly housing, child and adult day care, and the Eden Alternative® principles. Both traditional and online resources were used in their research. They also visited the site, read blueprints, and measured the spaces. Finally, interior design and gerontology students conducted research to collected data regarding needs of the elderly.

In the schematic development phase, students developed the design concept.

The concept reflected the focus of the Eden Alternative® Principles. The title of the design was "The Village," and the design concept statement was, "If it takes a village to raise a child, then that village shall be composed of many generations." With this in mind, students created sketches of ideas for a space that would house a variety of ages from infants to the elderly. This project challenged students with the layout of both residential and nonresidential spaces for elderly housing and day care that included the application of concepts and inclusive design. Because the landscape design students were not familiar with the ADA and inclusive or universal design, interior design students worked closely with them to create an accessible atrium and inclusively designed entrance. To facilitate compliance with the ADA and building/fire codes, one student was designated to examine the plans and work with other students in completing the code check.

In the design development phase, drawings were finalized. Students created a model to demonstrate the three-dimensional aspects of their assigned space. A sample board was created for all interior materials. After presenting the project, students, along with the instructor, evaluated the projects.

Results

The focus of the space was to create a living environment for the elderly. Thus, the following were included in the design: assisted living apartments, a childcare facility, an adult day care facility, congregate and private dining, residential apartments, and an atrium space. Case

Study Figure 8.1a is the floor plan based on the one completed by the students.

Assisted living apartments were designed for the elderly who were still independent but were in need of assistance with meal preparation, medication or therapy. Near these apartments were a nurses' station and a therapy room.

To create easy access for parents, a childcare facility was placed near the main entrance. This facility also was adjacent to the assisted living apartments and easily accessible to adult day care, which allowed interaction between the elderly and the children.

An adult day care facility was an important aspect of the design. In this section, shops, an activity room, a kitchen, a workshop, and a quiet room were included. The shops were designed to simulate a main street of any town and included the facilities offices, an ice cream parlor, a library, and a beauty shop. The activity room, which could be divided into two spaces, was designed to accommodate small and large groups of people for activities or entertainment. A kitchen and wood workshop were provided for an individual or a group to continue their skills of cooking or woodworking. The quiet room allows for a resting area for an adult. All of these spaces were designed to accommodate adults who lived in the assisted living facility, on second floor, or in the community.

On the first floor, a congregate dining area was available to the adults residing in the facility or participating in the adult day care and the children in the child day care facility. The dining area overlooked the atrium and included a private

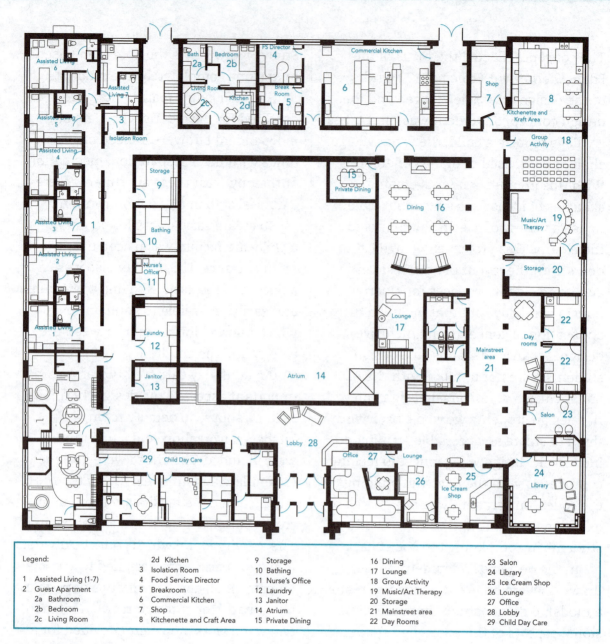

Legend:

		2d	Kitchen	9	Storage	16	Dining	23 Salon
1	Assisted Living (1-7)	3	Isolation Room	10	Bathing	17	Lounge	24 Library
2	Guest Apartment	4	Food Service Director	11	Nurse's Office	18	Group Activity	25 Ice Cream Shop
	2a Bathroom	5	Breakroom	12	Laundry	19	Music/Art Therapy	26 Lounge
	2b Bedroom	6	Commercial Kitchen	13	Janitor	20	Storage	27 Office
	2c Living Room	7	Shop	14	Atrium	21	Mainstreet area	28 Lobby
		8	Kitchenette and Craft Area	15	Private Dining	22	Day Rooms	29 Child Day Care

Case Study Figure 8.1a

Floor plan completed by students. The plan includes an office area, assisted living apartments, childcare facility, adult day care facility, congregate and private dining, and an atrium space. The residential apartments are located on the second floor (not shown). © Precision Graphics/based on a drawing by Kristin L. Mellema, Jessica Magnussen, and Cameron Serk

dining area. A commercial kitchen where meals were prepared was adjacent to the dining room.

The second floor housed apartments that would be available to any age. Located on this floor was an exercise room that overlooked an atrium below. This atrium in the center of the building was accessible

through elevators and used by the child day care facility as well as adults. See Case Study Figure 8.1b for a drawing based on those provided by landscape students.

The entrance on the exterior and the interior spaces were designed to incorporate concepts of inclusive design. Case Study Figure 8.1c shows the plan view

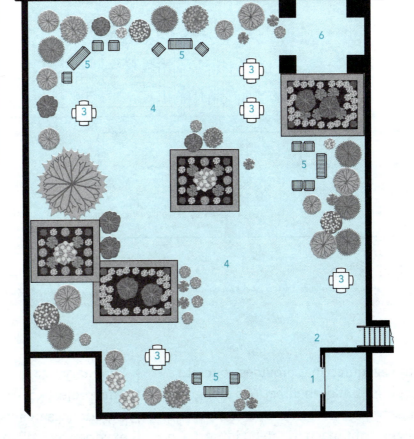

Case Study Figure 8.1b

The atrium area provides a place for people to exercise, play games, or visit and feel a sense of outdoors in the interior. Activities include all ages (e.g., children from the day care, assisted-living residents, adult day care participants, friends, and family). The space provides an inclusive environment for all ages and a variety of activities. © Precision Graphics/based on a drawing by Kristin L. Mellema, Jessica Magnussen, and Caeron Serk

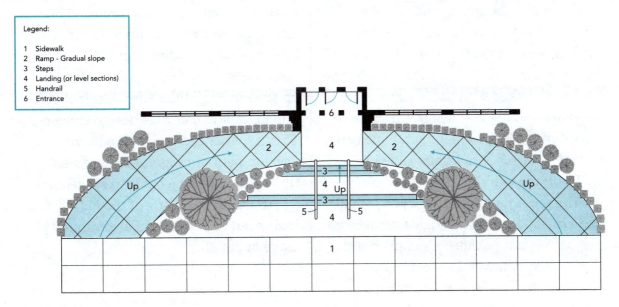

Case Study Figure 8.1c

The sketches show an elevation and plan view that provides inclusivity to the entrance. Although steps are at the center, the gradual slope and landscape encourage people to use the ramp rather than the steps thus creating an inclusive entrance into the building. © Precision Graphics based on a drawing by Kristin L. Mellema, Jessica Magnussen, and Caeron Serk

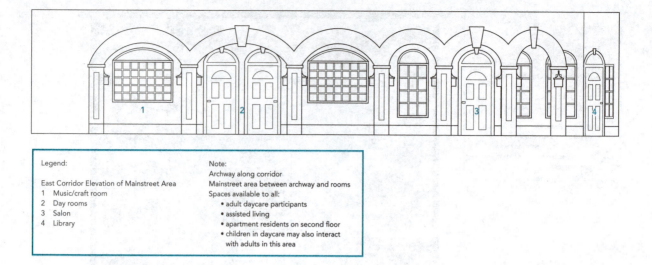

Legend:

East Corridor Elevation of Mainstreet Area
1 Music/craft room
2 Day rooms
3 Salon
4 Library

Note:
Archway along corridor
Mainstreet area between archway and rooms
Spaces available to all:
• adult daycare participants
• assisted living
• apartment residents on second floor
• children in daycare may also interact
  with adults in this area

Case Study Figure 8.1d

This sketch of the east corridor depicts the streetscape. Columns provide a separation between the corridor and walkway to the various activity rooms, day rooms, beauty salon, and library. This creates a homelike atmosphere as well as an inclusive environment for all © Precision Graphics based on a drawing by Kristin L. Mellema

of the entrance that provides concrete ramping from both directions along with landscaping to provide an inclusively designed approach to the building. Case Study Figure 8.1d depicts the streetscape.

Students worked separately yet as a team on the project. Interior design students were assigned portions of the project. The gerontology students assisted interior design students in the research of the elderly and their needs. The landscape students worked with the interior design students to integrate the atrium space to the interior design and integrate inclusive concepts into the landscape and sidewalks on the exterior.

The presentation of the project included various graphic and electronic formats. The graphic formats included a sample board, models, and contract documents. For the electronic format, students scanned pictures of the exterior, inserted CAD drawings and, then, using PowerPoint, they presented the project to guests and instructors.

Summary

This project gave students great learning experiences in a variety of ways. They experienced collaboration with other disciplines, which helped them appreciate what others have to offer to a project, and input from other disciplines was vital to the success of the project. They learned to work as a team with other interior design students and other disciplines. They developed a better understanding of the Eden Alternative® Principles and inclusive design concepts. They experienced ownership in the development of program requirements. Ultimately, the project aided students in a better understanding of the elderly and their need to be a part of a community (large or small).

Source: Eden Alternative®. (2009). *Eden Alternative®: Our 10 principles.* Available online: http://www.edenalt.org/our-10-principles.
Kayser-Jones, J. (2002). The experience of dying: An ethnographic nursing home study. *The Gerontologist*, 42(3), 11–19.
Nussbaumer, L. L. & Rowland, L. (2007). Transforming nursing homes into… homes? *Journal of Family and Consumer Sciences*, 99(4), 15-20.

of the physical as well as the social environment and are working to create responsive, adaptable, and secure environments for those with dementia. However, the greatest change in research has shifted from a nearly exclusive to a more inclusive approach. The ultimate goal is to provide quality of life for individuals.

According to Calkins (2009), some research evidence regarding Alzheimer's disease and related dementia supports positive benefits of private bedrooms. Benefits include the satisfaction of residents, families, and staff; reduction in infections; and better quality of life. Other research evidence found that some residents prefer having a roommate while yet another research study found that having roommates within a small unit may cause expressions of anger. Interestingly, an increase of "ambient light seems to provide the most consistent positive impacts on behavior, agitation, and sleep" (p. 152).

Calkins (2009) also notes that evidence shows that the design of the built environment impacts the emotional and probably the physical health of individuals with Alzheimer's disease and related dementia. Studies also suggest that the traditional institutional setting (e.g., multibed rooms, long corridors, and multipurpose dining/activity rooms) produce negative outcomes; therefore, long-term care facilities should not be built in this manner. Instead, all facilities must be built with the occupant in mind. They should follow inclusive design criteria—developing an accessible environment, adapting the environment to the resident, providing a secure environment, and using concepts such as the Eden Alternative® Principles to provide a positive living environment.

Gardens Can Be Restorative Environments

With the application of evidence-based design, healthcare facilities are designed through thorough research. Evidence has been found that art or gardens provide a positive distraction and have **restorative** properties, and as new hospitals are designed or renovated, this evidence is being applied to the design.

Until recently, healthcare design did not focus on outdoor environments or the specific needs of those with Alzheimer's disease. This has changed, however, and research has found that outdoor environments can provide safe, secure spaces for fresh air and sunshine, encourage walking and other types of exercise, offer beneficial exposure to natural light levels, improve psychological well being, and reduce depression. In particular, gardens as well as other outdoor spaces provide opportunities for socialization, stimulation, and recreation (Brawley, 2002).

An interior designer specializing in environments for aging adults, Elizabeth C. Brawley, IIDA (2002) states that gardens must be planned to be successful. This means that a garden must be incorporated into the plan for residents' care with programmed activities within the garden setting by coordinating them into the early stages of the design process. In that way, outdoor activities should be developed and used based on the design of the outdoor space. To facilitate this process, a professional landscape architect must be included on the design team at the beginning. This professional can provide interesting walking paths that meander through the garden and bring residents back to the beginning. They can facilitate selection of smooth surface materials that will reduce glare. Brawley (2002) provides several tips in garden design:

1. Assess to the garden: The outdoor space must be highly visible to the residents from the interior, which will encourage them to go outdoors. The entrance to the garden must be available (not locked), but the garden must be a secure space that is safe and encourages independent movement.

2. Overall layout: The garden's overall layout must be easily understood to minimize confusion. Larger gardens can be divided into areas of varied sizes and levels of privacy. Some spaces may be designed for socializing and a higher level of activity. Some spaces may be designed for residents, family, and visitors to sit comfortably and in private.

3. Spaces for activities: A sheltered pavilion is a space where programmed activities can take place, especially activities that may have been planned for the outdoors on what turned out to be a cold or rainy day. Space should be provided for active participation exercise such as Tai Chi, gardening, or other activities that include staff participation. Porches may be used as an active transitional space for lunch, supper, or snacks to encourage residents to ease their way outside.

4. Supporting exercise: The activity director can create strategies to encourage mobility, exercise, and walking. If they are able, residents may be given the opportunity to mow grass, rake leaves, participate in gardening, or hang clothes on a line. These activities can stimulate long-term memory from home or professional life.

5. Falls: Some residents may fear falling and, thus, limit mobility. However, the lack of exercise can decrease bone strength and, consequently, increase the risk of fractures from a fall. Therefore, many activities must be created as protective exercises that improve balance and strength and also reduce depression and loneliness as well as improve sleep, alertness, and energy. Selecting walking surfaces that are slip-resistant, glare-free, and uniform texture and color can also minimize falls.

6. Finding solace in privacy: In some long-term care facilities, living spaces including bedrooms are shared; therefore, private areas in a garden can provide places of solitude for the resident as well as for family visits. For families, outdoor spaces also provide a choice in places to visit, for privacy, to stimulate conversation, and to walk (p. 9–10).

Clearly, the benefits of a well-designed outdoor environment fulfill physical and psychological needs for the resident as well as visitors. Figure 8.5a–b shows paths leading to a gathering area for visiting with residents and family members and par-

Figure 8.5a

Landscape architect Brian Bainnson designed these gardens to serve Alzheimer's patients, their families, and caregivers. The gardens were part of a project to create 100 such gardens around the country to celebrate the American Society of Landscape Architects' 100th anniversary. Brian Bainnson, Quatrefoil, Inc.

Figure 8.5b

A private area for solace, covered areas, plant life, and smooth walking surface provide a natural, comfortable, and restful environment for residents in this park by landscape architect Brian Bainnson. Brian Bainnson, Quatrefoil, Inc.

ticipating in activities. Shelters are provided, and surfaces are even, smooth, wide, and safe for residents. A variety of plant life is found throughout the garden. All of these features give a natural, comfortable, and restful environment for residents. Providing opportunities to enjoy outdoor environments also connects to the Eden Alternative's® quality of life principles and are an inclusive design as well.

The Seven Principles that Connect Eden Alternative® and Inclusivity

A YouTube video by USC Architecture (2008, October 14) presents "The Academic Work of Victor Regnier, FAIA," who is a pioneer in the design of noninstitutional housing for older people who are frail. His designs have been informed by research he conducted in Northern Europe, where many of the first facilities for older adults began.

Victor Regnier's work has focused on making the building more attractive. His facilities combine residential aesthetic with special services and features to allow older adults to live more independently and with more autonomy. His designs were based on the following seven principles:

1. The environment should compensate for physical disability and mental frailty.
2. The environment should ensure privacy as well as stimulate social exchange.
3. The environment should facilitate choice, control, autonomy, and independence.
4. The environment should challenge residents to do as much for themselves as possible.
5. The environment should encourage physical movement and exercise.
6. The environment should invite family members to visit and participate.
7. The environment should connect residents to the surrounding neighborhood community.

Long-term care facilities can be designed as a positive environment and to recognize the older person's need for independence, familiarity, and self-worth. This can occur by applying the Eden Alternative® principles, Victor Regnier's principles, and ideas for restorative environments. All principles and ideas, used in part or the whole, will provide an inclusive space that shows concern for the older adult and their needs.

Clearly, the principles of the Eden Alternative® and Victor Regnier are similar. Both recommend that long-term care facilities develop into neighborhoods—small housing units (see Figure 8.6). In doing so, many of the other principles fall into place. With the example shown in Figure 8.6, a home-like residential atmosphere is created

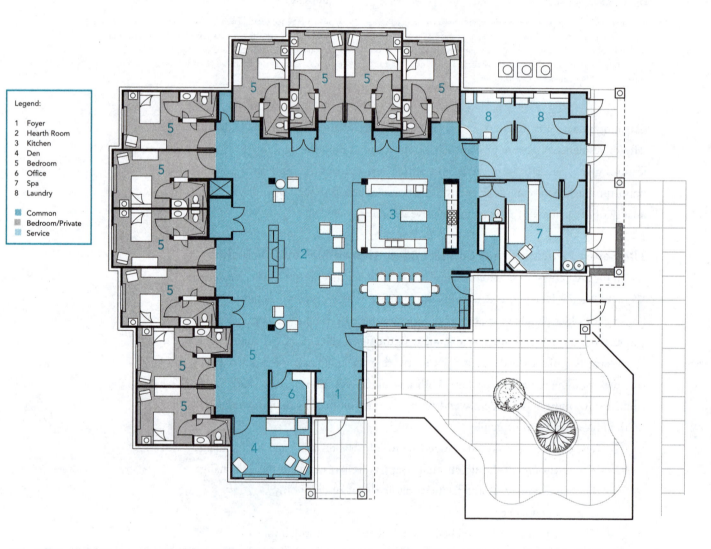

Legend:

1 Foyer
2 Hearth Room
3 Kitchen
4 Den
5 Bedroom
6 Office
7 Spa
8 Laundry

■ Common
■ Bedroom/Private
■ Service

Figure 8.6

An Eden Alternative® facility may be made up of several neighborhoods with a maximum of ten residents residing in each neighborhood. Within each neighborhood, the residents have separate bedrooms, and small visiting areas are provided for more intimate conversation. The living room and dining room provide a residential appeal and a place for all residents to congregate. The residentially designed kitchen is open to allow residents to participate in food preparation. An Eden Alternative® facility provides a residential atmosphere to a long-term care facility. © Precision Graphics

with a residential kitchen, dining room, and living room. For quiet living, a den is located in a separate room. To continue the residential environment, nursing staff is located in an office rather than a nursing station in the living space.

Such facilities provide a higher quality of life where individuals choose the activity in which to participate, live in a residential environment, and feel respected by staff and administration for ideas and opinions. It is an environment that provides a responsive, secure, comfortable setting for all residents.

ASSISTED LIVING AND INDEPENDENT LIVING

As a comparison, assisted living facilities involve a different type of care and service than long-term care facilities. These facilities have a greater residential feel with one-bedroom apartments that offer choices in personal care and health-related services. They provide enough help for an older person to keep a more independent lifestyle. Residents usually have complete control to choose whether or not to participate in a facility's services or programs (ALFA, 2009). In both types of facilities, compliance with the ADA is required. Both can also apply inclusive design criteria to accommodate all residents.

Institutional

Institutional facilities vary in design type (e.g., educational, government, libraries) as well as design needs and requirements. Some facilities are public; others are privately owned. For example, public facilities include government buildings, libraries, and schools; private facilities may also include private schools. Some facilities are designed for specific age groups (e.g., elementary schools), or specific user types (e.g., prisons) (Nussbaumer, 2009).

EDUCATIONAL FACILITIES

Educational facility types may be related to age groups (e.g., preschool, elementary, high school, and college), characteristics of study (e.g., technical institutes, community college, and university), or special circumstances (e.g., school for the blind or for the deaf). Libraries, studios, laboratories, and research facilities are often integrated into various educational types (Nussbaumer, 2009).

Acoustics in the Open Classroom

Some classrooms are designed in open environments. In those cases, the acoustics within the space are of special concern. For some children, noise is a deterrent that makes it difficult to comprehend and learn. Because these classrooms are designed with open areas, it is possible to select the appropriate ceiling or wall finishes that can absorb or mask the sound. What these spaces need for teaching to be effective is **high speech intelligibility**, which "means that the classroom must have low reverberation time, low background noise, and low sound transmission from adjacent spaces" (AWI, 2010, para. 1). This can be accomplished in the following three ways:

- Use a suspended ceiling to absorb and contain sound within the classroom.
- Use proper wall construction that extends above the ceiling to the deck to lessen transmission through the ceiling plenum.
- Add wall treatments to further reduce reverberation and improve sound isolation between classrooms (para. 2).

Special Educational Facilities

Children with disabilities (e.g., visual, hearing, physical, developmental, or emotional) have often been separated in special education classrooms or facilities, whereas other children are taught in general classroom. Although many of these children are "mainstreamed into the general population school" (Perkins & Bordwell, 2010, p. 73), there is still a need for special schools, and to design these schools, studying and understanding these children's special characteristics and needs is essential.

Architects, Bradford Perkins and Raymond Bordwell suggest the following points to consider when designing for these special schools:

- The design team must become extremely knowledgeable about the characteristics of the children's specific disability. Most special schools require unique and creative design solutions.
- Classrooms in these schools tend to have a lower student-to-teacher ratio.
- Nonambulatory children touch and view their environment and perceive space from a different height than other children. The design should not follow typical standards for mounting heights, windows, and other building elements.
- Toilet rooms should be part of or adjacent to classroom spaces to reduce distance and time without supervision.
- Travel distance to core functions should be minimized.
- Tactile surfaces are important to children who are missing other senses.
- Rooms or spaces apart from the general classroom should be provided for working with students one on one.
- Finishes, wall construction, and systems must be designed to withstand unusually heavy maintenance demands (p. 73–74).

Figure 8.7 shows a floor plan designed by Perkins Eastman for children with multiple disabilities. The design exhibits many special features that include adjacent toilet facilities, soft floor surfaces, and wheelchair storage.

Legend:

1 Classroom
2 Wheelchair Storage
3 Restroom
4 Access to outdoors

Figure 8.7

The Elizabeth Seton Pediatric Center in Yonkers, New York, is designed for children with multiple disabilities. The open space and flooring materials create an accessible and adaptable environment for various abilities and ways of teaching. Features include full wheelchair accessibility, soft material and rounded edges to minimize hazards, flexible yet small classrooms to accommodate wheelchairs and a variety of equipment, and bathrooms convenient to each classroom. © Precision Graphics/based on a drawing from Building Type Basics for Elementary Schools, Perkins, B. & Bordwell, R. (2010). Hoboken, NJ: Wiley, p. 75

Perkins & Bordwell (2010) also suggest that the following be included:

- Provide full wheelchair accessibility.
- Select materials and systems that minimize hazards (e.g., sharp corners, exposed heat elements, hard surfaces, etc.).
- Select floor surfaces for easy wheelchair movement.
- Select lighting levels that are sensitive to the visually impaired.
- Design flexible classroom spaces (a warm floor, low windowsills, and other special features).
- Provide small classrooms; however, they must accommodate wheelchairs and various special equipment.
- Provide bathrooms that are convenient to all program areas.
- Provide outdoor play area designed to facilitate appropriate exercise and play in a very safe setting.
- Combine educational environments with therapy areas (p. 75).

Applying these general suggestions will create an accessible and inclusively designed educational environment for children with disabilities. Specific educational environments have been designed for specific needs such as those with visual limitations.

Educational Facilities for Children with Visual Limitations

A facility for visually impaired children must provide many ways to stimulate the senses. Anchor Center for Blind Children was designed to do just that and is described in Case Study 8.2, "Designing for Children with Visual Limitations: Anchor Center for Blind Children." (Photos of the Anchor Center also appear in the color pages of this book.)

Supportive Classrooms for Children with Autism

According to InformeDesign research summary (2009, April 15), autism has become increasingly common, and yet the ADA and inclusive design do not consider the specific needs of autistic users. There are many challenges and needs for individuals with autism and that may be a reason comprehensive guidelines do not exist. Thus, this summary describes a study that tests children with autism in a classroom setting.

From this study, criteria related to architectural features and spatial characteristics were identified as supporting learning and developmental needs of children with autism. Some preliminary guidelines to design for users who are autistic have been developed. Briefly, these include minimizing noise, using various acoustic properties, creating areas with minimal sensory stimulation, compartmentalizing activities, separating areas for high stimulation, and locating buffers in transitional zones. Greater detail is found in Study Sketch 8.2: "Supportive Classrooms for Children with Autism."

Behavioral Interventions for Improving School Ventilation Performance

When airtight buildings are constructed using synthetic building materials, contaminants may be trapped and affect indoor air quality (IAQ). Poor IAQ and ventilation rates have been linked to adverse health conditions such as communicable respiratory illnesses or sick building syndrome. Because school-aged children are more susceptible to pollutants than adults, IAQ in school environments is a concern. To create inclusive school environments, the air quality must be healthy for everyone.

An InformeDesign research summary (2010, March 31) describes a study that examined the effect of different types of natural ventilation interventions on ventilation in 81 primary school classrooms in the Netherlands. With three different experimental groups and a control group, CO_2 concentrations and ventilation behaviors were recorded for each classroom at different monitoring weeks. One experimental group received more instruction than the others. Results from the study revealed that the combination of providing good ventilation and educating students helps improve IAQ. Unfortunately, the improvement in CO_2 levels was not significant. Although the study did not indicate the reason, specifying materials that are nontoxic may have a greater affect on CO_2 levels.

Assessing Classroom Indoor Air Quality

In the InformeDesign research summary (2007, November 3) "Assessing Classroom Indoor Air Quality," results were different than the study mentioned in the previous section. This study determined that VOC rates were higher in special use classrooms (e.g., art, science) and tested higher for specific VOC. It also determined that ventilation rates were poorer in classrooms with higher VOC levels; thus, to lower VOC levels, proper ventilation is necessary. To be inclusive for all users, proper ventilation is important in all classrooms but most important in special use classrooms (art and science).

CHILDCARE FACILITIES

Prior to kindergarten, children may spend their days in a type of childcare facility (e.g., nursery school, day care, or a type of early childhood development program).

In-home childcare providers must also comply with the ADA and cannot discriminate against children with disabilities; therefore, the portion of the home used for the childcare is covered by the ADA. As may be expected, many of these providers are concerned because altering their homes with ramps and accessible bathrooms may be difficult. However, this is not necessarily the case as the law states that they would not have to make structural alterations if these are not "readily achievable" or without much difficulty or expense (Pacer, 2010).

Churches and other religious entities operating childcare centers are exempt from complying with the ADA, as long as the church itself operates the childcare program. If the church leases space to a privately operated day care center, the private childcare center (within the church) must comply with the ADA. However, some states have laws that extend beyond the ADA. For example, in Minnesota, a church-operated childcare center must comply with the ADA (Pacer, 2010).

Going beyond ADA compliance, the application of inclusive design criteria in childcare facilities responds to children of various ages and abilities. This is accomplished by specifying fixtures and elements to be mounted at different heights and/or to be adjustable as well as creating secure, safe, and healthy environments (Easter Seals, n/d).

According to Vicki L. Stoecklin, education and child development director, and Randy White, CEO of White Hutchinson Leisure and Learning Group (2010), the design of a childcare facility greatly impacts children's learning and behavior as well as the teacher's ability to teach efficiently. The design and layout considers the building and outdoor spaces, room arrangement, selection of equipment, and interior finishes. It also must be an "age-appropriate physical environment to support and promote child-directed and child-initiated play" (para.2).

Unfortunately, problems have occurred in designing these facilities to meet inclusive design criteria and needs of children with various physical and cognitive abilities. Stoecklin and White (2010) point out the following problems:

STUDY SKETCH 8.2: Supportive Classrooms for Children with Autism

According to InformeDesign research summary (2009, April 15), autism has become increasingly common, and yet the ADA and universal design do not consider the special needs of the autistic user. There are many challenges and needs for individuals with autism, which may be the reason that comprehensive guidelines do not exist. Thus, this summary describes a study that provides preliminary guidelines to design for the autistic person and tests them in a classroom environment.

Method

A survey was conducted among 58 primary caregivers and 25 teachers of autistic children in a middle-class community of Egyptians and Western Americans. A voluntary questionnaire was then completed, either found on the Families for Early Autism Treatment (FEAT) website, or provided by the Advance Society for Developing Skills of Special Needs Children in Cairo, Egypt. "Subjects ranked architectural features (i.e., colors and patterns, textures, acoustics, lighting, and olfactory) and spatial characteristics (e.g., spatial sequencing) from most to least influential on autistic behavior" (para. 4).

Based on the survey results, design interventions were implemented. Twelve children (nine boys, three girls) with autism, ages 6 to 10 years old were observed: six in a control and six in a study group. Observations were conducted at a school for children with special needs in Cairo during two semesters in one school year. During the first semester, researchers developed a baseline by which they would compare subjects' progress and allowed subjects to be comfortable with the researcher in their classrooms. During the second semester, InformeDesign (2009, April 15) summarized the way interventions were implemented:

1. Echoing and external noise reduced in an intervention classroom with soundproofing to the floor, walls, and ceiling.
2. An intervention classroom was divided into spatial zones, including an escape zone—a space with less stimuli (para. 4).

Observations were conducted between February and June for 45 minutes and completed at 3-week intervals during a 12-week period. Researchers measured progress based on behavioral indicators such as behavioral temperament, attention span, and response time. Researchers and teachers collected data by behavioral mapping and direct observations. The following was measured for each child:

1. Behavioral temperament: How often self-stimulating behavior (e.g., head banging, hand biting, rocking) took place and how often it decreased indicated progress.
2. Attention span: Number of seconds s/he stayed on task before being distracted.
3. Response time: Number of seconds s/he took to respond to a verbal question or command.

Findings

Autism is a developmental disorder. For this reason, it may result in difficulty with social skills and communication skills, repetitive behavior, and sensory malfunction from the surroundings. Findings from the study revealed the following information:

- Architectural features that influenced behavior in children with autism:
  1. Acoustics ranked most significant
  2. Spatial sequencing ranked second
  3. Lighting, colors and patterns, texture, and smell
- After 12 weeks, the following was determined:
  1. Fewer self-stimulating behavior occurrences
  2. Longer attention spans

3. Faster response times

4. Improvements less significant with spatial sequencing

Criteria

Architectural features and spatial characteristics can support learning and developmental needs of children with autism. The following preliminary guidelines will aid the design for children with autism:

- Minimize noise from other areas, echo effects, and other distractive noises in spaces where children need longer attention spans, faster responses, and greater focus (e.g., one-on-one instruction, speech, and computer rooms).
- Incorporate rooms with various acoustical properties to prevent children from relying on soundproof rooms.
- Create a space within classrooms where there is minimal sensory stimulation.
- Compartmentalize classrooms by activity, which may be with furniture or visual cues.
- Locate spaces for high stimulation (e.g., gymnasiums, cafeterias) away from classrooms.
- Locate transition zones to provide buffers between areas of high and low stimuli.

Implications

Organize spatial layout and design architectural features by considering the effects of noise and overstimulation.

Source: InformeDesign. (2009, April 15). "Supportive Classrooms for Children with Autism." Retrieved on July 12, 2010, from http://www.informedesign.umn.edu/Rs_detail.aspx?rsId=3296

1. Some architects and designers have little knowledge of child development and the operation of childcare centers. Although anthropometric charts help create design elements at the appropriate heights and depths, adjustable and age-specific design elements and fixtures may not be specified. For example, toddler sinks specified may be too high, which would make them unsafe for a smaller child.

2. Some directors and teachers who understand children and their needs find it difficult to translate their teaching and administrative skills to the design of spaces and the language of the architect and designers.

3. The design process itself may cause problems. At each stage, the design can "squeeze" the stage that follows by closing off options to improve quality, reduce costs, and speed up construction. The architect, designer, or engineer may have a picture of their area of expertise rather than a united vision (p. 4–8).

However, when all parties involved work together, the design will meet needs of all children who may possibly use the facility. Stoecklin and White use what they call **concurrent design**. Concurrent design brings together all experts who design the facility and those who operate it. From the beginning, everyone works together as a multidisciplinary, cross-functional design team. The design and creation of a high-

Children with visual limitations deserve the same opportunities as children with good eyesight. With the Julie McAndrews Mork Building (Denver, Colorado), this is a reality; it is a facility that is uniquely designed for teaching very young children who have visual limitations. However, it embraces all senses and makes the building itself a teaching tool. The facility includes textures, lights, sounds as well as the Sensory Garden, Braille Trail, and Cane Walk Lane. It is also designed with a large, open Grand Hallway that provides a sense of security as children maneuver down it. Additionally, the building's wayfinding methods help children locate classrooms and give them confidence in their ability to navigate other places as well.

The architect, Maria Cole, was with Davis Partnership Architects during the design and construction of Anchor Center. Her concept behind the design was to create a building that would teach by embracing all senses. To accomplish this, the building has special acoustics, light, and textures that enhance the child's understanding of the world.

When children and families arrive at the facility's entrance, concrete "rumble strips," tell children that vehicles are turning into the parking lot. The concrete at the building entrances are scored closer together as children approach, as a guide for children using canes that they are nearing the front entrance. At the entrance to the facility, there is an area to store strollers and car seats as well as a quiet area where parents and children connect.

When inside the facility, the Grand Hallway directs the children to all classrooms and provides them with multiple wayfinding tools. For example, the hallway flooring alternates between wood and tile. The tile floor covering alerts children that they are entering a classroom pod. As children move down the hallway, they are able to feel the texture as well as hear the sound change from canes and footsteps on the two different surfaces (hardwood or tile) (see Color Plate 31 in the color pages of this book). Other guides in the hallway include the Trail Rail on one side of the hallway. Notches along this trail alert children that they are nearing a classroom. Another guide in the hallway floor, the Light Walk (see Color Plate 32 in the color pages of this book), simulates natural light by illuminating the way for children who can see some light. Above the hallway, skylights provide subtle blue, yellow, and red lights that alert children to the three classroom pods—each designed in the different colors.

The first pod is blue and includes the Quiet Room, Infant Classroom, Sibling Care Room, and Children's Kitchen and Dining Room (see Case Study Figure 8.2).

The Quiet Room has rules of "silence," whereas in the Infant Classroom next door, parents and their babies participate in a program to learn about early motor and play skill development. Across the hallway is the Sibling Care Room, where siblings of infants and toddlers play together. Also, on this side in the Children's Kitchen and Dining Room, preschoolers eat lunch at a dining table in chairs sized for them. Here children can also participate in cooking, and cleaning up as well. Adjacent to this pod is the entrance to the Sensory Garden that features meandering trails, fragrant flowers, a small bridge, a dry streambed, water sounds, and sculptures (see Color Plate 33 in the color pages of this book). Also in

the garden is a gazebo—a landmark structure for the building. This structure offers open air, sunshine, and a sand area for children to play.

The second pod is yellow and has two classrooms (one with a stage) on one side of the hallway; the Light Room, Fine Motor Work/Art Room, Literacy Room, and Eye Exam Room are located across the hallway (refer to Case Study Figure 8.2). The Stage Classroom features a small stage that provides an area for acting out stories. The Light Room features optimal lighting sources and high contrast that encourages the use of vision in play. Work/Art Room is the place where children create as well as clean up when their work/art is completed. In the Literacy

Our Building Is a Teacher

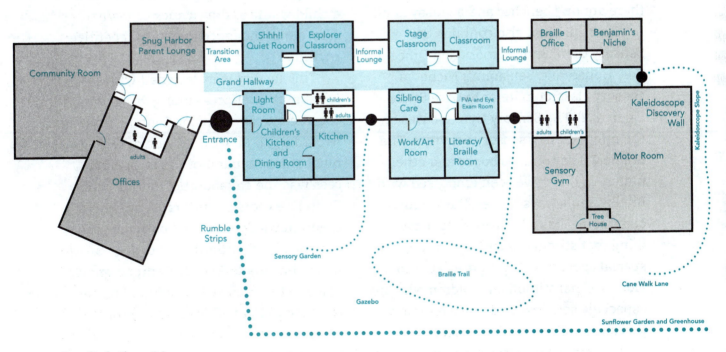

Case Study Figure 8.2

The floor plan shows various spaces in the building. To the left of the entrance are the offices, community room, and parents' lounge. Going down the Grand Hallway to the right are the classroom pods. Access to the Sensory Garden is located beyond the Pre-School Kitchen, Braille Walk is located beyond the Eye Exam Room, and Cane Walk Lane is located at the end of the Grand Hallway. © Precision Graphics

Room, children are exposed to and begin to read in Braille. In the Eye Exam Room, staff checks children's functional vision, and pediatric ophthalmologists provide eye exams. Near this pod, children can travel outside to the Braille Trail where a circular path provides a place to stroll or tricycle and features the Braille alphabet and numbers.

The third pod is red and features a large Motor Room with two types of floor covering (refer to Case Study Figure 8.2). One area is hardwood for tap dancing; another area is soft rubber for crawling, rolling, running, jumping, and scooting. On the east wall is the Kaleidoscope Discovery Wall, which has colored glass along with nooks and crannies that encourage children to explore and learn about the room and its space. Kaleidoscope concept continues on the outside with a Kaleidoscope Slope where there are tiny benches and a grassy knoll.

This third pod also contains the Sensory Gym, Braille Production Office, Tree House, and Benjamin's Niche—a sensory classroom (refer to Case Study Figure 8.2). The Sensory Gym focuses on the integration of sensory activities. The Braille Office contains books and other materials that have been embossed with Braille. Benjamin's Niche—the sensory classroom—has a hardwood floor covering that stimulates children through its special acoustics. Its purpose is to provide external stimuli for children who are especially sensitive and make learning less stressful and more focused.

Located between the classroom pods are two sets of cubbies that were designed by the architect, Maria Cole.

Different than prefabricated cubbies, the custom-design cubbies are large enough so that canes do not protrude and have notches on them to help children identify their own. Within each cubby is a bench, making it possible for a child to sit in his/her own space and begin to understand spatial concepts—child sized.

The Sunflower Garden and Greenhouse are located in the nature playground (refer to Case Study Figure 8.2). This area includes wheelchair accessible picnic tables under a shade structure allowing for sensory play in any season. Within this garden, there are trees, shrubs, plants, and grasses that were specifically selected for their sensory quality. A slatted fence surrounding the playground provides a play on light and shadow and gives children another tactile experience. A three-panel design repeats throughout the length of the fence, so if a child wants to drag a stick or his/her cane along the fence there is a repetitive rhythm.

This facility was designed with collaborative efforts among designers, contractors, and Anchor Center. According to Maria Cole, one of the most amazing parts of the design process was the collaboration with Anchor Center's expert educators. They shared their knowledge, showed patience, and provided great attention to detail—all of which has made Anchor Center a great place to teach as well as a joyful place to be a child. It is this collaboration to which the design team and Anchor Center educators are most proud and to which successes can be attributed. This participatory design (e.g., designers, contractors, educators) was the reason for its successful outcome.

The executive director, Alice Applebaum adds that whenever any decision was to be made, Anchor Center's educators would ask, "How does this impact the children?" "Is it in their best interest?" She also states that as a result (of these questions), changes needed to be considered carefully. For example, the main change that impacted the children was in the Sensory Classroom. Anchor Center's educators wanted the floor to be suspended (like a dance floor) that would give more vibration. However, they settled for hardwood, which still gives some vibration, but not as much as they would have preferred. They also cut back on the amount of colored glazing above the classroom pods because clear glass is less expensive. Clear glazing makes the pod color less brilliant, but it is still beautiful at the right time of the day. Also, value engineering resulted in smaller office spaces, a basement under only part of the building, and the mechanical room outside. These impacted only the staff and other adults related to the facility's function, however, and did not impact the children and families.

JC Greeley, a teacher and the program coordinator, describes the advantages of the building related to distance and spatial awareness for children with low vision. For example, hallways are kept clear of busy art and the planes and lines from floor to ceiling are clear. This allows the child to see the form of a moving person from the other end of the hallway as he/she becomes larger or smaller—denoting moving toward or away from the observer. The hallways are wide and without protuberant obstacles such as water fountains; children are safe in moving—even running—down the hallway. JC also adds that every child needs to have a chance to run free and they have it at Anchor Center.

The child focus was the guiding principle for the design, and everyone on the team bought into that principle. It has served the center well. In fact, the center received the Workspace Award from the Colorado Business Committee for the Arts (CBCA) that recognizes exceptional design advancing business objectives. In the acceptance speech, Anchor Center team stated that its premise is child-focused—in the design as well as in the decision-making process. In fact, the contractor firmly agreed that everyone focused on the children before anything else, and then, the rest fell in place.

Because the design was focused on the children and their needs, it is a great place—a magical, wonderful, fun, and joyful place for children with visual limitations to learn about the world around them. It is a place that gives children confidence—a confidence for their transition to public school and to life beyond—an inclusion into society.

Sources: Anchor Center for Blind Children. (n/d). *Julie McAndrews Mork Building*. Retrieved on October 27, 2010, from http://www.anchorcenter.org; and Anchor Center for Blind Children. (2007). Seeing life differently. *Commemorative Book. Julie McAndrews Mork Building at the Anchor Center for Blind Children.* Retrieved on October 27, 2010, from http://www.anchorcenter.org

quality childcare facility is complex, and all concerned parties (architects, designers, engineers, staff, parents, and the community) should be involved at all phases of the project to meet the children's needs and create the best facility possible.

Inclusively Designing Childcare Facilities

As noted earlier, most childcare facilities are not required to be entirely inclusive. To become an inclusive facility, however, questions presented in Chapter 5 may help create inclusive environments. The following additional or specific questions have been added:

- Outside to inside
  - Is designated accessible parking available for parents who have a child in a wheelchair, a mother who is pregnant, or others with mobility limitations?
  - Is the parking lot safe and secure for small children while exiting or entering vehicles?
- Circulation
  - Is the circulation easy for children to understand?
- Seating
  - Are there a variety of seating heights?
- Various types of rooms (sleeping, classrooms, and so on)
  - Are surfaces adjustable or adaptable to various age groups?
  - Are the restrooms equipped with fixtures for various ages?
- Outdoor spaces
  - Are all areas adaptable to children with mobility limitations?

PLAYGROUNDS

Children learn as they play, and outdoor playgrounds provide opportunities for learning that can aid in physical, cognitive, and social development.

Playground areas can encourage play that is functional (repetitive muscle movement), constructive (building spaces) and dramatic (creative and pretend activities). Summarized in InformeDesign (2010, June 18), "Children's Use of Different Playground Features" studied "how the addition of loose parts (i.e., moveable items that children can manipulate to play with in different ways) to fixed playground equipment affected children's play behavior" (para 1). The results of this study determined that playgrounds should be designed with loose parts, as well as nodes and connectors such as thresholds and platforms that are easily moved, to encourage constructive play and also lead to increase in dramatic play. Highly visible areas such as bridges and spaces should also be included to allow two to three children to engage in dramatic play. (See Figure 8.8 and Color Plate 26 in the color pages of this book.)

Because playgrounds provide children with opportunities to develop motor skills and social behavior, children with disabilities should have the same opportunity.

Figure 8.8

Boundless™ playgrounds are designed to be inclusive of children and adults. The gentle sloped ramp (not visible) provides access to areas of equipment and is easy to navigate for children with limited mobility. This playground is located at Grand Park Community Recreation Center in Fraser, Colorado. © Salvador III Manaois/Alamy

InformeDesign (2009, July 21) summarized a case study that examines play behaviors of children with disabilities and related design features at Shane's Inspiration, a Boundless™ Playground, which is designed to accommodate children with physical disabilities in Los Angeles, California.

Findings revealed that there were accessible paths and soft surfaces to accommodate children with mobility disabilities. Even though the playground was 90 percent accessible for assisted devices, there were limited opportunities for children with disabilities to be involved in active play. Children in wheelchairs were able to explore the playground, but they were not able to "exit their wheelchairs for any play equipment except swings" (para. 3). For further details on this study, see Sketch 8.3: "Children's Use of Accessible Playgrounds."

Groundbreaking took place on May 19, 2011 in Round Rock, Texas, on a park (Play for All Abilities) designed to accommodate children of all abilities. The park will be divided into five areas: (1) Boundless™ Playscape, (2) Brushy Creek Village, (3) Rock Band Pod, (4) Sensory Fun Pod, and (5) Island Retreat. Kathryn Eakens is executive assistant to the mayor and Council at City of Round Rock and was the former market editor at Round Rock's Community Impact Newspaper. Eaken (2009) describes the conceptual plans for each area of this playground:

The playground in the Boundless™ Playscape (Pod 1) area will be accessible to children who are able-bodied as well as those in

STUDY SKETCH 8.3: Children's Use of Accessible Playgrounds

Playgrounds help children develop motor skills and social behavior. InformeDesign (2009, July 21) summarized a case study that examines "play behaviors of children with disabilities and related design features at Shane's Inspiration, a Boundless™ playground (i.e., designed to accommodate children with physical disabilities) in Los Angeles, California."

Method

At Shane's Inspiration, their playground's design features (e.g., presence of wheelchair accessible paths, maneuverable flooring, obstructions) were evaluated through field observations. In two-hour sessions twice a week for three months, researchers observed children with disabilities, as well as interactive play between children with and without disabilities, and recorded their social, functional, dramatic, and exploratory play.

Findings

Shane's Inspiration has accessible paths (e.g., wide concrete paths) and soft surfaces (e.g., rubber cushion or matting) that provide access to children with mobility disabilities. Even though the playground was 90 percent accessible for assisted devices, children with disabilities were given limited chances to participate in active play; and only a smaller percentage of children with disabilities engaged in active play. On the other hand, children in wheelchairs were able to discover areas of the playground, but they were not able to exit their wheelchairs to access play equipment except swings. For the most part, children with disabilities engaged in passive rather than active play.

Criteria

From these findings, the following criteria were determined:
- Design playgrounds to be accessible for all children regardless of their ability
- Design playgrounds to provide children of all abilities the opportunity to participate in a variety of activities
- Design playgrounds to exceed the ADA's minimum accessible requirements
- Include areas (tables, play houses, water play) to foster social interaction among children with and without disabilities
- Understand how children with disabilities can play and interact with others
- Include play elements for functional play (repetitive muscle movement)

Implications

Playgrounds designed for accessibility must go beyond the ADA requirements. Additionally, it is important to look at the design from the perspective of children with disabilities.

Source: InformeDesign. (2009, July 21) "Children's Use of Accessible Playgrounds." Retrieved on July 12, 2010, from http://www.informedesign.com/Rs_detail.aspx?rsId=3333

wheelchairs (see Figure 8.9). It will be equipped with ramps as well as rubber fall surfaces that are safe for all children.

Brushy Creek Village (Pod 2) was designed with several play buildings such as a gas station, stores, and a post office; and its roads will be lined with streets signs to teach children riding tricycles to obey the rules of the road.

The Rock Band Pod (Pod 3) will also be accessible and equipped with instruments such as drums, xylophones, and bells. This area will offer children an opportunity to express their creativity through music.

The Sensory Fun Pod (Pod 4) will have low-sitting walls made of various textures to offer sensory experiences. The pod will include learning panels, a table-height sandbox area, and a fountain. Surrounding the pod will be aromatic plants to engage children's sense of smell. Color Plate 27 in the color pages of this book shows an example of a sensory wall that is inclusive of children of all abilities.

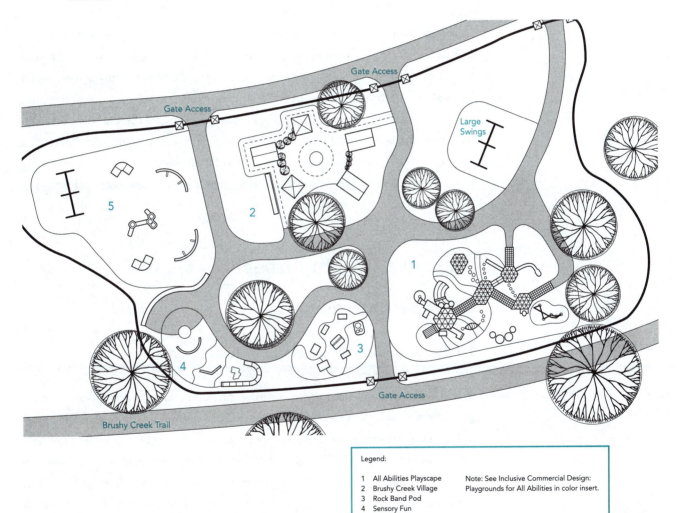

Legend:

1 All Abilities Playscape
2 Brushy Creek Village
3 Rock Band Pod
4 Sensory Fun
5 Island Retreat

Note: See Inclusive Commercial Design: Playgrounds for All Abilities in color insert.

Figure 8.9

Preliminary Concept Plan for Park for All Abilities is divided into five areas. (1) All Abilities Playscape—a traditional playground designed to exceed accessibility standards; (2) Brushy Creek Village—play buildings and street signs with roads for tricycles; (3) Rock Band Pod—wheelchair-accessible outdoor instruments; (4) Sensory Fun Pod—materials of various textures for sensory experiences; and (5) Island Retreat—a quieter, calmer play experience with less clutter. This conceptual playground is planned for Round Rock, Texas. © Precision Graphics

Island Retreat (Pod 5) will provide a quieter, calmer play experience. It will be less cluttered and located away from the remainder of the park. Tunnels, climbing equipment, and various adaptive swings will be found in the Island Retreat and are designed for children of various abilities. When built, children of various abilities will have the opportunity to play side-by-side and to enhance learning through play (Eakens, 2009).

Summary

Healthcare and most institutional facilities must comply with the ADA, but are not required to create an invisible inclusive design. A few examples were presented in this chapter such as single-patient rooms in healthcare facilities, headwall systems for hospital rooms that consider ergonomics of the caregiver as well as a noninstitutional look, furniture that accommodates people of varied shapes and sizes, housing for long-term care that adds to quality of life, adaptable playgrounds that allow children of all abilities to participate in activities, and so on. Thus, to meet inclusive design criteria facilities must respond to user needs, be adaptable as well as accessible, and provide a secure environment for everyone.

Inclusive Design Projects

EXPERIENTIAL PROJECTS

1. How do medical offices create inclusive environments?

Not all of us look forward to seeing a doctor, but when it is necessary the experience should be positive and occur in an inclusive environment. Although these offices are generally accessible, however, they are not always inclusive. To realize this, a field trip to a medical clinic may be revealing. (This project should be a planned class field trip to lessen the burden on medical staff and at a time when few or no patients are present. Your instructor should also ask a staff member to provide a tour, which will let everyone view all parts of the office from the entrance to the exam rooms.) During and after the visit, complete the following:

1. Sketch the entrance, waiting area, pathways, and rooms. (This could be a shared experience in which you and others are given specific areas to sketch.)
2. Take copious notes as your tour guide speaks.
3. Note areas of concern for inclusivity.

4. State findings in a written report.

5. State findings and determine solutions through in-class discussion.

6. Develop sketches to create an inclusive environment.

2. Can connecting the Eden Alternative® and inclusivity create a better, more home-like atmosphere?

Although the design of many nursing homes and other long-term care facilities meets the ADA accessibility guidelines, these environments often feel cold and institutional. This raises the question, "Can connecting the Eden Alternative® and inclusivity create a better, more home-like atmosphere?" To answer this question, begin with a field trip to a long-term care facility. This will provide you with a first-hand experience. As you tour these facilities:

1. Sketch the entrance, waiting area, pathways, and rooms. (This could be a shared experience in which you and others are given specific areas to sketch.)

2. Note the following features of the facility:
   a. Facility size (approximate)
   b. Number of residents in one building
   c. Lobby
   d. Size of public or social areas
   e. Number of social areas
   f. Dining areas
   g. Private meeting areas
   h. Resident rooms (single or double) and amount of space
   i. Nursing area(s) and offices

3. Note areas where residents congregate and note the following:
   a. Are they alert and active?
   b. Are they sitting in wheelchairs sleeping?
   c. Are they visiting with others or alone?

4. Visit with a staff person and ask if the residents are on rigid or flexible schedules (eating, sleeping, activities).

5. Note if the facility goes beyond the ADA and applies inclusivity.

6. State findings in a written report.

7. State findings and determine solutions through in-class discussion.

8. Develop ideas for an inclusive environment:
   a. Administrative suggestions
   b. Sketch of ideas for the facility

APPLICATION PROJECTS

1. How can educational facilities be inclusive for children with developmental challenges?

When children are diagnosed with autism, muscular dystrophy, Down syndrome, or other developmental challenges, they may be separated from others in the classroom. Although separation may be necessary for learning, mainstreaming children into the classroom aids their ability to function as adults in society.

This project involves research into a developmental disability to learn ways of including these children with others. To complete the exercise, the following steps should be taken:

1. Research a variety of childhood developmental problems.
2. Select one developmental problem to research in greater depth and locate the following information:
   a. The cause
   b. Symptoms
   c. Behavior
   d. Learning challenges
3. Locate information regarding ways these children have been mainstreamed.
4. Sketch a space that will facilitate these children into the classroom.
5. Write a reflection paper about what was learned from the research project.

CHAPTER 9

Hospitality, Retail, and Other Commercial Design

KEY TERMS

> audible instructions
> color coding
> compost
> illumination
> keycard
> nonchlorinated pool
> no-VOC paint
> organic
> symbol identification
> transgenerational

"Architecture should speak of its time and place, but yearn for timelessness."

—Frank Gehry

OBJECTIVES

▼ Discuss wayfinding in various commercial environments

▼ Discuss creating a secure environment

▼ Explain ways for various designs to integrate sustainability with inclusive design

▼ Discuss challenges faced when designing inclusively for various design types, including hospitality design (lodging, food and beverage), retail, and transportation (airport terminals, aircraft, and others)

From hotel to shopping center, church to airport, every commercial (or otherwise public) facility presents its own set of accessibility requirements and needs for user inclusivity; each offers unique challenges to the interior designer.

Hospitality

Hospitality design combines commercial design with aspects of residential design such as guest rooms as well as commercial such as restaurants and retail (Jones & Allen, 2009). Hospitality design includes lodging as well as food and beverage facilities.

Whether a small coffee shop or large conference center or casino, everyone must have access, but not all are inclusive without drawing attention to any type of impairment. To create an inclusive hospitality environment, it is important to apply inclusive design criteria (e.g., responsive, adaptable, accessible, and secure results) during the design process as well as paying special attention to the following areas (refer to Chapter 5 for questions in each category):

- Outside to Inside
- Circulation
- Entering and exiting
- Wayfinding
- Seating
- Lighting and acoustics
- Thermal comfort
- Information systems

LODGING

Together, accessibility and inclusive design concepts create environments appropriate for all people within various hospitality design types. Although places of lodging have improved over time, some still have minimum accessibility with little or no thought to creating inclusive environments. Some areas of particular concern are wayfinding, guest rooms and other areas (e.g., lobbies, registration desk, restaurants, and so on), security, and sustainability.

Wayfinding is Inclusive

Wayfinding is often an important and critical issue for hotel guests and must be considered to be inclusive. To help people to maneuver in large hotels, wayfinding methods must be incorporated into the design. This may be with directories, signage, audible instructions, and more. Although audible information will work for people with visual limitations, international symbols must be included for those who speak a different language. A creative method of accommodating a variety of people would be to have different themes or color schemes for each floor. This would provide familiarity and inclusivity to all.

When entering a hotel lobby, registration should be obvious; however, if not, signage should immediately provide directions to registrations as well as elevators, restaurants, conference or meeting room areas or floors. This signage should be large and above eye level to be seen by all. For larger hotels, a directory (see Figure 9.1) should include an audible interactive directory, hotel directories listing areas, map of the building, contact information, and more. For example, the visitor begins by touching the interactive directory, and a map of the building appears. When touching various rooms on the screen, information about each of them appears. A hotel directory should list areas or rooms and their location. Providing an interactive directory, sufficient signage, and a color-coded floor scheme at a minimum creates inclusive wayfinding. For those who are color blind, three-dimensional images representing each floor with signage may be helpful.

Many hotels in metropolitan areas are located above ground level and require guests to enter an elevator that takes them to a lobby and registration. Therefore, at ground level, signage must be sufficient and clearly inform guests. This should

Figure 9.1

Interactive directories are wayfinding methods that allow people with multiple abilities or disabilities to access them. Photo courtesy of Redyref

include signage as well as an audible announcement when guests enter the area. This informs guests with visual or hearing limitations as well as the able-bodied. Elevators should accommodate all abilities.

Issues Related to Guest Rooms

Hotel guest rooms have become more accessible over time, but generally, the minimum number of accessible rooms is provided within most hotels. Guest bathrooms are often designed with minimum accessibility. The assistant director at the Center for Inclusive Design and Environmental Access (IDEA Center) located at the University of Buffalo, in Buffalo, New York, Danise Levine and her team have researched new universal (inclusive) design concepts that go beyond the ADA. Levine states that "most hotel bathrooms now accommodate enough space for a wheelchair, but often, that still is not enough room" (Crowell, C. 2009, July 13). In this case, the bathroom is not an inclusively designed space that is usable for everyone. In most hotels, bathrooms are accessible in only "accessible" rooms and, therefore, all rooms are not inclusive of all (see Figure 9.2).

Concerns in Other Areas of a Hotel

Rosemarie Rossetti, who has been paralyzed from the waist down since 1998, led a seminar on universal design at the Hospitality Design Exposition and Conference in Las Vegas in 2009. During this seminar, she states that hotels can do better than applying the ADA as a minimum. In fact, she believes that although there is a standard with the ADA, it is not being followed very well. The following are her assessments (Stoessel, 2009, August 18):

- Carpets in public spaces and hallways are often too dense, or the padding underneath is too thick, which challenges not only those in wheelchairs but also people with strollers or luggage carriers.
- Most doors should work with just five pounds of pressure, but they seem heavier and are hard to open and close.
- Furniture in guest rooms often needs to be moved to access temperature or light controls, which would be difficult for someone with limited mobility. Also, controls are often placed about five feet above finished floor, and this is difficult for someone in a wheelchair or short in stature.
- Bathrooms need more thought in shower design—walk-ins are better for wheelchair transfers than tubs.
- Mirrors and vanity space should be placed so that all guests are able to access them (para. 7).

If the entire hotel were an inclusive facility, people without disabilities would not notice accessible design features. These facilities would not only be accessible, but inclusive to all.

Concerns with Security

Security in public buildings has become more important since 9/11, and hotels are no exception. The hotel entrance must provide a sense of security to all through personnel, cameras, and even entrance devices. Additionally, hotel staff and/or a **keycard** provide access to elevator lobbies in many hotels. A combination of proper **illumination**, **symbol identification**, **color coding**, **audible instructions** in more than one language, or other methods may be used to identify the location to insert the card, especially for those with various limitations or a language barrier. When in the room, a keycard may also turn on the power within the room—a cost-saving and sustainable practice (see Figure 9.3).

Benefits to Applying Sustainability Practices

The hotel industry has been slow to adopt sustainable practice in building and operations. The InformeDesign research summary (2009, December 18) "Benefits of Sustainable Hotels" points out that the hotel industry should apply sustainable practices and also provides ideas to be applied. For example, sustainable features (e.g., daylighting, low-emitting paints and adhesives) may have health benefits by reducing

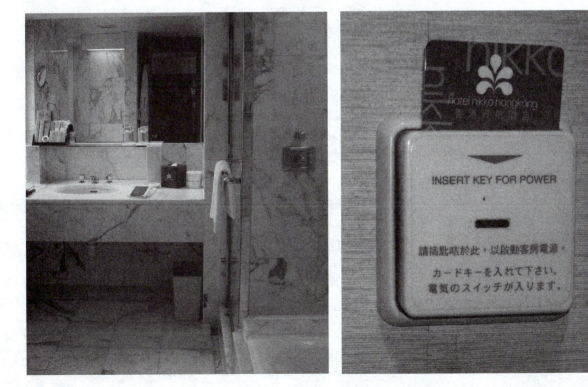

Figure 9.2

Bathrooms in hotel rooms are not accessible unless specifically identified as accessible rooms. In this hotel bathroom, the shower is one step up, and a person in a wheelchair would find it difficult to use the sink. Photo courtesy Linda L. Nussbaumer

Figure 9.3

Hotel key card that can also turn on the power in the hotel room. Photo courtesy Linda L. Nussbaumer

illness and absenteeism in workers. Such practices also provide a healthier, inclusive environment for everyone—guests as well as workers. For further details, see Study Sketch 9.1: "Benefits of Sustainable Hotels."

Examples of Sustainable Hotels

Some hotels such as St. Julien in Boulder, Colorado, have fully implemented sustainable practices into their hotel beyond those listed in the InformeDesign research summary "Benefits of Sustainable Hotels." They also use local **organic** food and beverages, **compost** food waste, have a **nonchlorinated pool**, use a green line of cleaning products, utilize **no-VOC paint** for all paint projects, and many other sustainable practices. A full description of their environmental commitment (energy conservation, waste reduction, material re-use, nontoxic practices, transportation, and more) can be downloaded from their website at http://www.stjulien.com/environmental-commitment (St. Julien, n/d).

FOOD AND BEVERAGE FACILITIES

There are many types of food and beverage facilities, and some are quick such as the coffee shops or fast-food establishments. Some serve a variety of clients that may include families (cafeteria, quick-dining, and more) whereas others offer a dining experience (an evening out) for a couple to a group of people. Whichever it may be, accessibility to all is expected; however, they may not be inclusive environments. Color Plate 36 in the color pages of this book illustrates an accessible dining room; however, it may become congested with a wheelchair and movement of wait staff.

To be inclusive, several features must be in place. Levine (2003) suggests ways to create inclusion within a food and beverage facility:

- Adequate maneuvering clearances provided at the entrance
- Adequate maneuvering clearances and space provided for service lines to prevent congestion and accommodate groups of people
- Unobstructed, easily maneuverable circulation allowed between tables
- Lifts or elevators provided to connect all levels
- Movable and removable seating provided to offer the greatest flexibility
- A comfortable eating environment provided for all guests
- Circulation paths installed with nonslip flooring (p. 103)

A combination of these suggestions, questions from Chapter 5, and the inclusive design criteria will aid in creating an inclusively designed environment for all patrons.

Color Plates 34 and 35 illustrate two different solutions to a restaurant design. Both provide easy access into the restaurant and maneuverable space; however, both have limited seating for wheelchairs. In Color Plate 34, within the dining area, a large number of booths limit access for wheelchairs at the end and only a few tables. In

STUDY SKETCH 9.1: Benefits of Sustainable Hotels

In InformeDesign (2009, December 18), a position paper discusses consequences of sustainable design and the possibility of its becoming a standard for the hotel industry. Even though the United States Green Building Council's (USGBC) Leadership in Energy and Environmental Design (LEED®) certification standards have been applied to many building industries, few hotels have met LEED standards.

Discussion
The position paper emphasized the following:
- Costs to apply sustainable practice have decreased.
- Sustainably designed hotels indicated a 25 to 30 percent energy savings.
- Savings have been connected to using LEED standards for energy costs.
- Federal and some state and local governments require public buildings to be LEED-certified or offer incentives to green developments.
- Hotel industry may be faced with increased cost of goods for manufacturing, construction, and energy because of emissions or energy regulations.

Criteria
The following sustainable practices can be applied to or affect buildings in the hotel industry:
- Install low-flow shower systems in hotel rooms to decrease water consumption.
- Install compact fluorescent lamps (CFLs) to decrease energy consumption.
- Limit unsustainable procedures (e.g., individual shampoo bottles, heavily chlorinated pools).
- Constructing a new hotel to meet sustainable building standards may be more cost effective and efficient than to retrofit a hotel.
- Project costs may be higher for energy and resources.
- Sustainable design incentives such as energy credits and tax incentives may have short-term availability.
- Sustainable features such as daylighting and low-emitting paints and adhesives may have health benefits by reducing illness and absenteeism in employees.

Source: InformeDesign. (2006, May 18). "Benefits of Sustainable Hotels." Retrieved on August 2, 2010, from http://www.informedesign.org/Rs_detail. aspx?rsId=3363

Color Plate 35, a greater number of tables allow flexibility; however, even with good circulation, there are still limitations for wheelchairs. To provide full inclusion of all, further manipulation of this plan should continue. Color Plate 36 illustrates a similar configuration and has similar concerns.

Pubs Designed to Ease the Demands on Pub Workers

These concepts are reinforced in InformeDesign research summary (2006, May 18) "Designing Pubs to Avoid Injury Among Workers." This summary was a case study that evaluated the tasks of waitresses, bartenders, and cooks in a pub to determine possible risks for physical injuries. The criteria developed focused on the demands of the tasks, use of raised platforms and flooring materials, design of layout and circulation, specifying of tables, and so on. Clearly, issues can arise with heavy lifting and pulling, improper clearances, obstructed circulations, and improper materials. Observing as a participant (e.g., wait staff) that involves being the worker would help designers better plan or organize an inclusive space. For further details see Study Sketch 9.2: "Designing Pubs to Avoid Injury Among Workers."

Restaurants must meet the ADA Accessible Guidelines (ADAAG), and yet, restaurants often seem crowded and difficult for servers to maneuver. As noted in the research summary "Designing Pubs to Avoid Injury Among Workers," poor design may have a greater affect on physical well being of workers than restaurant patrons. Regardless, restaurant layout and design must go beyond the ADA compliance and create invisible inclusively designed spaces.

Retail

Retail establishments range from a small grocery store or boutique to super stores such as Walmart and Target. These establishments must be accessible, but as inclusively designed spaces, they will better serve the public and make shopping more pleasurable for everyone.

WAYFINDING

When entering a shopping mall or large department store, signage should immediately provide directions to various shops, restaurants, elevators, and more. To be inclusive, a directory should include an audible interactive directory with a list of shops (see Figure 9.4a), location of elevators or escalators, an interactive map of the building, contact information, and so on. For example, the visitor begins by touching the interactive directory and a map of the building appears (see Figure 9.4b). When touching various rooms on the screen, information about each will then appear. Beyond the directory, signage for areas within the mall or department store should be above eye level (see Figure 9.4c). Providing an interactive directory, sufficient signage is a minimum for creating inclusive wayfinding.

ACCESSIBILITY TO PRODUCTS AND SERVICES

All are required to be accessible—entrance, circulation, wayfinding, checkout area, and so on. But to be inclusive, items must be accessible to the reach of an individual in a wheelchair. Susan S. Szenasy of *Metropolis* magazine shares a story that points out the need for greater compliance with the ADA and the application of inclusivity.

> I'm at Duane Reade in Manhattan's Port Authority bus terminal, the hub for New Jersey–New York commuter traffic. It's Christmas Eve, and the place is buzzing with last-minute travelers and shoppers.

STUDY SKETCH 9.2: Designing Pubs to Avoid Injury Among Workers

Local neighborhood pubs in Canada are an important part of the community and culture. They serve as gathering places. However, pub workers' tasks are physically demanding and may lead to injuries and costs related to worker's compensation. For this reason, governmental regulations in British Columbia, Canada, require studies to evaluate the potential for injury and work factors. This InformeDesign research summary (2006, May 18) describes a case study that evaluated tasks of waitresses, bartenders, and cooks in a pub to determine possible risks for physical injuries.

Method and Subjects

To comply with government regulations, neighborhood pub owners in British Columbia, Canada, who provided food and beverage services in buildings constructed in 1980, requested a study to evaluate the potential injuries related to employee tasks. Subjects in the study included five female bartenders (average 37.4 years of age), seven female waitresses (average 32.3 years of age), and five male cooks (average 40 years of age). A physical therapist observed workers on site for a two-hour period. As part of this observation, the therapist performed the following:

- Measured objects that were lifted, pulled, or moved
- Recorded age and anthropometric measurements of workers
- Conducted interviews at three follow-up visits
- Photographed typical postures while tasks were performed
- Identified (by participants) the three most demanding tasks

Findings

Findings indicated tasks that created excessive back strain and could lead to injury. These tasks include: lifting and pulling kegs and heavy bags or buckets, stooping to serve food, and performing bartending and server-related tasks.

Criteria

The criteria developed focuses on ways to lessen physical demands of tasks and, thus, minimize the potential for injuries as follows:

- Use nonslip flooring for raised platforms.
- Design layout of tables to increase efficient movement for servers.
- Specify two-thirds of tables with high tops to limit bending and stooping.
- Specify long beer lines and a high-power air compressor to dispense beer to minimize lifting and pulling to reposition kegs.

Implications

Issues can arise with heavy lifting and pulling, improper clearances, obstructed circulations, improper materials, and so on. Following the previously mentioned criteria can minimize the potential for injury to pub workers.

Sources: InformeDesign. (2006, May 18). "Designing Pubs to Avoid Injury among Workers." Retrieved on August 2, 2010, from http://www.informedesign.org/Rs_detail.aspx?rsId=2378; and University of Michigan (UM). (2010). 3D Static Strength Prediction Program. Retrieved on August 4, 2010, from http://www.engin.umich.edu/dept/ioe/3DSSPP/index.html

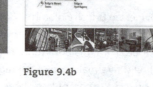

Figure 9.4a

Interactive directory with list of spaces.

Figure 9.4b

When a visitor touches the interactive directory, a map of the building appears. The visitor can then touch various rooms on the screen to access more information about each of them. Courtesy of Redyref

Figure 9.4c

Overhead signage with symbols, words, and directions. Oxford Properties - Southcentre Mall, Calgary, Alberta, Canada.

Pushing my way past those gathered around cosmetics, baby stuff, and paper products, I arrive at my destination—the painkiller aisle. I scan the boxes placed at eye level, looking for my brand. No luck. Finally, I find it on the bottom shelf. As I reach down to retrieve the container with its bold, colorful logo and tiny instructional type-face, a man with a cane approaches me. "Miss, would you mind getting those pills for me, right there?" he asks, pointing to where my hand is now. And again, pointing with his cane to the opposite shelf: "Could you grab that foot powder too?" Both of these items are displayed on the lowest rung of a tall shelf, difficult to find and clearly out of reach for the man with the cane. As I do my neighborly duty and hand him the boxes, I wonder if the store's manager has heard of universal design, design for the aging, **transgenerational** design, or any of the other phrases that have been bandied about since the Americans with Disabilities Act was signed into law, by Bush the elder, nearly two decades ago. A lot of care seems to have been expended to find just the right eye-level spot for lip gloss, but those in pain, those who can't bend down to retrieve things, and those who would benefit from considerate product placement seem to have been ignored or simply forgotten (p. 14).

From this article, it seems that the design of many retail environments focuses on the younger generation and the able-bodied. As baby boomers (the greatest consumers) need products to be more accessible, retail owners must pay more attention, listen, and even observe their consumers' needs. In this way, the retail environment will become inclusive to all. Figure 9.5 illustrates merchandise being displayed for purchase. Some products can be found on shelves at all levels; however, some are found only at the top or the bottom. To be inclusive, all products must be available to those in wheelchairs.

EXEMPLARY INCLUSIVE DESIGN

There are retail stores that do apply inclusive design criteria. When Suzy Regitz (2009, September) was shopping in an Apple® store, she found it easy to maneuver through the space and mused that not only would a wheelchair user be able to experience the store, but inclusive design criteria abounded.

- All counters were sleek and broad, and all were mounted at 34 inches above the floor.
- There was ample space between the parallel counters that held the high-tech products with easy access and passage for several people at a time.
- Flooring was smooth, even, and with no jarring changes in height.
- There were no transition strips or other obstacles to cause tripping or struggles with wheels.
- The store was inviting, brightly illuminated, clean, and included graphics.

Figure 9.5

Some products can be found on shelves at all levels; however, some are found only at the top or the bottom.
© Ian Dagnall / Alamy

These characteristics demonstrate the application of inclusive design criteria in such a way that it was invisible, but it was also a safe and comfortable place to be.

BEHAVIOR OF SHOPPERS

To create an inclusively designed space, it is important to understand the behavior of shoppers and ways to improving shopping environments. Summarized in the InformeDesign (2005, December 7) review "Satisfying Environments for Shoppers," a review of environment-behavior research for shopping environments was conducted to understand how physical aspects of shopping environments might affect shoppers' psychological needs. The review determined that a positive shopping experience is one that provides stimulus to excite shoppers and is easy to maneuver; however, it also must be an environment that is not crowded, is devoid of loud noise, and does not use scents as a lure. Following these guidelines will provide a more comfortable and safe environment that meets inclusive design criteria. For further details see Study Sketch 9.3: "Satisfying Environments for Shoppers."

Retail establishments impact many users and, therefore, must be designed to meet the ADA. To create a comfortable, functional space for everyone, however, inclusive design criteria must be applied.

Transportation

Transportation facilities include many types such as airports, heavy and light trains (including subways), buses, ships, and so on. All are required to comply with the ADA, although some (such as airplanes, buses, and trains) may find it difficult to apply inclusive design criteria. Terminals, particularly airport terminals, can be considered hospitality industries with their food and beverages facilities. Airplanes have food and beverage service and, especially with international flights, passengers recline to rest as they travel.

AIRPORT TERMINALS

Since 9/11, airports have gone through tremendous changes related to security. When checked in, passengers must wait in line for their security check—for themselves and their belongings. In larger airports, there are separate security checks for those in wheelchairs, which separate those with disabilities—not an inclusive practice.

For people who have visual and hearing limitations, communication may be challenging as they check in, navigate through security, and travel toward the gate. Travel companions would make the travel experience easier; however, this may not always be practical.

STUDY SKETCH 9.3: Satisfying Environments for Shoppers

Understanding shopper's motivations for choosing a specific environment is valuable information. InformeDesign (2005, December 7) summarizes a review of literature on consumers' responses to retail environments that may determine the way these environments affect various shoppers' needs.

Method

The review of literature focused on environment-behavior research (e.g., psychology, sociology, marketing, retailing, and human-computer interactions) of shopping environments. Additionally, a conceptual framework was developed to aid the understanding of physical features of retail environments that may influence shoppers' psychological needs.

Findings

Findings from the study that relate to universal design included the following:

- Shoppers prefer environments that provide information, are safe and comfortable, and allow social interaction.
- Most types of shoppers are categorized as task-oriented or leisure-oriented shoppers.
- Shoppers generally select a particular shopping venue based on individual needs (i.e., social, physical, and cognitive).
- Indoor shopping malls fulfill shoppers' needs for convenience, safety, and comfort.
- Low preference for a shopping environment may be associated with level of crowding and noise.

Criteria

From the findings, the following criteria were identified:

- Provide stimulus and new information to excite and involve shoppers as they move through a mall.
- Create an easy-to-understand building floor plan and circulation path.
- Provide wayfinding signage that includes universal pictographs.
- Plan the interior with acoustical features to isolate stores from loud noise from entertainment located within the mall.
- Provide opportunities for shoppers to touch products or materials.
- Specify smooth floor finishes for easy maneuvering of wheelchairs.
- Avoid the use of scents to lure people to shop.
- Avoid or remove irritants such as crowding and loud noise.

Implications

Criteria identified relate to a positive shopping experience, provide stimulus to excite shoppers, and are easy to maneuver. However, it also must be an environment that is not crowded, devoid of loud noise, and does not use scents as a lure. Following these guidelines will provide a more comfortable and safe environment.

Source: InformeDesign (2005, December 7) "Satisfying Environments for Shoppers." Retrieved on July 12, 2010, from http://www.informedesign.umn.edu/Rs_detail.aspx?rsId=2220

People with visual limitations may use a cane or a seeing eye dog, and airport personnel would then recognize their need for assistance. On the other hand, deaf people may experience challenges because their limitation is not visibly apparent, and they may find it difficult to communicate their needs without using paper and pencil. One of most problematic issues is hearing announcements for gate changes or delays. Some airports have announcement screens; however, if all airports were equipped with screens, it would be more inclusive to the deaf person.

Applying Inclusive Design Criteria in an Airport Terminal

It is possible to apply inclusive design criteria to airport security checks. An example is the Rygge Sivile Lufthavn (RSL)—in English, the Moss Airport Rygge (2008)—located in southeastern Norway. When they reconstructed the terminal, the RSL collaborated with the Norwegian Association of Disabled Persons through the building process to design an airport terminal that was user friendly for everyone, but especially for those with physical impairments. The following are solutions for the terminal building.

- Floor areas have guide lights in the floor tiles to assist those with visual limitations to find their way to check-in, counters, toilets, and airport facilities.
- Signs were designed for people who have visual limitations.
- Service counters for check-in are designed so that wheelchair users do not arrive at a high counter, but have their own lower counter integrated into the public service desks.
- Parking areas are designed especially for handicapped parking at spots closest to the entry door in the parking garage.
- A separate room inside the terminal building was established where air passengers can park their private wheelchair while traveling. Bench seating is also provided in this room for passengers to rest before traveling on through the terminal.
- An elevator was installed inside the terminal building just beside the escalator and a standard stairway, so that wheelchair users can follow the normal passenger flow to and through the security check area.
- When a passenger with a physical limitation is inside the travel zone within the airport (the security zone), all airport design functions will ensure that these persons' and wheelchair users' needs for mobility in the terminal area are cared for.
- A large number of toilets in the travel zone and public areas are handicapped accessible.

Solutions established for entering and exiting the airplanes include:
- Passengers with physical limitations who arrive at the gate have two possible ways of entering planes: Some can take the stair down to the

airplane area, whereas others can take the elevator. There are three elevators servicing the departure area.

- Passengers with physical limitations do not need to be carried into the airplanes. A special lift was installed to raise individuals up into the airplane entryway. The lift has roof and wall barriers so that one enters the airplane safely, without having to be carried around.

- Inside the airplane, cabin personnel have been trained to place these passengers in their seats, and care for correct onboard placement.

Additionally, Moss Airport Ryyge trains employees to understand and care about all passengers' needs as well as to apply inclusive design in various areas of the facility.

An Airport Wheelchair

Another challenge for the individual with physical limitations is the transition from their personal wheelchair to the airplane. Because the standard wheelchair is not sufficient for an airplane, individuals must transfer up to four times prior to being seated on a plane. In fact, according to Martin C. Pedersen (2005, September 19) a passenger may: (1) arrive at curbside in their own wheelchair; (2) be placed in an airport wheelchair at check-in; (3) be transferred to a boarding chair; and (4) be brought inside the aircraft and placed in a standard airplane seat. During the flight, if the person needs to use the bathroom, a traveling companion or flight attendant would assist him/her to an in-flight chair to navigate the aisle.

However, according to Pederson (2005, September 19), there could be a solution—a chair was designed by Sondra Frances Law, a graduate student at Parsons School of Design in 2005—in which an "accessible seat combines the structural and ergonomic aspects of four chairs—the basic wheelchair, a boarding chair, an in-flight chair, and the regular airplane seat—into a single mechanism that eliminates at least two transfers" (para. 4). Though still on the drawing board, this type of chair means only one transfer is needed at curbside, from the individual's own wheelchair to the accessible wheelchair. This chair has a braking system that is controlled by a pair of handles in the back. If the passenger needs to use the lavatory, the flight attendant can pull up the handles and slide the chair out. Caster-type wheels allow the seat to pivot 360 degrees as well as lock into the standard track system of the airplane (see Figure 9.6).

The best location to position the chair within the aircraft is near lavatories. Because first-class is already generally accessible, the chair would be placed in the back row to allow the flight attendant to easily stand behind the chair to engage or release the lock system. Unfortunately, this wheelchair is still in the design phase; if eventually available, this chair could be an excellent solution to creating an inclusively designed chair from curbside to aircraft.

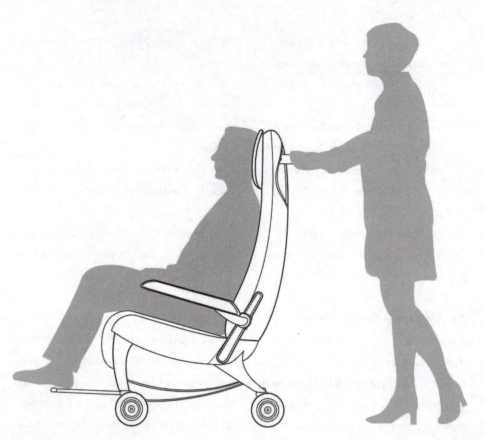

Figure 9.6

This chair was sketched by Sondra Frances Law, a graduate student at Parsons School of Design in 2005. It allows only one transfer at curbside and can be used as an airline seat as well. It is a basic wheelchair, a boarding chair, an in-flight chair, and a regular airplane seat. Once on the airplane, the chair's braking system locks it into place. © Sondra Law

BUS TRANSPORTATION

The Department of Transportation regulates and mandates accessibility of public transit vehicles and facilities. Requirements include the following:

- All new fixed-route public transit buses must be accessible.
- Supplementary paratransit services must be provided for individuals with disabilities who are not able to use fixed-route bus services (ADA, 2008).

Examples of accessible services can be found in cities around the country. In particular, Sun Tran (n/d) in Tucson, Arizona, provides bus service for people with physical limitations. In fact, all of their buses are equipped with lifts or ramps and are able to carry two wheelchairs per bus. Each bus has annunciators to announce bus stops, which aid those with hearing limitations. Additionally, for those eligible for ADA assistance, Sun Tran provides paratransit service. Clearly, since all Sun Tran buses are accessible with annunciators, their service not only provides accessible services but is also inclusive to those with physical and hearing limitations.

Remodeling for Accessibility or Inclusivity

Renovating existing or historic buildings is a challenge, especially when providing accessibility and even more when designing for inclusivity. Many church congregations, in particular, find it difficult to remodel for inclusivity. In Case Study 9.1, "Comparison of Religious Facilities in a Midwestern Town," two are partially accessible and one is not only accessible but exhibits inclusive concepts.

Summary

This chapter discusses ideas and ways to provide inclusive environments that begin during the design process. Some areas of concern for hospitality are wayfinding, accessible guest rooms, security, sustainability, and workers' needs. For retail, access to products and services can be a challenge for those with physical limitations. A design was shared that is exemplary. Airport terminals must be accessible, but they are not necessarily inclusive. In particular, for those in wheelchairs, moving from curb to the airplane is the greatest challenge.

For the most part, hospitality and retail design are accessible to the public and, therefore, are accessible to individuals with physical, cognitive, visual, and hearing limitations. Creating inclusive environments is not always a priority, however. And yet, with knowledge, these spaces can become inclusive environments and open to all regardless of ability.

Inclusive Design Projects

EXPERIENTIAL PROJECT

1. How can I find my way around this mall?

Shopping malls come in all sizes, from the strip mall to the Mall of America. In large malls, it is easy to get lost or confused. Image the challenge for someone who has mobility, visual, and hearing limitations. How can designers alleviate the problem? It is about creating inclusive wayfinding. To learn how this may be a problem for these individuals, a first-hand experience demonstrates an understanding and compassion. Use similar techniques from Projects 1, 2, or 3. Then, a team of three will visit a mall and find a store within this mall. Consider the following:

CASE STUDY 9.1 Comparison of Religious Facilities in a Midwestern Town

Churches have yet to be required to make their entire facilities accessible, particularly historic buildings or those that may have a difficult time raising funds for an elevator. Even where portions of a church are made accessible, however, they may not pass as inclusive with access through all entrances and for all activities. This is the case of churches located in Lake Crystal, Minnesota.

The Methodist church has two ways to access the sanctuary—via a ramp, and up the stairs off the street to the main entrance (see Case Study Figure 9.1a and Color Plate 39 in the color pages of this book). The ramp allows those with limited mobility access into the sanctuary through a door to a side room. When inside the sanctuary, the side room with its folding chairs provides the best area for a wheelchair. It would be difficult, however, for a wheelchair to maneuver beyond the side room. Although moveable, a piano limits access to the altar, and solid wood pews fill the sanctuary. Using the main entrance means ascending a flight of steps to the sanctuary or descending a flight of steps to the basement kitchen and fellowship hall (Case Study Figure 9.1b). For someone with limited mobility, the main entrance allows congregants to participate in activities that are located only in the church office and Sunday school wing, which are on the same level as the main entrance.

Case Study Figure 9.1a

Entrance ramp to the Methodist Church provides the only accessible entrance for persons with limited mobility or those who use a wheelchair. Photo courtesy Linda L. Nussbaumer

Case Study Figure 9.1b

The main entrance to the Methodist Church requires people to ascend ten steps to the sanctuary and descend ten steps to the basement. It does not provide access to the sanctuary or basement for persons with limited mobility or those who use a wheelchair. Photo courtesy Linda L. Nussbaumer

Additionally, nonaccessible restrooms are located in the Sunday school wing, and, therefore, access from the sanctuary or fellowship hall is only by taking a flight of steps.

Although the main entrance to the Presbyterian church is to ascend a flight of steps (Case Study Figure 9.1c), the church offers an optional second entrance with an elevator lift that travels up to the sanctuary or down the basement level—kitchen, fellowship hall, and some classrooms. Case Study Figure 9.1d shows the second accessible entrance. Within the accessible foyer is an area for coats and an accessible restroom; however, it is the only accessible restroom in the building. Thus, a person in the sanctuary or basement must use the elevator to access the restroom. Some additional problems occur within the building as well. For example, when in the sanctuary, the wheelchair user must stay in the back. To reach the altar, they can only use the main aisle because the side aisles are barely wide enough to walk through.

Case Study Figure 9.1c

The main Entrance to the Presbyterian Church is not accessible for someone with limited mobility or in a wheelchair. In fact, the last step in or out of the church is dangerous. Photo courtesy Linda L. Nussbaumer

Case Study Figure 9.1d

A zero-step entrance to the Presbyterian Church provides access. Within its foyer, an elevator lift provides access to the sanctuary or the basement fellowship hall. An accessible restroom is also located in this area. Photo courtesy Linda L. Nussbaumer

If the person using a wheelchair wanted to visit with the minister, they would use the accessible entrance, take the elevator lift to the sanctuary level, enter the sanctuary, travel down the main aisle toward the altar, turn to the left in front of the altar, and then, turn right into the secretary's office. To reach the minister's office, the parishioner must continue through the secretary's office into a hallway, and then, the minister's office. If the person using a wheelchair wanted to participate in Sunday activities (teaching or as a participant), they must maneuver through the sanctuary (as noted earlier) or, if on the basement level, travel through the fellowship hall to opposite end of the building. On either level, doorway widths are narrow; therefore, maneuvering beyond the sanctuary or fellowship hall is difficult.

When a Lutheran church in this small Midwestern town decided to remodel, it also planned for equal access into the

Case Study Figure 9.1e

The staircase to the church offices is not accessible. In order to access the offices, a person in a wheelchair must travel down the foyer to take the elevator, and then, when on the second level, he or she must travel back toward the office. Photo courtesy Linda L. Nussbaumer

building for people with limited mobility as well as provided some inclusive features. When approaching the entrance to the Lutheran church, there is a choice between two steps or a sloped concrete ramp. There is also a large level concrete pad with more than the minimum turning radius (Color Plate 37).

A zero-step entrance provides access to a large open foyer. Within the large foyer, there is ample room for coat storage, and toward the end of the hall, hangers are provided at a lower level for children or someone in a wheelchair.

To the right of the foyer, access is open to the sanctuary. Within the sanctuary, each pew is made up of separate moveable chairs. These provide seating that can easily be moved to allow access for a wheelchair. Thus, an individual in a wheelchair can sit most any place within the sanctuary (an inclusive feature) (Color Plate 38). Access to the altar is not only via two steps, but a ramp also provides special access (an accessible feature).

Continuing down the spacious hallway past the sanctuary takes the parishioner to an elevator, accessible restrooms, as well as a fellowship hall. Church offices are located on the second level and are accessed via steps near the entrance (see Case Study Figures 9.1e) or by taking the elevator. Although accessible, travel distance is greater for someone in a wheelchair or with limited mobility.

Each of these churches provides access to the sanctuary by various means: a ramp, an elevator lift, or a zero-step entrance. Certainly this creates accessibility; however, separate entrances via a ramp or elevator do not provide the same access that everyone else enjoys. They are "separated" from the able-bodied, and therefore, this type of access would not be considered inclusive.

Creating inclusive environments is difficult in existing buildings and can be costly. It is less intrusive and less expensive to install ramps than an elevator lift and, especially, to remodel an entire building. Additionally, religious facilities must depend on donations from their congregations to support a remodel. In these cases, congregations vary in size, and the larger congregation could afford a more inclusive remodel. Even other religious facilities (e.g., synagogues, mosques, and temples) or design types (e.g., hotels, restaurants, retail, educational facilities, and so on) must depend on sales, donations, occupancy, and more to afford small or large renovations. It is the designer's responsibility to see that renovations or changes (large or small) consider not just accessible design, but also inclusive design to give everyone the same opportunities to use and/or enjoy the spaces.

1. Was there a directory?
2. Was it interactive?
3. Did it have a variety of ways to locate the store?
4. Was the individual able to reach, hear, or see where the store was located using the directory?
5. Could the individual find the store in the mall?

After the experiment has been completed, state the findings and possible solutions in a written report.

2. Am I really safe here?

Safety has become a greater concern. For this reason, many buildings (e.g., shopping malls, hotels, office buildings, arenas, and other buildings) have systems in place to provide a sense of security. To the public, security may be visible or invisible through the use of cameras or plainclothed security people. To learn more about a building's security system, take a field trip to an office building or hotel and observe the visible and invisible security. Take notes and do the following:

1. Sit in the lobby.
2. Observe the movement of people.
3. Notice security cameras.
4. Notice security people.
5. Are you able to access the elevator lobby?
6. Can you use the elevator without a keycard?

Using observation notes, state the findings and possible solutions in a written report. Include a reflective paragraph that states the sense of security in the space observed.

APPLICATION PROJECT

1. How can I reach the product if it is too high or low?

For many people, it is not difficult to reach the lowest or highest shelves in a department store, grocery store, or pharmacy; however, it could be difficult for someone with limited mobility (e.g., has arthritic hands and arms, uses crutches or is in a wheelchair), a person who has dwarfism, or someone with poor eyesight (can read only large letters). For any one of these people, merchandise that is accessible only on the top or bottom shelves does not provide an inclusive environment. This project investigates how merchandise is organized for display and purchase.

1. Select the type of store (department store, grocery store, or pharmacy).
2. Note how merchandise is displayed and record on a notepad.
3. Take a photograph of the shelves (ask permission before taking a photograph).
4. Check a minimum of four aisles of the store for comparison.
5. Create a poster to display photographs and describe how the example was inclusive or not.
6. In written format, report the following:
   a. Findings (well-organized or problems)
   b. Solutions to make all merchandise reachable
   c. State ways this information will be used in your design solutions for retail spaces.

Part III

ADVOCATES OF
INCLUSIVE DESIGN

CHAPTER 10

The People

"The happiest people don't necessarily have the best of everything; they just make the best of everything."

—*John C. Maxwell*

OBJECTIVES

▸ Learn from others' personal experiences

▸ Learn about pioneers who became leaders in the area of inclusive or universal design

▸ Use this knowledge to become an advocate for inclusive design that meets universal needs

Inclusive design is for all kinds of people, and all kinds of people can be inclusive designers. In this chapter, we meet a diverse group of individuals whose inspiring stories and pioneering efforts make them role models for everyone who appreciates the social responsibility of inclusive design.

The voices in this chapter are those of architects, interior designers, innovators, motivational speakers, educators, and executives. Although their educational or professional fields differ, a common thread unites them—a concern that everyone is included in having access to products and environments.

Some individuals within this chapter experience daily challenges from a variety of limitations. Some of them design products and/or spaces to provide access and inclusion while others are leaders in their field with a concern for those with limited abilities. Some have found fame while others are notable among their peers. Regardless of their backgrounds or fame, they all work to make life better for others—they understand this to be their social responsibility. Whether or not they have a disability, they all promote good design that is inclusive.

The prominent architect and designer **Michael Graves** designs buildings that provide beauty, enjoyment, and access to many people. Since his illness and paralysis, he also designs products that make life easier for those with physical limitations. After **Rosemarie Rossetti**'s accident, her wheelchair experience gave her the opportunity to share her story and motivate those who may be discouraged by their limitations. She also encourages the design of inclusive products and environments. **Eric Weihenmayer**, an educator and world-class adventurer, encourage others with disabilities to reach new heights (literally) and to experience the world beyond themselves. **Tracy Bell** and **Jenny Stenner** work with the deaf and hard-of-hearing to make their lives better through education and services.

Sometimes people who have not experienced a disability personally feel a responsibility to design inclusive environments. After a family member experienced a disability, designer **Shirley Confino-Rehder** began creating spaces for safe access and inclusion. Designer, educator, and entrepreneur **Shashi Caan** advocates that all design should be inclusive. **Valerie Fletcher**, executive director for the Institute for Human Centered Design, believes that inclusivity is the heart of social sustainability. **Gregg Vanderheiden** has focused his life's work on providing inclusivity for technology.

All of these individuals have experienced nonaccessible environments as well as accessible and inclusive environments. Their compelling stories inspire attention and advocacy in others. Each has worked to improve lives in various ways. This chapter provides an opportunity to learn from these individuals and to become advocates for inclusive design.

MICHAEL GRAVES—EXPERIENTIAL DESIGN BY NECESSITY

In 2006, John Hockenberry, a journalist and wheelchair user, interviewed Michael Graves for *Metropolis Magazine*. Michael Graves' observations and interview proved that universal or inclusive design is not foreign to architects and interior designers. In fact, Michael Graves' story is a perfect example of its importance to the design profession.

In 2003, Michael Graves—the famous designer of iconic buildings and products—came down with a virus that destroyed nerves in his spinal cord causing paralysis from the mid-chest down. A few years later, Hockenberry visited Graves at his home; so when Hockenberry drove his car into Graves' parking lot, he expected to see outward signs of accessibility, such as a ramp. Instead, Hockenberry found that the house did not have a ramp but was still accessible. He observed that the house was built at ground level with wide doors and no step at the entrance. Hockenberry inquired how long Graves had lived there. "Michael's been here forever," said Karen Nichols, a principal of Michael Graves & Associates (MGA). "The amazing thing is how little needed to be done to make the house work for him." When inside, Hockenberry found it easy to maneuver with his wheelchair. The house was comfortable and filled with art and books. Corridors were flat, straight, and spacious, and they connected to well-appointed rooms (e.g., ornate colorful tile, sculptures, and household objects with an intriguing arrangement). The newly constructed elevator was also well appointed and opened onto the second floor that was filled with natural light.

The only changes Graves made to his home were to add the elevator and a roll-in shower, and remove balustrades to provide easier movement with the wheelchair. The floor plan in Figure 10.1 indicates where each is located. Figure 10.2 shows the roll-in shower appointed with Graves' infamous colors—blue and orange.

Flashback: In the Hospital

During his hospital stay, as Graves explains in the Hockenberry interview, he felt trapped in a world of ugly, mundane medical objects that lacked color and style. In fact, when his doctor was visiting Graves, he asked the doctor to step into the hospital bathroom while Graves was attempting to shave from his wheelchair. Graves asked the doctor who designed these bathrooms. The doctor replied, "Experts." Graves said, "Oh, really." Graves then had the doctor sit down and look at himself in the mirror that was too high and turn on the water that was out of reach. It took the doctor two seconds to understand the problem (Hockenberry, 2006, October 11).

Merging Utility with Elegance and Beauty

This was a particularly difficult experience for Graves, a designer who found beauty and purpose in everything he designed. Because of this hospital experience, Graves

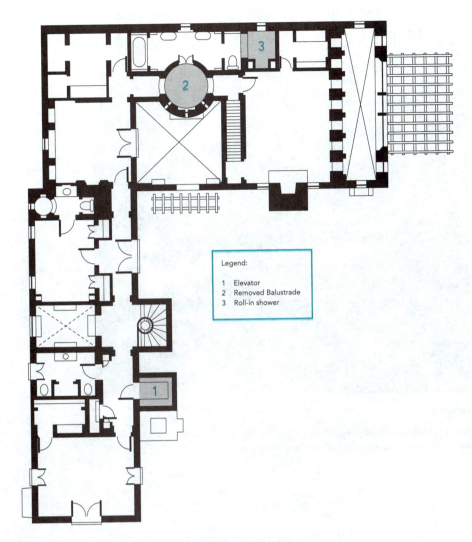

Figure 10.1

Floor plan for Michael Graves home. Note where the (3) roll-in shower was added; (2) the balustrades were removed; and (1) the elevator was installed. © Precision Graphics/based on a drawing courtesy Michael Graves & Associates

and his team developed medical products that combined medical utility with style, multifunctional elegance, and beauty. As they developed products, they experimented with color, style, and design improvements as well. The products include a shower seat, walking canes, and other devices (Hockenberry, 2006, October 11). Figure 10.3 shows a bathtub chair that is stable and easy to adjust. Figures 10.4a–f show various styles of collapsible walking canes.

Through Graves' experience, he found a deepening understanding for those with physical impairments and has become an advocate for functional products and interiors (see Figure 10.5). Clearly, Graves expresses the need for inclusive design in many areas—in hospitals and homes as well as products used—to make living easier for those with various impairments.

Figure 10.2

The roll-in shower Michael Graves designed and installed in his home is appointed with his trademark colors (blue and orange). Courtesy Michael Graves & Associates

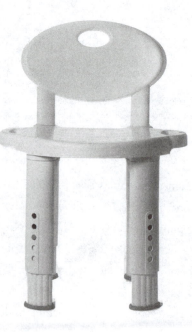

Figure 10.3

Michael Graves designed this white plastic bathtub chair to not only be sturdy but with a soft, rounded look to fit with other bathroom elements. The seat and back are wider, and a nonslip rubber end cup is attached to the blue feet with a patterned bottom surface that allows water to flow underneath. The seat was designed with a molded nonslip wave pattern. Orange buttons are used to adjust the seat, and the elliptical-shaped legs prevent twisting. Note how the orange buttons and blue feet are in keeping with Graves' colors. Courtesy Michael Graves & Associates

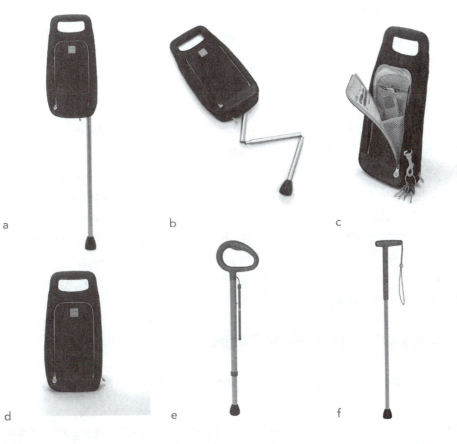

a   b   c

d   e   f

Figure 10.4a–f

Graves and his team designed three height-adjustable extruded-aluminum canes. The first (a and b) is a collapsible cane that (c and d) folds into a built-in padded nylon bag. This allows the user to hide the cane and have it out of sight. The second, the team designed (e) with an ergonomic hand and optional wrist strap. The third is (f) a folding cane with a wrist strip, which can be used to tie the collapsed parts together. Courtesy Michael Graves & Associates

Figure 10.5

The designer Michael Graves has become an advocate and expert on functioning equipment for inclusive access. Courtesy Michael Graves & Associates

ROSEMARIE ROSSETTI—MOTIVATION THROUGH EDUCATION

Rosemarie Rossetti, Ph.D. is an international motivational speaker and wheelchair user. On June 13, 1998, after a three-and-a-half ton tree came crushing down on her, Rossetti suffered a spinal cord injury that paralyzed her from the waist down. Her life changed dramatically. Nevertheless, Rossetti turned what must have appeared at first to be little more than an overwhelming challenge into an active and very productive lifestyle. Now she shares what she has learned and motivates and encourages others confronted with similar misfortune through education—speaking, writing, and more (Rossetti Enterprises Inc., 2010) (see Figure 10.6). The following websites provide further information about Rosemarie Rossetti and the Universal Design Living Laboratory: rosemariespeaks.com and udll.com.

A Q&A with Rosemarie Rossetti

What drew your interest to inclusive (universal) design?

My home was not meeting my needs. So my husband and I researched and learned about homes designed for those with physical limitations. We also learned that a home could be designed to make life easier for people with a range of abilities, sizes, and ages. As a couple, we illustrate the need for universality; Mark is 6'4" and I am 4'2" tall seated in a wheelchair.

Figure 10.6

Rosemarie Rossetti. Photo courtesy Roshunda Holloway

Because of our research of universal design and its transformation for our lives, we believed it was necessary to share this research and knowledge as well as our home to make a difference in the lives of others. We wanted to find a way to share what we had learned with others. We are building a home for ourselves, but it will also serve as the Universal Design Living Laboratory (UDLL) (www.udll.com). The UDLL will help people understand ways to create a more comfortable living environment that will enhance their quality of life. The UDLL will be a learning resource. The ranch–style home will be approximately 3,500 square feet that will incorporate sustainable practices, universal features, advanced automation technology, and feng shui design principles. For more on this home and garden, visit www.udll.com/the–home. (See Figure 10.7.)

Why is inclusive (universal) design important?

Inclusive (universal) design is a type of design that includes everyone—no one person is singled out. Whether or not in a wheelchair, everyone should have the same opportunities. Everyone should be able to use the same entrance, have equal access, go

Figure 10.7

The plan of this home incorporates inclusive design features. Some of these features include zero-step entrances, three-foot-wide doors, wider hallways, lever handles on doors and faucets, various counter heights, side-by-side refrigerators, front-loading washer and dryer, open knee space under all sinks, and more. © Precision Graphics/based on a drawing by Rosemarie Rossetti

through the same doors, be comfortable conducting various tasks (e.g., cooking), and so on. For those in a wheelchair, life can be frustrating when tasks are difficult.

What advice would you give students to encourage their application of inclusive (universal) design?

Interior design students can become "better" interior designers when they have experienced life like their clients. Unless students experience life in a wheelchair, it is difficult to understand how the person who uses a wheelchair lives. Students need to experience the wheelchair beginning in a parking lot; getting to the house; functioning in and around the home; and going to and shopping at the mall, in the grocery store, and beyond.

I suggest that students find a wheelchair, take it home, and live in it for a while (a day or more)—pretend that you cannot get out of the seat. Using a wheelchair gives you a different perspective. Then, students will become frustrated and gain a new understanding of universal design. They will be frustrated because just a quarter-inch really does make a difference in getting through a door and into the space beyond. They will learn that furniture designs do not accommodate a person in a wheelchair, such as the high bed design.

Here are some experiences students should be involved in to not only become frustrated but also to learn and design with this new knowledge. Students must ask the following questions as well as experience life in a wheelchair that begins in the parking lot:

- How can I get into a car?
- How can I get from the car to the house?
- How can I open or close doors? Does the door swing get in the way? Would a pocket door work better?
- How high is the carpet? Can I maneuver the wheelchair on the carpet?
- How do I fix a meal in the kitchen?
- How can I reach items in lower cabinets?
- How can I reach items in upper cabinets that are 18 inches above the counter?
- How can I get into the freezer portion when it is a top-freezer refrigerator?
- How can I peel potatoes at the sink?
- How can I make a sandwich or cut an apple on a 36-inch-high counter?
- How can I put cereal in a bowl, add milk, and transfer it to a table without spilling?
- How do I open the oven door to get a pizza inside?
- Where are the controls on the stove or cooktop? Can I reach across to turn it on or off without getting burnt?
- How can I see inside a pot on the stove?
- How do I do stir-fry or fry bacon without being spattered in the face or eyes? Will I need protective eyewear?

- How can I reach the miniblind to adjust it?
- Can I get into the bathroom?
- Can I get under the sink to use it?
- Are there grab bars by the toilet or shower to transfer myself from the wheelchair to the toilet or a shower chair?
- Can I reach a towel bar from the shower?
- How do I get into bed when furniture is blocking access?
- How can I reach clothes in the closet?
- How can I get out of a walk-in closet? (See Figure 10.8.)
- How can I use the wheelchair at a desk or table and work on a computer?
- Can I reach the light switch to turn it on/off, or is furniture in the way?
- How can I reach clothes in the washer and dryer?
- Can I set the HVAC thermostat?
- How can I be independent at home or anywhere else?
- Is there a five-foot turning radius in places where I need to turn around?
- Is there clearance on the latch side of each door?
- Are the hallways larger than three feet wide so I can turn around?
- Is there a 30" x 48" clear floor space for the wheelchair to get through in various locations such as the toilet or sink?

This experiential learning process will help students understand what it is like to live life in a wheelchair; they will understand that it is difficult and frustrating not being able to maneuver or not feeling independent. Experiential learning will help students realize the problems with planning and designing spaces and become designers who consider everyone's needs and apply their new knowledge to all projects.

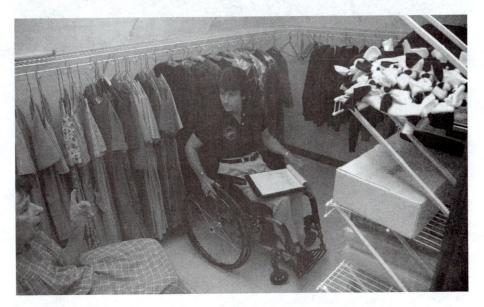

Figure 10.8

Rosemarie Rossetti researching a closet designed for easy access in a Cincinnati home.
Photo courtesy Rosemarie Rossetti (rosemarie@rosemariespeaks.com)

ERIK WEIHENMAYER—A WORLD-CLASS ADVENTURER

Erik Weihenmayer, a world-class adventurer, is the only blind man in history to not only reach the summit of the world's highest peak, Mount Everest, but also climb the Seven Summits—the highest mountains on each of the seven continents (see Figure 10.9). Fewer than 200 mountaineers have accomplished these feats, and yet his feats do not end there. He continues to take on new adventures and complete some of the toughest athletic events.

Figure 10.9

Erik Weihenmayer on his trek to Mount McKinley (also called Denali), the highest peak in North America. Here, Erik is traveling to the base camp and pulling a 70-pound sled as well as carrying a 50-pound backpack filled with enough supplies for three weeks on the mountain. Didrik Johnck—www.johnckmedia.com

A former middle-school teacher and wrestling coach, Erik is one of the most exciting and well-known athletes in the world. Despite losing his vision at age 13, Erik has become an accomplished mountain climber, paraglider, and skier who has never let his blindness interfere with his passion for an exhilarating and fulfilling life. Erik has also earned many awards, authored two books (*Touch the Top of the World* and *The Adversity Advantage*), produced award-winning films, shared his experiences through speaking engagements around the globe, and much more. It is clear that Erik's accomplishments show that one does not have to have perfect eyesight to have extraordinary vision. Here, he shares comments related to his world with visual limitations.

Q&A with Erik Weihenmayer

What challenges have you experienced or continue to experience with people, products, and spaces because of poor design?

A big challenge for someone who is disabled is often in wilderness areas. In the past, there's been a perception these places are not accessible to people with limitations in mobility, hearing, or vision. However, technology is beginning to make the wilderness accessible through talking GPS devices, audible tracking technology, better prosthetics, new innovative hand-cranked mountain bikes for paraplegics, and more. Technology is also changing how the world around us works. Technology is providing access to rugged exotic places, but it is the challenge of the everyday life that provides a mixed bag. For example, the new technologies such as flat screen TVs, flat panels on the microwave, or touch-screens are no longer tactile and make it difficult for a blind person to use. There are no raised areas or Braille to signify the start, clear, time, or other information. For this reason, many who are blind will purchase products using older technologies that still provide tactile controls. Another concern is that when new products are brought onto the market, their design has considered only the exciting new technology without consideration for those with limited vision, hearing, or mobility. For example, when the iPod and iPhone were introduced, a blind person could not use them; however, now, finally, these products have built-in audible software. The problem is that new technologies are introduced without thought to those with limitations. The question may be "why can't new devices, products, and the like be inclusively designed from the beginning?"

How do you maneuver a space that you have never been in before?

If good cane and mobility skills have been learned, the blind person can navigate any space, but some spaces are easier than others. I believe blind people appreciate predictable patterns that give them a clue of what's to come when they are navigating. For instance, in Denver International Airport, the bathrooms can be located in areas in which a hard surface is under foot, and the gates are located in areas where a carpet is under foot. Plus, the even number gates are on one side, the odd number gates on the other side.

Advancements such as technology, tactile applications, changes in surfaces, and more have made navigation easier and the environment safer for the blind person. For example, audible signal lights help a blind person know it is safe to cross the street, or strips at the edge of a track warn a person to stop before the train platform ends. However, if the blind person has developed good cane skills, they can feel the end of the train platform or use mobility skills to listen for cues from traffic to cross the street. The question may be "should we make the environment easier to maneuver, or is it more important for the blind person to develop good cane and mobility skills?"

What advice would you give students as they design for someone who is blind?

There are two competing schools of thought within the blindness community about designing for those who are blind. One is to change the world through design in order to help people who are blind; the other is for the blind person to use his/her mobility skills to maneuver through the world. I believe that, if we are to design the world to help a blind person, we must make sure that the design compensates for skills that can't be learned. Otherwise, the design may become a crutch, and then, the important learned skills are not used and people become dependent on the audible sound or surface changes. This could potentially limit a blind person's ability to branch out and face more challenging environments. It may be best to ask this question in design: "Can the design meet the challenge of the person's needs?"

TRACY BELL AND JENNY STENNER—HEARING BY SEEING

Tracy Bell is the regional manager for Deaf and Hard of Hearing Services at the Minnesota Department of Human Services; Jenny Stenner is also employed in the same office. Both Tracy and Jenny are deaf and, in conducting the interview, Sara Swanson was the interpreter.

Figure 10.10

Tracy Bell is preparing to use a videophone to place a phone call. Before she makes the call, her image is produced on the monitor. After she makes the call and the receiver answers, the person receiving the call will be visible on the screen and also able to see Tracy. They can use sign language or an interpreter to communicate. Photo courtesy Tracy Bell

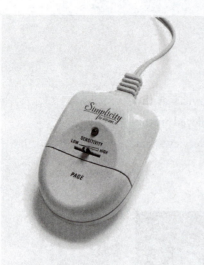

Figure 10.11a

This device detects everyday sounds, such as a baby's cry or an oven timer. Used by permission of Harris Communications, Inc.

Figure 10.11b

This alarm clock has several features to awaken the sleeper: loud alarm of up to 85+ decibels; a visual alarm indicator; a bed shaker; and a lamp flasher connection. Used by permission of Harris Communications, Inc.

A Q&A with Tracy Bell and Jenny Stenner

What do you use as hearing devices? (e.g., reading lips, hearing aids, TTY's, etc.)

To communicate, people with hearing loss need assistive devices such as videophones, computers, and cell phones, as well as sign languages and interpreters.

Videophones are the most common method of making phone calls; people who have hearing loss and use sign language use videophones to use the video relay service to call hearing people. With videophones, people can see one another as they communicate sign language to the hearing person; or two people will use sign language to communicate (see Figure 10.10).

Computers or cell phones, email and text messaging are excellent methods of communication. Another method is through the video relay service in which an interpreter interprets sign language. Another method is using the written word—a method that works whether deaf or not. However, sign language between deaf people or using an interpreter through sign helps communicate with nondeaf people. If an interpreter is not available, pen and paper is used when the deaf person must communicate with a nondeaf person; however, having an interpreter is the preference. Sometimes texting with a pager or phone is used; this allows the nondeaf person to read the communication.

The quality of communication through videophones is influenced by lighting, color, and visual distractions. It is helpful to not have background distractions but not a requirement. Videophones are used in offices and at home, even in the kitchen, like a regular phone. If privacy is required, then standard procedures would be used as if you were using a regular phone.

Deaf people's visual senses are stronger. They use their eyes to observe their surroundings, thus they depend on their eyes. The eyes are sensitive to light and color—similar to hearing people. But in particular, lighting (natural or artificial) can affect the ability to see flashing lights or obscure a video screen. Some deaf people prefer relaxing colors rather than loud colors such as lime green, yellow, orange, and neon colors.

What newer devices are available?

Many of the newer devices relate to phones such as the videophone. For example, WiFi aids connections to a phone through on-demand services. The new Android benefits hearing and deaf because it features a video chat on the phone; however, the connection depends on the strength of the signal. Videophones and texting are especially beneficial. Lastly, newer and important aids are Bluetooth hearing aids.

Beyond the phone, cochlear implants have benefited the hearing impaired for many years, but it is improving with digital technology by making the implant more efficient.

At home, what devices do you use for phone, alarms, etc.?

When at home, deaf people use light and vibrations for alerts or alarms (see Figure 10.11a). Light flashes replace the ring of the doorbell and the phone. The signal sets a specific flash for each.

Light can also be attached to the videophone, which works through electrical systems. Also, a special lighting system can be routed within the house and in some buildings. As an example, a wall sconce can be connected to an alerting system that lights up in the house. The problem with light is that it can be confused with natural light. For example, an alert can be missed because natural light is streaming through the window. For alerts (e.g., baby crying, smoke detector strobe light, phone signalers, doorbell signalers) the right light is needed, and the light must be in the right place to see it.

A morning alarm may be through flashing lights or vibrations (see Figure 10.11b). It could be a bed, BlackBerry, or phone that vibrates. Animals, especially dogs, also serve to alert the hearing impaired.

At work, how do you communicate with others and they with you?

Interpreters, sign language, videophones, and Video Relay Services (VRS) are the most common means of communication.

Interpreters are used when a nondeaf person is in the office. In particular, the interpreter's role is to facilitate communication between a deaf person(s) and a hearing nonsigner(s). However, among staff, sign language is used. Videophones or VRS are used to communicate by phone. Writing back and forth is a last resort. Interpreters and signing is most often used.

A new technology, Interpret on Demand, is an online feature that is being tested. Due to the lack of interpreters in some areas, technology is used to connect with a live interpreter online using interpreter-on-demand services. Individuals and service providers can schedule an interpreter ahead of time, or at the last minute. Both of these methods have varying rates. Being able to see an interpreter allows for signing or having an interpreter along with signing. This can be accomplished with the videophones or VRS, but today there are other excellent methods of face-to-face communication as well:

1. Laptops with built-in video cameras
2. The new iPod with a video system
3. Skype, OOVOO (like Skype), or Face-Time by Apple
4. An Interactive TV feature (iTV), a polycom system used for meetings where people are in several different locations

How do you manage in public spaces where the ability to hear is important?

At concerts, deaf people can sit and watch even though we don't hear. We can still enjoy concerts because we feel vibrations (especially the bass).

In malls, fire alarms are required to have flashing lights; however, we are observant of others' behavior. We don't use hearing but rather use our eyes; our eyes are very sensitive. We see more with our eyes than hearing people do. For example, in a restaurant we might notice the behavior in the corner of restaurant; we would also notice behavior of others looking toward a commotion. If something happens, it is not a noisy situation for us but a seeing situation. Sometimes, we take notice first because we see before others hear it.

Airports are difficult for us. At airport security, there are problems at scanners. There is no one to interpret for us, and this makes going through security more difficult.

Announcements are made over the loudspeaker system. In these situations, we must be assertive and ask. We might go to a help desk and ask, and they are often very helpful. For example, if the airplane is delayed, we do not hear the announcements, but we can observe behavior and, then, ask with a note to find out what is happening.

On the airplane, we must ask the attendant (using paper and pencil) about our location and other announcements. They are pretty good about helping us. Others go with the flow and enjoy the flight. Hearing people have advantages to find answers quickly through hearing; deaf people must seek answers.

Jenny (an employee at the regional office) shared this experience when shopping: "In small stores when clerks come up behind me, I cannot hear them and don't respond. So, they think I am rude. However, when they realize I am deaf, their attitude changes."

Hearing people can multitask—they can hear and work at the same time. Deaf people can also multitask; however, they cannot sign while typing or doing a task. Therefore, deaf people explain (by signing) before they do something.

Do you feel that we (designers) consider your needs when creating various environments?

Although this does not relate to design, deaf people would appreciate if hearing people had more awareness and patience with the deaf.

Related to interior design, deaf people are more sensitive to light and color, especially, light systems. In airports, there are many challenges as noted earlier. For example, when announcements are made regarding changes (e.g., gate changes, delays, and more), this information would be scrolled across the screen. Their system can have captioning just as it is on TV. Because all TVs have captioning capacity, this should be easy to do.

In public or even private offices, videophones would be helpful. However, when they are used, the background should be a single color and one that is less saturated.

More hospitals are now installing videophones in their systems. This is very helpful to the deaf person. However, not all public spaces have videophones and they may not be free.

In hotels, some have free Internet and others do not. When traveling, we need the Internet to connect through our computers; therefore, this influences the hotel and room we select. We try to find hotels that do not charge for Internet access because it is a necessity.

Clearly, deaf people have many challenges. But they also are more sensitive to happenings around them and are often more alert for this reason.

SHIRLEY CONFINO-REHDER—THE RESPONSIBILITY TO LISTEN, LEARN, AND ATTEND

Shirley Confino-Rehder, CID, AFFIL, AIA, is a certified interior designer and an ADA and universal design advocate, as well as a lecturer, teacher, author, and chair of the Norfolk, Virginia, Mayor's Commission for Persons with Disabilities. She shares her expertise and advocacy for universal design. (See Figure 10.12.)

A Q&A with Shirley Confino-Rehder

What drew your interest to inclusive (universal) design?

I started my career as an interior designer in 1970. The term, "universal design" was coined in 1990 by (the architect) Ron Mace. The very early realization as a designer that all people are happier if their environments are easier and safer to live and work in created the foundation of my practice in barrier-free design, the forerunner for universal design.

My niece was born with a genetic disorder while I was still attending New York School of Interior Design. Some of the manifestations of the disorder were scoliosis, no sense of hot and cold or pain, and no tear ducts, leading to suturing eyelids to heal ulcerations. These led to other problems that required special attention to design in their environment, including clean, nonallergenic personal environments for their poor breathing; safer environments for their poor senses of pain; and good lighting, color schemes, textured environments for their sporadic temporary loss of eyesight.

Figure 10.12

Shirley Confino-Rehder working on the stepless shower. Photo courtesy Shirley Confino-Rehder

In addition, one of my first clients was a couple of short stature (both about 4'8") who desired to have comfortable seating in their living room, where "their feet can touch the floor" and their guests could still sit comfortably. Another client shared a small apartment with one main common closet. He was 6'5", she 4'10". These clients, along with my work with my niece and her friends, whetted my enthusiasm to design creative solutions for safer, healthier environments for all without sacrificing aesthetics and gave me challenges that still keep my creative juices flowing. Thinking out-of-the-box continuously allows me to create solutions to meet real challenges so clients and nonclients can enjoy the world within their own personal abilities.

Why is inclusive (universal) design important?

Everyone has the right to participate in what this wonderful world has to offer to the best of their ability. Universal design, inclusive design, design-for-all principles, when followed, can make this happen. It is the designer's responsibility to demand that the politician, fabricator, developer, and the architect learn to listen and attend to the needs of the real world; the educator should understand the intent of all the principles of these design concepts; and the client should advocate for their own special needs without shame or guilt. The Americans with Disabilities Act and its Architectural Guidelines in the United States, and all of the other laws for accessible design around the world offer guidelines that can be applied in all aspects of design, for residential, commercial, and common space. The principles are starting points. Everyone is unique. People are the standard for design, not outdated, out-of-the box standards, rules, and regulations. And of course, sustainability and "green" design must be included. Our planet is our client, too.

What advice would you give students to encourage their application of inclusive (universal) design?

Your responsibility as future architects and designers of our built environment is far more important than your ego and your own dreams of creativity. Your responsibility is not only to attend to the needs of your clients to fill their present needs and dreams, but to attend to their safety, health, and their own human frailties, whether they recognize it or not. Whether you are involved in home design, city planning, or commercial planning your responsibility is to attend to needs of all people, and the footprints they make in our environment. You can make a difference in the life of one person, one family, one community by using your creative juices to listen, learn, and attend. Our responsibility to each other is to eliminate barriers of attitude and architecture through the concepts of universal design so that everyone can take part in the social and economic opportunities this wonderful world offers.

SHASHI CAAN—PROVIDING SMART SOLUTIONS TO LIFE'S PROBLEMS

Shashi Caan is a multidisciplinary designer with degrees in architecture, industrial design, and interior design. She is the founding principal at Shashi Caan Collective, 2009–2011 president of International Federation of Interior Architects/Designers (IFI) (see Figure 10.13), and a member of the executive committee at the International Design Alliance (IDA). She also held the position of chair of interior design at Parsons School of Design and design director and associate partner at Skidmore, Owings, and Merrill LLP (SOM). Shashi Caan has also been recognized for her firm's work—including some international projects.

A Q&A with Shashi Caan

What drew your interest to inclusive (universal) design?

Design, pervasive in all facets of life, exists to improve the human condition and quality of life. A combination of art, science, and common sense, design is simply an intention with a purpose. Design provides smart solutions to all of life's problems. Design must perform and is only successful when it satisfies the desired outcomes. As such, design inherently touches all people. Ideally and by design, whether experienced individually

Figure 10.13

As IFI president, Shashi Caan presides over the DFIE Brazilian Think Tank in Sao Paolo, Brazil in October 2010. Photo by Heather Zinger. Courtesy Pacific Northwest College of Art, MFA in Applied Craft and Design

or by the collective, design supports, enhances, and uplifts human behavior and the human spirit. Therefore, design is fundamentally egalitarian and inclusive in its essence.

Believing in the previous statements, for me, there was never a question of being "drawn toward or becoming interested in universal design." The universal outreach of design is a fundamental criteria and at the heart of design. Therefore, it is an inherent design requirement that must always be satisfied.

Why is inclusive (universal) design important?

It is not a question of why universal design is important, but the fact that *design* is by nature universal. Design is the most successful when it enables our full and democratic participation in society. This requires intentionally designing for ease of access and mobility and for all people regardless of gender, age, economic status, nationality, ability, or education. This also requires designing with sensitivity and responsibility for the needs and optimization of participation by all of humanity.

For design to produce solutions that universally address human concerns, three distinct categories of needs must be envisioned, developed, and met:

1. The broadest and first pertaining to all humans includes the innate physiological requirements that form our mutual, programmed inheritance. Social and ecological responsibilities are very much a part of these needs, which can be best described simply as human nature.

2. The second is a more fluid set of culturally specific needs, which can vary widely according to geography, over time, and through history.

3. Thirdly, the narrowest range of human needs consists of those that are specific to the individual, such as having a sense of belonging, trust, and pride.

These layers of needs require that the designer is always cognizant of core human requirements, and must be fluent in the language of culture and sensitive to the unique demands of individuals. A great challenge because these demands are often competing—the approach for bodily measurements needs to be imbued with a comprehensive understanding of the immaterial measures of human needs.

What advice would you give students to encourage their application of inclusive (universal) design?

I would encourage design students to personify design and to embrace the depth of responsibility inherent to design thinking and manifestation. Stylistic and visual aspects of design are only the surface coating that provides a superficial window into personality. This personality must have depth of character, values, principles, and goals. Often this is lacking in design articulation, thereby providing hollow and unsatisfactory design contributions to all society and culture.

VALERIE FLETCHER—INCLUSIVITY AT THE HEART OF SOCIAL SUSTAINABILITY

Valerie Fletcher has been the executive director of the Institute of Human Centered Design since its inception in 1998. She oversees a wide range of projects, such as a web-based collection of universal design case studies and community development initiatives that connect universal design and environmental sustainability, focusing people with sensory or brain-based functional issues. She also makes presentations, gives keynote addresses, and presents with panels at many conferences (see Figure 10.14).

A Q&A with Valerie Fletcher

What drew your interest to inclusive (universal) design?

My career has been divided between design and social justice work in public mental health and in racial and economic equality. Although I knew that design was the work that made my blood run faster, that engaged me fully and made me happy, it felt indulgent and insufficiently meaningful. In 1997, I had left government after a satisfying stint as the deputy commissioner for the Massachusetts Department of

Figure 10.14

Valerie Fletcher makes many presentations on human-centered design, of which inclusive design is a part. After her presentations, she takes time to visit with attendees. Here she thoughtfully visits with Kyuho Ahn, assistant professor of interior architecture at the University of Oregon, who attended the IDEC 2011 conference in Denver. Photograph provided by krsitynivey.com

Mental Health where I had the opportunity to lead a process of closing four institutions and redirecting 74 million dollars in community program expansion through a participatory planning process. An old friend who was on the board of directors at what was then the Adaptive Environments Center asked me to look at the posting for a new executive director to replace co-founder Elaine Ostroff. Although the organization was small, I quickly connected to the extraordinary power of the ideas of inclusive design and to Elaine, and I pursued the opportunity. This was the ideal melding of my passion for design and need to invest fully in work that made a difference for people. I've never looked back.

Why is inclusive (universal) design important?

Design matters in a particular way to people at the edges of the spectrum of ability, age, and culture. Too often, design is a negative experience in which bad or thoughtless design constrains experience and compromises opportunity. With the increasing diversity of the world's population, we can't afford to forfeit attention to the positive power and potential of design to make human diversity work. Being able to use design as a tool of enhancing life is at the heart of the World Health Organization's contextual definition of disability. Designers are makers of the human context and we have the potential of doing transformative work that changes people's lives for the better. An investment in thinking about the full range of physical, sensory, and brain-based abilities can stimulate creativity and generate solutions that seamlessly integrate esthetics and function. Design is a social art that realizes its full potential in relation to its positive impact on people.

What advice would you give students to encourage their application of inclusive (universal) design?

Think of inclusive design as the heart of social sustainability. Environmental sustainability has become an urgent priority for most design students and a defining characteristic of a good career in design. I would suggest that a commitment to environmental sustainability is the baseline for anyone choosing a responsible course as a designer. There is also an urgent need to think practically about what constitutes social sustainability in design. It is not another leg of the stool but rather a next step in a holistic vision of sustainability that acknowledges and celebrates human diversity. Given the reality of diversity of age and ability worldwide in the 21st century, inclusive design is at the core of a socially sustainable practice. Thus, applying social sustainability, which encompasses environmental sustainability and inclusive design, designers can promote the potential for building a better world.

GREGG C. VANDERHEIDEN—PIONEERING INCLUSIVITY FOR THE PC AND BEYOND

Gregg C. Vanderheiden, PhD, is the director of Trace Research and Development Center as well as professor of the Industrial and Systems Engineering and Biomedical Engineering departments at University of Wisconsin-Madison. He shares his extensive background in universal design and provides encouraging words to students (see Figure 10.15).

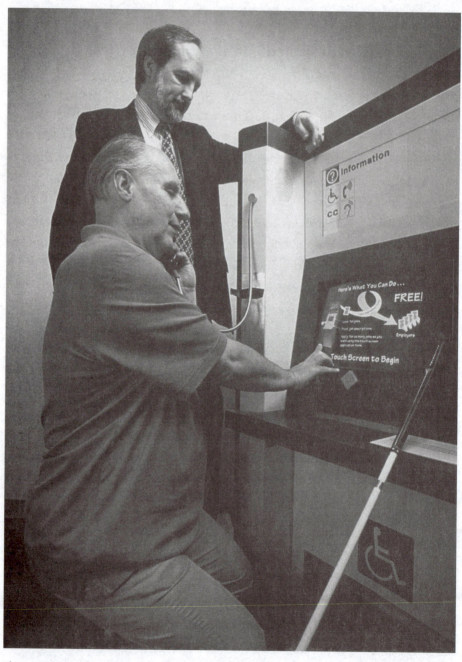

Figure 10.15

Dr. Gregg C. Vanderheim (standing). Photo courtesy Dr. Gregg C. Vanderheiden

Inclusive Technology Out of the Box

My early work (1970s) was in assistive technology (AT) used for communication and control. The Trace Center pioneered in the new field of augmentative communication (a term that I coined). When PCs were invented, we began to focus on how to make them accessible for people with disabilities (especially those with physical and vision impairments). Initially, the approach was through AT, but I began to see that if aspects of the design of the human interface on PCs was altered, the PC could be accessible "out of the box" to many people with disabilities.

In the early 1980s, I was a leader in the development of guidelines for the PC industry for making this technology more accessible and usable for people with disabilities. This work led to guidelines for both hardware and software. Ultimately, our Center developed a suite of accessibility features that have been built into Windows, Mac OS, Linux, and other operating systems for over the last 10 years.

Building on our success with computer access, we have applied the same approach to other emerging information and communication technologies. We developed the first Web accessibility guidelines, which became the basis for the W3C's Web Content Accessibility Guidelines 1.0, and provided leadership in development of WCAG 1.0 and 2.0. When touchscreen-based kiosks appeared, we developed the EZ Access techniques and features (hardware and software) to provide a means for developers of those types of systems to make them accessible. These techniques have been adapted and implemented on systems as diverse as electronic voting systems, self-service postal kiosks and ticket machines, airport paging, and building information directories. We also developed a set of more generic guidelines for more accessible consumer (electronic) products.

After doing a study of the practice of universal design across industries, we concluded that government regulation and industry standards are important means of ensuring that companies are motivated to include accessibility considerations in the design of their mainstream products and systems. We have, therefore, devoted a significant amount of time and effort to working on federal advisory committees and industry standards groups to develop accessibility guidelines in support of regulation such as Section 508 and 255, and also to infuse accessibility into IT and telecommunications industry standards.

My primary motivation for working to make mainstream products and systems more accessible (universally designed) is that:

- AT alone cannot provide accessibility to the increasingly ubiquitous information and communication technologies.
- AT is essential when it is essential (wheelchairs, prosthetics, etc.), but it is not feasible to require that people purchase adaptations or adapt every bit of the world around them to meet their needs. Most individuals cannot afford such an approach. And, in the case of shared or public devices, it is not

possible to install AT modifications. AT will always be needed at the edges where we don't know how to build in sufficient accessibility.

■ We have an aging population, so we need to do this for them (soon, us!).

We began to refer to this approach as "universal design" in the late 1990s, when the term became widely used. I was one of the participants in the development of the original principles of universal design. However, we have found that term less useful in recent years for ICT (information and communication technology). Many ICT companies have trouble with term *universal design* because they are afraid of having to make their products work for everyone. In the world of ICT, it is more common to refer to this simply as *inclusive design* or *accessibility*, which is sometimes viewed as another aspect of *usability*.

Summary

These leaders in their fields offer their advice to encourage you to consider everyone as you design. Being inclusive may not mean that everyone can use the same item equally; however, it does mean that everyone is considered and can use spaces, products, and/or services without having attention drawn to them.

Inclusive Design Projects

EXPERIENTIAL PROJECT

1. Adopt a virtual mentor.

The people who shared their stories in this chapter are advocates for inclusivity. To deepen your understanding of their challenges or knowledge, conduct further research on one of these individuals and write a reflection paper on ways their stories have impacted you and ways this will change or improve how you will design in the future.

APPLICATION PROJECTS

1. Design an inclusive product or environment for someone you know.

The greatest learning experiences are personal. Everyone knows a friend or acquaintance that has or has had difficulty using products or moving through an environment. For this project, locate someone you know who has physical, mental, visual, or hearing limitations and interview them. Set up an appointment for the interview, and if you want to videotape them or take photographs, ask permission. A list of questions should be prepared prior to the interview. Begin with the following list of questions and add additional questions that will help you understand their situation. If possible, share the questions with the interviewee prior to the interview. Initial questions include:

1. How did you acquire the disability or limitation?
2. Describe difficulties you have encountered due to this disability or limitation.
3. What advice can you share that will help me as an interior designer?

Take copious notes during this interview along with the videotape. From these notes, make a list of issues found. State the issues that were revealed (e.g., entrance to buildings, shelving in the grocery store, entering a church, or other issues). Determine how these problems can be solved in your future designs.

2. How will you bring inclusivity into your own designs?

There are many individuals who have experienced the world in a different way (from a wheelchair, by seeing through hearing, or by hearing through seeing). For those without these challenges, it is difficult to image what their world is like. Throughout this book, you may have conducted observations, participated in first-hand experiences, taken field trips, and much more. Now it is time to put this knowledge to practice. In a reflection paper, explain the process by which you will create inclusively designed environments. At a minimum, this paper should consider the design process, research, experiences, and inclusive design criteria.

Glossary

A

accessible design Products and environments are designed and constructed so that people with disabilities may access and use them.

active adult community Life-stage housing in communities for those ages 55 and older that contains health clubs, college classrooms, and computer labs.

affordable housing A term used to describe housing units with costs that are considered affordable for those with moderate income.

age-related macular degeneration A medical condition that generally affects older adults and results in a loss of vision at the center of the visual field. It is caused by damage to the retina.

age-restricted or **active-adult community** A life-stage housing in communities for those ages 55 and over that contains health clubs, college classrooms, and computer labs.

aging in place Remaining in one's home while growing old and modifying the home to accommodate the aging process.

Air Carrier Access Act (ACAA) A law enacted by the U.S. Congress that prohibits discrimination based on a disability in air travel and requires air carriers to accommodate passengers with disabilities.

Alzheimer's disease A form of dementia, which is an incurable, degenerative, and terminal disease.

American National Standards Institute (ANSI) A private nonprofit organization that oversees voluntary standardization systems for products, services, processes, systems, and personnel.

Americans with Disabilities Act (ADA) A law that was enacted by the U.S. Congress in 1990 and signed into law on July 26, 1990 that prohibits discrimination based on disability.

Americans with Disabilities Act Accessibility Guidelines (ADAAG) A document that provides the scope and technical requirements for access to buildings and facilities set forth through the Americans with Disabilities Act (ADA).

Americans with Disabilities Act Amendments Act of 2008 Amendments to the Americans with Disabilities Act (ADA) were signed into law on September 25, 2008 that clarified and reiterated who is covered by the law's civil rights protection.

analysis The study of the parts (e.g., data) and their interrelationships in making up a whole.

anthropometric Measurements of the size, weight, and proportions of the human body.

Architectural Barriers Act (ABA) of 1968 Enacted into law in 1968, the Architectural Barriers Act (ABA) required facilities that were designed, built, altered, or leased with federal funds to be accessible to the public.

accessibility specialist A professional whose specialty is the application of the ADA law, who determines if a part of the building environment is compliant with the Americans with Disabilities Act and state laws.

assisted listening system (ALS) A method or device used to provide hearing ability for people in a variety of situations.

assistive technologies A general term for assistive, adaptive, and rehabilitative devices (e.g., hearing aids, canes, wheelchair) for people with disabilities.

audible instructions Verbal directives provided for those who are unable to read the written material.

automated teller machine (ATM) Also known as automated banking machine (ABM) or cash machine, the ATM is a computerized telecommunications device providing clients of a financial institution with access to financial transactions in a public area without needing a cashier or bank teller.

autism A neurological condition that disrupts perceptions and relationships.

B

baby boomer The largest population group; those born between 1946 and 1964.

bariatric(s) A term related to obesity, including products and treatment for individuals who are overweight.

Braille A method used to read and write by people who have visual limitations.

brownstone Brown sandstone used as a building material; buildings with this material were called "brownstones."

C

case study An in-depth investigation of a single site (e.g., office, residence, hotel), behavior, or individual.

cataracts A clouding that develops over the eye and obstructs the passage of light.

cerebral palsy A general term covering a group of disorders that involve the brain and nervous system functions that can causes physical disability.

Civil Rights Act of 1964 A law that made discrimination based on race, religion, gender, national origin, and other characteristics illegal.

closed captioning Systems developed to display text on a television or video screen that allows a person with hearing disabilities to have access to programming.

cohousing A type of collaborative housing where residents are actively involved in the design and operation of the community that is composed of private homes.

color coding A method providing or displaying information by using different colors.

compost Organic material from plant and animal matter that is allowed to decompose.

concurrent design A method that brings together all experts who design the facility and those who operate it.

congregate housing Similar to independent living except that the facility usually provides conveniences and support services (e.g., meals, housekeeping, and transportation).

content analysis A research technique used to analyze text (e.g., books, websites, newspaper articles, speeches, paintings, laws) for the presence of a particular word(s) or phrase; objectively and systematically identifying the form and content of written or spoken material.

continuing care retirement community (CCRC) A community that offers several levels of assistance; these include independent living, assisted living, and nursing home care.

contract administration phase Administration of a design project takes place during this phase of the design process and involves the execution of the project-ordering, constructing, installing, and supervising a project to completion.

contract document phase Contract documents are prepared and approved by the client during this phase of the design process.

contrast glare An issue with light level changes in which the person is unable to focus from one light level to another.

critical regionalism An architectural style that intends to oppose placelessness and lack of identity in modern architecture through the use a building's geographical context.

cultural regionalism A culture within a geographical area or region that may be definite or specific to a group of people.

cultural sensitivity Considering cultural differences in the needs of others.

D

daylighting The practice of admitting natural light into a space through windows.

dementia/Alzheimer's care A specialized skilled nursing care for individuals with dementia/Alzheimer's.

design development phase Final design decisions for plans, specifications, and preparation of final presentation documents are made during this phase of the design process.

designing for all A concept that refers to all products, environments, and services that can be used by many people without the need for adaptation.

design process A systematic, logical step-by-step process by which a design is executed.

disabilities A lack of ability related to physical, sensory, developmental, cognitive/mental, emotional, or a combination.

E

epilepsy A chronic neurological disorder characterized by sudden and recurrent seizures.

Education for All Handicapped Children Act (EAHCA) A law that provides equal access to education for children with physical and mental disabilities.

ergonomics The applied science of equipment design that reduces operator fatigue and discomfort to maximize productivity.

evidence-based design (EBD) A process for the conscientious, explicit, and judicious use of current best evidence or findings from research and practice to making critical decisions.

evidence Objects and information that are helpful in forming a decision; results, or findings from research or investigation.

exclusion The act of excluding something or someone.

experiment A research procedure carried out to determine the effect of an independent variable (an action or treatment) on a dependent variable (a behavior) under controlled conditions; experiments are usually conducted in a laboratory setting.

F

fact finding Locating information.

Fair Housing Act (FHA) Prohibits discrimination based on race, color, national origin, religion, sex, familial status, and more in the sale, rental, and financing of dwellings, or in other housing-related transactions.

FF&E An acronym for furniture, fixtures, and equipment.

focus group A qualitative research method in which a group of people are asked questions about their opinions, attitudes, beliefs, and perceptions toward a particular topic (e.g., concept, service, advertisement, product, idea, and more).

formaldehyde An organic compound or chemical used by industry to manufacture building materials and many household products.

furniture, fixtures, and equipment (FF&E) See *FF&E*.

G

GenXers Generation X (also known as Gen X or gen-Xers) is the generation born after the baby boom, after 1964.

glaucoma A condition in which the optic nerve is damaged and leads to progressive, irreversible loss of vision.

global positioning system (GPS) A space-based global navigation satellite system that gives location and time information.

H

Habitat for Humanity housing Housing built through the nonprofit organization Habitat for Humanity. Houses are built in partnership with communities and families in need.

heating, ventilation, and air conditioning (HVAC) Refers to indoor environmental comfort. See *HVAC*.

high speech intelligibility High-level ability to hear in the presence of noise or distortions.

hot-desking See *hoteling*.

hoteling Also called free address, just-in-time, guesting, or hot-desk (hot-desking). It is an unassigned office approach—no personally assigned office, workstation, or desk. The employee calls ahead for a work area or desk and is assigned a work area or desk upon arrival.

Housing and Urban Development (HUD) HUD administers federal programs that deal with housing and urban renewal. One of its main functions is in the role of lending facilitator. Although it is not a lending institution, HUD helps people of low and mid-level income obtain loans to purchase housing.

Huntington's disease A progressive neurodegenerative genetic disorder affecting muscle coordination.

HVAC The acronym for heating, ventilation, and air conditioning. See *heating, ventilation, and air conditioning*.

I

iChat An instant messaging Apple® software application.

illumination Supplying light or being illuminated.

impairment Also referred to as limitation. A disability that may be physiological, psychological, cognitive or mental, sensory, or a combination of these and they may be permanent or temporary.

inclusive Including people of all kinds—age, sizes, abilities, and more.

inclusive design A place or product that is planned, designed and built, managed and used with all people in mind.

Individuals with Disabilities Education Act (IDEA) A federal law enacted in 1990 and reauthorized in 1997 that was designed to protect rights of students with disabilities to ensure that everyone receives a free public education.

indoor air quality (IAQ) The content or quality of indoor air that could affect the health of building occupants.

InformeDesign A research and communication tool for designers that summarizes research articles from a large variety of journals.

International Classification of Functioning, Disability, and Health (ICF) A classification of health and health-related domains related to body, individual, and societal perspectives.

interview Collecting data with a survey instrument that utilizes verbal questions.

iPhone An Apple® cell phone with high-resolution display, video calling, FaceTime, HD video recording, a camera, and more.

iPod An Apple® portable media player.

ischial tuberosity Bony area that bears the weight of the body while sitting.

K

keycard A plastic card with a magnetically coded strip that is scanned to operate a mechanism (e.g., hotel door, security entrance door), or one that stores a digital signature used to electronically access a control lock.

L

Landmarks Preservation Commission (LPC) An agency (within a city) that is responsible for identifying and designating a city's landmarks and buildings in the historic district.

Leadership in Energy and Environmental Design (LEED) A third-party certification program that is a nationally accepted benchmark for the design, construction, and operation of a green building.

lifespan design See *transgenerational design*.

limitation A word used in place of impairment.

M

major life activities Activities that are of central importance to most people's daily lives, such as walking, talking, seeing, hearing, breathing, caring for oneself, and so on.

McMansion A term used to describe a large house that is considered pretentious, tasteless, or badly designed for its neighborhood.

Millennials Also known as Generation Y (GenY). Birth dates range from 1981 to the present.

multifamily housing A building that contains multiple separate housing units.

multiple chemical sensitivity (MCS) An illness in which the individual becomes sensitive to numerous chemicals at low concentration levels that affects multiple organ systems.

multiple sclerosis An autoimmune disease that affects the brain and spinal cord (e.g., central nervous system).

musculoskeletal disorder (MSD) A disorder that affects muscles.

N

neurological disorders Diseases or disorders that affect the nervous system.

nonchlorinated pool A pool that uses a chemical-free, nonchlorine method of purifying the water.

no-VOC paint Paint that does not contain volatile organic compounds.

O

observation Watch or view in a casual or methodical manner.

occupational therapist A professional who helps people improve their ability to perform tasks in the living and working environment.

organic Develops naturally.

P

Parkinson's disease A degenerative disorder of the central nervous system that impairs motor skills, cognitive processes, and more.

participatory design An approach to design that strives to include all stakeholders (e.g., employees, managers, end users, customers, citizens) along with specialists and a design team.

photovoltaic Solar cells that convert sunlight into electric energy.

physiological impairment Physical limitations.

polyvinyl chloride (PVC) A chlorinated plastic that is widely used for a variety of products such as tubing, clothing, upholstery, flooring, and more.

population A number or group of people.

post-occupancy evaluation (POE) After a building is completed and occupied, a systematic method of assessing the performance of a building during a site visit.

prefabricated (prefab) house: *Prefab* is an abbreviation for *prefabricated*. The word *prefab* is often used to describe any type of home that is made from easy-to-assemble building parts that were manufactured off-site. Manufactured homes and modular homes are types of prefab housing. They are also known as factory-built, factory-made, pre-cut, panelized, manufactured, modular, mobile home, and more.

productivity A measure of output from a work completed.

programming phase The information-gathering phase of the design process.

psychological impairment A disability affecting the human mind.

proxemics The study of the cultural, behavioral, and sociological aspects of spatial distances between humans.

punch list A form where notations are made to record any errors or omissions during a walk-through (site inspection) near the completion of a project.

Q

quality lighting Light that produces an aesthetically pleasing environment and also provides comfort and safety.

quantity of light Measurable amount of light used within the space and includes both artificial and natural lighting for visual comfort and security.

R

Rehabilitation Act of 1973 A law that prohibits discrimination based on disability in programs conducted by Federal agencies.

research To study something through scholarly or scientific investigation or inquiry.

reasonable accommodations A modification or adjustment to the job or workplace that allows someone with a disability to apply for a job or perform essential tasks on the job.

restorative Something being restored, healed, given new strength.

reverberation Sound that echoes or bounces back.

role-playing A participant observation method of collecting data.

S

schematic (or concept) development phase The ideation phase of the design process where ideas for details, sections, elevations, and plans are sketched. It is also the phase where preliminary design decisions and documents are prepared.

sink The absorption of chemicals or energy into materials and later released back into the air.

sustainable design An environmentally responsible design that integrates energy-conscious and environmentally friendly elements, products, and materials into a construction or design project.

symbol identification Use of symbols to identify a direction, building, or area.

T

telecommunications device for the deaf (TDD) See *text telephone (TTY)*.

telecommunications relay services (TRS) A telephone service that uses operators called communications assistants to facilitate telephone calls between people with hearing or speech limitation or a person without the limitation.

TeleTYpewriter (TTY) See *text telephone (TTY)*.

text telephone (TTY) A telephone that uses text rather than voice to communicate over telephone lines. It may also be referred to as a TeleTYpewriter or Telecommunications Device for the Deaf (TDD).

toxins Substances that are produced by living cells or organisms; they are capable of causing illness when introduced into the body.

trackpad A touch pad on a laptop designed to work by allowing the user's finger to control the computer.

traditionalists Born in 1945 or before.

transgenerational Acting across multiple generations.

transgenerational design Making products and environments compatible for physical and sensory limitations that may limit major life activities.

typology (typologies or **types)** A system of groupings that are identified by specific attributes (characteristics) or similarity of use. For example, an art museum is a type of museum design or a department store is a type of retail design.

U

universal Related to the whole world; applying to everyone.

universal design The process of creating products (devices, environments, systems, and processes) that are usable by people with the widest possible range of abilities, operating within the widest possible range of situations (environments, conditions, and circumstances).

V

veiling reflection or **veiling glare** A reflection on a visual task into the viewer's eyes that obscures visibility by reducing contrast.

virtual office The office of the future that senses and responds to occupant's arrival or an office that is not found in one physical location but is virtual and accessed through the computer.

visitability The extent to which a house can be visited by a person with a disability, without barriers (e.g., stairs) to a bathroom and bedroom (or room to sleep in).

Voice Carry Over (VCO) Allows the person with a hearing limitation to use his or her own voice to speak directly to the called party but receive text responses.

VoiceOver Voice is used to control a computer or another device.

Video Relay Service (VRS) TRS-mediated call. See *telecommunications relay services (TRS)*.

volatile organic compounds (VOCs) Organic chemical compounds that vaporize when they enter the atmosphere.

W

wayfinding A process of navigating through unfamiliar territory.

References

CHAPTER 1

Accessible Journeys. (2011). *Air Carrier Access Act*. Retrieved on March 13, 2011, from http://www.disabilitytravel.com/airlines/air_carrier_act_details.htm

Americans with Disabilities Act (ADA). (2008a). *ADA best practices tool kit for state and local government: Chapter 1: ADA basics: Statute and regulations*. Retrieved on September 16, 2010, http://www.ada.gov/pcatoolkit/chap1toolkit.htm

Americans with Disabilities Act (ADA). (2008b). *Questions and answers*. Retrieved on September 16, 2010, from http://www.ada.gov/q&aeng02.htm

Americans with Disabilities Act (ADA). (2009). *The Americans with Disabilities Act (ADA) of 1990, as amended*. Retrieved on May 24, 2010, from http://www.ada.gov/pubs/adastatute08.htm

Americans with Disabilities Act (ADA). (2010). *Enforcing the ADA: A status report from the Department of Justice April-September 2009*. Retrieved on May 24, 2010, from http://www.ada.gov/aprsep09.htm#litigation

Americans with Disabilities Act Technical Assistance (ADATA). (2010a). *ADA document portal*. Retrieved on September 16, 2010, from http://www.adaportal.org/adadoc-General/ADAOverview.aspx#title4

Americans with Disabilities Act Technical Assistance (ADATA). (2010b). *New amendments to Titles II and III*. Retrieved on September 16, 2010, from http://www.adata.org/Static/TitlesIIandIIIAmends.aspx

Americans with Disabilities Act Technical Assistance (ADATA). (2010c). *What is a disability?* Retrieved on September 16, 2010, from http://www.adata.org/Static/Disability.aspx#1

Disabled in Action. (n/d). *Facts About Disability in the U.S. Population*. Retrieved on September 16, 2010, from http://www.disabledinaction.org/census_stats.html

Federal Communications Commission (FCC). (2010). *Telecommunications relay services: FCC consumer facts*. September 16, 2010, from http://www.fcc.gov/cgb/consumerfacts/trs.html

InformeDesign. (2003, November 1). "Issues of Disability and Building Access." Retrieved on September 18, 2010, from http://www.informedesign.org/Rs_detail.aspx?rsId=1484

Jobs Accommodation Network (JAN). (n/d). *About JAN*. Retrieved on September 17, 2010, from http://askjan.org/links/about.htm

Jones, L. (2010). "Accessible, universal, inclusive design: Have the horses reached the finish line?" In Martin, C. S. & Guerin, D. A., Eds. *The State of the Interior Design Profession*. New York: Fairchild Books.

Rhodes, M. A. (2010). *The ADA companion guide.* New York: Wiley.

U. S. Access Board. (2005). *Americans with disabilities act accessibility guidelines for buildings and facilities.* Retrieved on May 27, 2010, from http://www.access-board.gov/ada-aba/final.cfm

U. S. Access Board. (2009) *The Americans with Disabilities Act (ADA) of 1990, as amended.* Retrieved on May 27, 2010, from http://www.access-board.gov/about/laws/ADA.htm

U. S. Access Board. (2011). *Guide to the updated ADA Standards.* Retrieved on September 12, 2011, from http://www.access-board.gov/ada/guide.htm

U. S. Census Bureau. (2009). *Facts for features: Americans with Disabilities Act* (July 26). Retrieved on May 24, 2010, from http://www.census.gov/newsroom/releases/archives/facts_for_features_special_editions/cb09-ff13.html

U. S. Census Bureau. (2010). *Population profile of the United States: Disability.* Retrieved on September 16, 2010, from http://www.census.gov/population/www/pop-profile/disabil.html

U. S. Department of Justice (US-DOJ). (2005). *A guide to disability rights laws.* Retrieved on September 16, 2010, from http://www.ada.gov/cguide.htm

U. S. Department of Justice (US-DOJ). (2008). *Issues: Historically significant facilities.* September 18, 2010, from http://www.ada.gov/comprob.htm

U. S. Department of Justice (US-DOJ). (2010). *Enforcing the ADA: A status report from the Department of Justice April-September 2009.* Retrieved on June 8, 2010, from http://www.ada.gov/aprsep09.htm#litigation

U. S. Equal Employment Opportunity Commission (EEOCa). *The Americans with Disabilities Act Amendments Act of 2008.* Retrieved on September 16, 2010, from http://www.eeoc.gov/laws/statutes/adaaa_info.cfm

U. S. Equal Employment Opportunity Commission (EEOCb). *Title VII of the Civil Rights Act.* Retrieved on September 16, 2010, from http://www.eeoc.gov/laws/statutes/titlevii.cfm

U. S. Equal Employment Opportunity Commission (EEOCc). *Title I and V of the Americans with Disabilities Act of 1990 (ADA).* Retrieved on September 16, 2010, from http://www.eeoc.gov/laws/statutes/ada.cfm

U. S. Equal Employment Opportunity Commission (EEOC). (2009a). Notice of Proposed Rulemaking (NPRM). *Notice Concerning The Americans with Disabilities Act (ADA) Amendments Act of 2008.* Retrieved on September 16, 2010, from http://www.eeoc.gov/laws/statutes/adaaa_notice.cfm

U. S. Equal Employment Opportunity Commission (EEOC). (2009b). Question and answer on the NPRM. *Notice Concerning The Americans With Disabilities Act (ADA) Amendments Act of 2008.* Retrieved on September 16, 2010, from http://www.eeoc.gov/laws/statutes/adaaa_notice.cfm

U. S. Equal Employment Opportunity Commission (EEOC). (2009c). Summary of the NPRM changes. *Notice Concerning The Americans With Disabilities Act (ADA) Amendments Act of 2008.* Retrieved on September 16, 2010, from http://www.eeoc.gov/laws/statutes/adaaa_notice.cfm

World Health Organization. (2010). *International classification of functioning, disability, and health (ICF).* Retrieved on September 16, 2010, from http://www.who.int/classifications/icf/en/

CHAPTER 2

Adaptive Living. (n/d). *The ErgoChair for Little People.* Retrieved on October 4, 2010, from http://www.adaptiveliving.com/

Administration on Aging (AoA). (2009). *Projected future growth of the older population: By age 1900-2050—older population as a percentage of the total population.* Retrieved on June 11, 2010, from http://www.aoa.gov/AoARoot/Aging_Statistics/future_growth/future_growth.aspx

Center for Universal Design. (1997). *The principles of universal design, Version 2.0.* Raleigh, NC: North Carolina State University. Retrieved on August 18, 2010, from http://www.ncsu.edu/www/ncsu/design/sod5/cud/about_ud/udprinciples.htm

Center for Universal Design (CUD). (2008). *What is universal design: Principles of universal design.* North Carolina State University: The Center for Universal Design. Retrieved on June 17, 2010, from http://www.design.ncsu.edu/cud/about_ud/udprinciples.htm

Center for Universal Design (CUD). (2010). *About universal design.* North Carolina State University: The Center for Universal Design. Retrieved on June 9, 2010, from http://www.design.ncsu.edu/cud/about_ud/about_ud.htm

Coleman, R., Clarkson, J., Dong, Hua., & Cassim, J. (2007). *Design for inclusivity: A practical guide to accessible, innovative, and user-centred design.* Aldershot, Hampshire, England: Gower.

Commission for Architecture and the Built Environment (CABE). (n/d). *Inclusive design.* Retrieved on September 16, 2010, from http://www.cabe.org.uk/inclusion/inclusive-design

Commission for Architecture and the Built Environment (CABE). (2008). *The principles of inclusive design.* Retrieved on September 16, 2010, from http://www.cabe.org.uk/publications/the-principles-of-inclusive-design

Design Council. (n/d). *Inclusive design education resource.* Retrieved on September 19, 2010, from http://www.designcouncil.info/inclusivedesignresource/

Design for All Foundation. (n/d). *Design for all, What is it?* Retrieved on September 20, 2010, from http://www.designforall.org/en/dfa/dfa.php

Digital Accessibility Team. (2009). *Inclusive Design.* Retrieved on September 21, 2010, from http://www.tiresias.org/research/guidelines/inclusive.htm

EDeAN. (2007). *European Design for All e-Accessibility Network.* Retrieved on September 20, 2010, from http://www.edean.org/central.aspx?sId=64I160I327I323I259530&lanID=1&resID=1&assID=99&inpID=3&disID=1&famID=3&skinID=3

EDeAN. (2010). *DfA@eInclusion: Description.* Retrieved on September 20, 2010, from http://www.dfaei.org/description.html

Eden Alternative®. (2009a). *Eden Alternative®: Our 10 principles.* Retrieved on June 17, 2010, from http://www.edenalt.org/our-10-principles

Eden Alternative®. (2009b). *Our mission, vision, values.* Retrieved on March 20, 2011, from http://www.edenalt.org/mission-vision-values

English Partnership. (2008a). *About us.* Retrieved on March 21, 2011, from http://collections.europarchive.org/tna/20100911035042/http://englishpartnerships.co.uk/about.htm

English Partnership. (2008b). *Inclusive design.* Retrieved on September 19, 2010, from http://www.englishpartnerships.co.uk/inclusivedesign.htm

English Partnership. (2010). *English Partnership.* Retrieved on March 21, 2011, from http://www.homesandcommunities.co.uk/english-partnerships.htm

Green House (n/d). *The green house project.* Retrieved on June 17, 2010, from http://www.ncbcapitalimpact.org/default.aspx?id=146

Inclusive Design and Environments Center (IDEA). (2009). *What is universal design.* Retrieved on September 19, 2010, from http://www.udeworld.com/

Inclusive Design Toolkit. (2010). *Definition of inclusive design.* Retrieved on September 19, 2010, from http://www.inclusivedesigntoolkit.com/betterdesign/whatis/whatis3.html

Institute for Human Centered Design (IHCD). (2010). *Universal design: What is universal design?* Retrieved on June 9, 2010, from http://adaptenv.org/index.php?option=Content&Itemid=3

Leibrock, C. A. & Harris, D. D. (2011). *Design details for health: Making the most of interior design's healing potential, (2nd Ed.).* New York: Wiley.

Levine, D. (2003). *Universal design New York 2.* Center for Inclusive Design & Environmental Access, University at Buffalo, The State University of New York. Retrieved on July 28, 2010, from www.nyc.gov/html/ddc/downloads/pdf/udny/udny2.pdf

Little People of America (LPA). (n/d). *Welcome.* Retrieved on October 4, 2010, from http://www.lpaonline.org

MetLife Mature Market Institute (2009). *Mature market news: New housing trends report.* Retrieved on June 9, 2010, from http://www.metlife.com/about/press-room/us-press-releases/2009/index.html?SCOPE=Metlife&MSHiC=65001&L=10&W=HOUSING%20NEW%20REPORT%20TRENDS%20&Pre=%3CFONT%20STYLE%3D%22background%3A%23ffff00%22%3E&Post=%3C/FONT%3E&compID=12912

Myerson, J. (2007). In Coleman, R., Clarkson, J., Dong, Hua., & Cassim, J., eds. *Design for inclusivity: A practical guide to accessible, innovative, and user-centred design.* Aldershot, Hampshire, England: Gower.

National Association of Home Builders (NAHB). (2010). *Mature-market home buyers look beyond buildings, desire services.* Retrieved on June 15, 2010, from http://www.nahb.org/news_details. aspx?newsID=10259

National Association of Home Builders (NAHB). (2010). *Where are builders building and what do buyers want?* Retrieved on June 15, 2010, from http://www.nahb.org/generic.aspx?sectionID=8 26&genericContentID=123833

National Center on Accessibility (NCA. (2003). *An Eden Alternative®: A Life Worth Living.* Retrieved on June 17, 2010, from http://www.indiana. edu/~nca/ncpad/eden.shtml

Null, R. L. & Cherry, K. F. (1996). *Universal design: Creative solutions for ADA compliance.* Belmont, CA: Professional Publications.

Nussbaumer, L. L. (2009). *Evidence-based design for interior designers.* New York: Fairchild.

OXO International (n/d). *Universal design.* Retrieved on August 23, 2010, from http:// www.oxo.com/UniversalDesign.aspx

Pirkl, J. J. (1994). *Transgenerational design: Products for an aging population.* New York: Van Nostrand Reinhold.

Rains, S. (2009). *What is universal or inclusive design?* Retrieved on September 19, 2010, from http:// www.changemakers.com/en-us/node/52208

Reed Construction Data (RCD). (2007). *Universal design ideas for style, comfort, and safety.* Kingston, MA: RSMeans.

Rhoads, M. A. (2010). *The ADA companion guide.* New York: Wiley.

Salmi, P. (2007). "Wayfinding design: Hidden barriers to universal access." *Implications 5(8).* Retrieved on February 5, 2008, from www. informedesign.umn.edu

Sitmatic. (n/d). *Custom fit measuring.* Retrieved on July 22, 2010, from http://sitmatic.com/ Administrivia.html

The Little Office (2006). *Product information.* Retrieved on October 4, 2010, from http:// www.thelittleoffice.com/products.htm

U.S. Access Board (2005). *Americans with disabilities act accessibility guidelines for buildings and facilities.* Retrieved on May 27, 2010, from http://www. access-board.gov/ada-aba/final.cfm

Vanderheiden, G. C. (1996). *Universal design: What it is and what it isn't.* Madison, WI: University of Wisconsin-Madison, Trace Research and Development Center. Retrieved on September 20, 2010, from http://trace.wisc.edu/docs/ whats_ud/whats_ud.htm

Vanderheiden, G. C. (2009). "Accessible and usable design of information and communication technologies." In Stephanidis, C., Ed., *The Universal Access Handbook.* Boca Raton, FL: Taylor & Francis.

Waller, S. & Clarkson, P. J. (2009). "Tools for inclusive design." In Stephanidis, C., Ed., *The Universal Access Handbook.* Boca Raton, FL: Taylor & Francis.

CHAPTER 3

Commission for Architecture and the Built Environment (CABE). (2008). "The principles of inclusive design." Retrieved on September 16, 2010, from http://www.cabe.org.uk/publications/the-principles-of-inclusive-design

Computer Professionals for Social Responsibility (CPSR). (n/d). "Participatory design." Retrieved on June 19, 2010, from http://cpsr.org/issues/pd/

Guerin, D., & Dohr, J. (2005). Research 101—Part III: Research Methods. *A research tutorial by InformeDesign.* Retrieved on November 23, 2007, from http://informedesign.umn.edu/Page.aspx?cId=182

InformeDesign. (2005, December 28). "Outdoor Accessibility Preferences of Assisted Living Residents." Retrieved on June 19, 2010, from http://www.informedesign.umn.edu/Rs_detail.aspx?rsId=2247

InformeDesign. (2007, March 17). "Nursing Staff Involvement in Design." Retrieved on June 19, 2010, from http://www.informedesign.umn.edu/Rs_detail.aspx?rsId=3276

InformeDesign. (2008, October 8). "Confusing Images Made Clear for Colorblind Individuals." Retrieved on June 19, 2010, from http://www.informedesign.umn.edu/Rs_detail.aspx?rsId=3153

InformeDesign. (2009, April 15). "Supportive Classrooms for Children with Autism." Retrieved on June 21, 2010, from http://www.informedesign.umn.edu/Rs_detail.aspx?rsId=3296

InformeDesign. (2010, April 5). "Neighborhood Open Space Impacts Older Adults' Quality of Life." Retrieved on June 21, 2010, from http://www.informedesign.umn.edu/Rs_detail.aspx?rsId=3153

Leedy, P. D. & Ormrod, J. E. (2005). *Practical research: Planning and design, (9th Ed.).* Upper Saddle River, NJ: Pearson Prentice Hall.

Null, R. L. & Cherry, K. F. (1996). *Universal design: Creative solutions for ADA compliance.* Belmont, CA: Professional Publications.

Nussbaumer, L. L. (2009). *Evidence-based design for interior designers.* New York: Fairchild Books.

Pile, J. F. (2003). *Interior Design* (3rd ed.). Upper Saddle River, NJ: Prentice Hall.

Piotrowski, C. M. (2002). *Professional practice for interior designers,* (3rd ed.). New York: Wiley.

Rayfield, J. K. (1994). *The office interior design guide: An introduction for facilities managers and designers.* New York: Wiley.

Wang, D. (2004). "Diagramming research methods." *Journal of Interior Design, 33*(1), 33–43.

CHAPTER 4

Apple, Inc. (2010a). *Accessibility comes standard.* Retrieved on July 1, 2010, from http://www.apple.com/macosx/accessibility/

Apple, Inc. (2010b). *iPhone.* Retrieved on July 1, 2010, from http://www.apple.com/iphone/features/accessibility.html

Apple, Inc. (2010c). *Literacy and Learning.* Retrieved on July 1, 2010, from http://www.apple.com/accessibility/macosx/literacylearning.html

Apple, Inc. (2010d). *Physical and motor skills.* Retrieved on July 1, 2010, from http://www.apple.com/accessibility/macosx/physical.html

Apple, Inc. (2010e). *Vision.* Retrieved on July 1, 2010, from http://www.apple.com/accessibility/macosx/vision.html

Bellingar, T. A., Beyer, P., & Wilkerson, L. (2009). "The research behind Zody." *Haworth Ergonomics White Paper.* Retrieved on July 3, 2010, from Haworth.com

Delta (2010a). *Delta single hole electronic lavatory faucet.* Retrieved on October 15, 2010, from http://www.deltafaucet.com/bath/details/590-LGHGMHDF.html

Delta (2010b). *Pilar® pull-down with touch20™ technology.* Retrieved on June 30, 2010, from http://www.deltafaucet.com/newproducts/980T-DST.html?room=&filter=

Garmin. (2010). Nüvi® 1390T https://buy.garmin.com/shop/shop.do?cID=134&pID=32700

InformeDesign. (2006, April 12). "Designing Usable Products for Everyone." http://www.informedesign.umn.edu/Rs_detail.aspx?rsId=2380

InformeDesign (2007, April 30). "How Alternative Keyboards Affect Arm Position." Retrieved on July 2, 2010, from http://www.informedesign.umn.edu/Rs_detail.aspx?rsId=2758

InformeDesign. (2010, February 11). "Understanding Seated Reaching Abilities." Retrieved from http://www.informedesign.umn.edu/Rs_detail.aspx?rsId=3388

Merriam-Webster Dictionary. (2010). "Ischial tuberosity." Retrieved on June 24, 2010, from http://www.merriam-webster.com/medical/ischial%20tuberosity

Motorola, Inc. (2010). *DROID by Motorola.* Retrieved on July 2, 2010, from http://www.motorola.com/Consumers/US-EN/Consumer-Product-and-Services/Mobile-Phones/ci.Motorola-DROID-US-EN.vertical

Microsoft Corporation. (2010). *Accessibility.* Retrieved on July 2, 2010, from http://www.microsoft.com/enable/guides/vision.aspx

Nussbaumer, L. L. (2009). *Evidence-based design for interior designers.* New York: Fairchild Books.

Occupational Safety & Health Administration (OSHA) (n/d). *Computer workstations: Good work positions.* Retrieved on March 5, 2011 from http://www.osha.gov/SLTC/etools/computerworkstations/positions.html

Risedale. (2010). Retrieved on June 30, 2010, from http://www.risedalechair.com/

Stephanidis, C. (2009). "Universal access and design for all in the evolving information society." In Stephanidis, C. (Ed.). *The Universal Access Handbook*. Boca Raton, FL: Taylor & Francis.

Steelcase, Inc. (2010). Retrieved on July 3, 2010, from http://store.steelcase.com/go/products/detail/ATP2454/

Target. (2010). *Clear Rx*. Retrieved on June 30, 2010, from http://sites.target.com/site/en/health/page.jsp;jsessionid=XLBPM0FMLWYPJLARAAV5YAQ?contentId=PRD03-003977&ref=sc_iw_r_l_1Clear

TOTO USA. (2010, October 4). *Q&A: Investing in the future of architecture*. Retrieved on October 15, 2010, from http://www.totousa.com/Press/PressReleases/FutureOfArchitecture.aspx

Vanderheiden, G. C. (2008). "Ubiquitous accessibility, common technology core, and micro assistive technology: Commentary on 'computers and people with disabilities.'" *ACM Transactions on Accessible Computing. 1*(2), pg. 10.1-10.7.

Vanderheiden, G. C. (2009). "Accessible and usable design of information and communication technologies." In Stephanidis, C. (Ed.). *The Universal Access Handbook*. Boca Raton, FL: Taylor & Francis.

CHAPTER 5

About.com. (2010). *Architecture: What is a prefab house?* Retrieved on September 6, 2010, from http://architecture.about.com/od/housetypes/g/prefab.htm

Association for the Advancement of Retired Persons (AARP). (2010a). *Home and community glossary*. Retrieved on September 1, 2010, from http://www.aarp.org/relationships/caregiving/info-12-2009/women_glossary_home_community_terms.html

Association for the Advancement of Retired Persons (AARP). (2010b). *2009 New York livable communities surveys of AARP members 50+: Fact sheets, annotations, and methodology*. Retrieved on September 2, 2010, from http://www.aarp.org/home-garden/livable-communities/info-12-2009/ny_livcom_09.html

American Occupational Therapy Association, Inc. (AOTA). (2007). *Modifying your home for independence*. Retrieved on August 29, 2010, from http://www.aota.org/Consumers/consumers/Adults/HomeMods/35182.aspx

American Society of Interior Designers (ASID). (2010). *Accessible bathroom case study*. Retrieved on August 30, 2010, from http://www.asid.org/designknowledge/aa/accessible/Accessible+Bathroom.htm

Center for Universal Design (CUD). (2006). *Universal design in housing*. Retrieved on August 30, 2010, from http://www.ncsu.edu/www/ncsu/design/sod5/cud/pubs_p/phousing.htm

Cohousing. (2011). *What are the 6 Defining Characteristics of Cohousing?* Retrieved on March 23, 2011, from http://www.cohousing.org/six_characteristics

Concrete Change. (2008). *Visitability.* Retrieved on August 30, 2010, from http://www.concretechange.org/

The Eye Digest. (2009). *Eye changes with age.* Retrieved on October 7, 2010, from http://www.agingeye.net/visionbasics/theagingeye.php

FabCab. (2011). *FabCab provides homes for better living.* Retrieved on June 10, 2011, from http://fabcab.com/products/fabcab-kit/

Habitat for Humanity. (2010). *What are Habitat houses like?* Retrieved on September 6, 2010, from http://www.habitat.org/how/whatlike.aspx

Habitat for Humanity. (2011). *How to apply for a habitat for humanity house.* Retrieved June 10, 2011, from http://www.habitat.org/getinv/apply.aspx

Hadjiyanni, T. (2003, January). "Culturally sensitive housing." *Implications, 3*(1). Retrieved on October 9, 2010, from http://www.informedesign.org/NewsletterArchive.aspx

Improve Your Vision.com. (2009). *Senior eyes.* Retrieved on October 7, 2010, from http://www.improveyourvision.com/understanding-vision/senior-eyes.html

InformeDesign. (2006, July 17). *Impact of Critical Regionalism.* Retrieved on July 12, 2010, from http://www.informedesign.umn.edu/Rs_detail.aspx?rsId=1502

InformeDesign. (2006, June 22). *Japanese Research on Environments and Aging.* Retrieved on July 12, 2010 from http://www.informedesign.umn.edu/Rs_detail.aspx?rsId=2459

InformeDesign. (2008, June 25). *Aging in Place Housing Options.* http://www.informedesign.umn.edu/Rs_detail.aspx?rsId=3074

InformeDesign. (2008, November 5). *Affordable Accessible Homes in Rural Areas.* Retrieved on July 12, 2010, from http://www.informedesign.umn.edu/Rs_detail.aspx?rsId=3178

InformeDesign. (2009, August 4). *Preferred Housing among Older Adults in Thailand.* Retrieved on July 12, 2010 from http://www.informedesign.umn.edu/Rs_detail.aspx?rsId=3336

Levine, D. Ed. (2003). *Universal design New York 2.* Center for Inclusive Design and Environmental Access (IDEA). Buffalo, New York: University at Buffalo, The State University of New York.

Leibrock, C. A. (2000). *Design details for health.* New York: John Wiley & Sons.

Mack, S. (2006, March/April). "Universal design: don't buy, build, or remodel without it." Ultimate Home Design, 2, 50-53.

Mansueto Ventures. (2010). *FabCab builds universal design prefabs for "aging in place."* Retrieved on September 6, 2010, from http://www.fastcodesign.com/1662127/fabcab-builds-universal-design-prefabs-for-aging-in-place

Mullick, A. (2010). "Universal bathrooms." In Preiser, W. F. E. & Smith, K. H., Eds, *Universal Design Handbook* (2nd Ed.). New York: McGraw Hill.

National Eye Institute (2010a). *Facts about age-related macular degeneration*. Retrieved on October 7, 2010, from http://www.nei.nih.gov/health/maculardegen/armd_facts.asp#1a

National Eye Institute (2010a). *Facts about cataracts*. Retrieved on October 7, 2010, from http://www.nei.nih.gov/health/cataract/cataract_facts.asp

National Eye Institute (2010c). *Facts about glaucoma*. Retrieved on October 7, 2010, from http://www.nei.nih.gov/health/glaucoma/glaucoma_facts.asp#1a

Peachy Green. (2011). *Downsizing homes is a big idea*. Retrieved on March 23, 2011, from http://www.peachygreen.com/going-green/downsizing-homes-is-a-big-idea

Preiser, W. F. E. & Smith, K. H., Eds. (2010). *Universal Design Handbook, 2nd Ed*. New York: McGraw Hill.

Preservation Iowa. (2010). *Step by step*. Retrieved on July 31, 2010, from http://preservationiowa.org/programs/awardsItem.php?id=137&year=2010

Rosenfeld, J. P. & Chapman, W. (2008). *Home design in an aging world*. New York: Fairchild Books.

Sandler, L. A. (2009). *Universal design & green home survey checklist*. Iowa City, Iowa: University of Iowa Clinical Law Programs. Online at http://www.homemods.org/resources/PDF/UDGreenHomeChecklist061609-FINAL.pdf

Senior Resource. (2010). *Housing choices*. Retrieved on September 1, 2010, from http://www.seniorresource.com/house.htm#apts

Senior-site. (n/d). *Congregate housing for senior citizens*. Retrieved on September 1, 2010, from http://seniors-site.com/housingm/congrega.html

Susanka, S. (2001). *The Not So Big House*. Newtown, CT: Tauton Press.

U.S. Department of Housing and Urban Development (HUD). (2006). *Disability rights in housing*. Retrieved on August 31, 2010, from http://www.hud.gov/offices/fheo/disabilities/inhousing.cfm

Universal Design Products. (UD Products). (n/d). *Accessible household: Automatic coatlift*. Retrieved on September 2, 2010, from http://universal-design-products.com/automatic_coat_lift.htm

Utah State University (USU). (2010). *Utah House*. Retrieved on September 2, 2010, from http://theutahhouse.org/htm/house

CHAPTER 6

American Occupational Therapy Association, Inc. (AOTA). (2010). "About occupational therapy." Retrieved on August 29, 2010, from http://www.aota.org/Consumers.aspx

Beane, G. (2010, March 4). "Accessibilitiy watch: Navigating New York's building code." *Metropolis.Mag.* Retrieved on September 27, 2010, from http://www.metropolismag.com/pov/20100304/accessibility-watch-navigating-new-yorks-building-code

Edwards, L. & Torcellini, P. (2002). *A literature review of the effects of natural light on building occupants.* Golden, CO: Natural Renewable Energy Laboratory.

Havemeyer III, Horace. (2009, October 13). "Preservation vs. accessibility." *MetropolisMag.com.* Retrieved on July 31, 2010, from http://www.metropolismag.com/pov/20091013/preservation-vs-accessibility#more-10508

InformeDesign. (2009, June 9). "PVC Emissions Higher in Completed Buildings." Retrieved on July 28, 2010, from http://www.informedesign.org/Rs_detail.aspx?rsId=3320

InformeDesign. (2010, July 7a). "Comparing Environmental Research in Office and Health Care Environments." Retrieved on July 22, 2010, from ttp://www.informedesign.org/Rs_detail.aspx?rsId=3445

InformeDesign. (2010, July 7b). "VOC Levels in Retail Settings." Retrieved on July 30, 2010, from http://www.informedesign.org/Rs_detail.aspx?rsId=3432

Institute of Human Centered Design. (2010). *Wesleyan University Performing Arts Center.* Retrieved on September 28, 2010, from http://www.dev.ihcdstore.org/?q=node/146

Levine, D. (2003). *Universal design New York2.* Center for Inclusive Design & Environmental Access, University at Buffalo, The State University of New York. Retrieved on July 28, 2010, from www.nyc.gov/html/ddc/downloads/pdf/udny/udny2.pdf

National Lighting Bureau (NLB). (2010). *Case history: Federal building and courthouse save taxpayers money.* Retrieved on July 21, 2010, from http://www.nlb.org/index.cfm?cdid=10374

Noise Reduction Coefficients (NCRs). (1998). *Sound absorption.* Norlite Corporation. Retrieved on November 12, 2007, from www.norliteagg.com/maps/sound.htm#nrc

Nussbaumer, L. L. (2009a). *Evidence-based design for interior designers.* New York: Fairchild Books.

Nussbaumer, L. (2009b). "The role of textiles in indoor environmental pollution: Problems and solutions." In Rowe, T., ed. *Interior Textiles: Design and Development.* Oxford: Woodhead Publishing Limited.

Piotrowski, C. (2007). *Professional practice for interior designers.* New York: Wiley.

Texas Registered Accessibility Specialists Association (TRASA). (2010). *Mission statement.* Retrieved on September 29, 2010, from http://www.trasatexas.com/

U. S. Environmental Protection Agency. (2010). "Three basic strategies." *The Inside Story: A Guide to Indoor Air Quality.* Retrieved on September 27, 2010, from http://www.epa.gov/iaq/pubs/insidest.html#Improve5

Winchip, S. (2005). *Designing a quality lighting environment.* New York: Fairchild Books.

Winchip, S. (2011). *Fundamentals of lighting, (2ᵈ Ed).* New York: Fairchild Books.

CHAPTER 7

Advameg, Inc. (2010). *Facility management.* Retrieved on September 24, 2010, from http://www.referenceforbusiness.com/encyclopedia/Ent-Fac/Facility-Management.html

America.gov. (2007). *Religion in the workplace is diversity issue for U.S. companies.* Retrieved on July 15, 2010, from http://www.america.gov/st/peopleplace-english/2007/November/20071128173019xlrennef0.1781427.html

CBS Interactive, Inc. (2010). *BNET Business Dictionary.* Retrieved on July 7, 2010, from http://dictionary.bnet.com/definition/Virtual+Office.html?tag=col1;rbDictionary

Center for Disease Control and Prevention (CDC). (2000b). *Ergonomic checklist.* Retrieved on November 2, 2007, from www.cdc.gov/od/ohs/Ergonomics/compergo.htm

Denslow, L. (2006). *World wise: What to know before you go.* New York: Fairchild Books.

Herman Miller. (2006, July 12). *Worker types, worker wants, worker comfort.* Research Summaries: People. http://www.hermanmiller.com/DotCom/jsp/research/researchResults.jsp?navId=29&topicId=2

Herman Miller. (2007). *It's all about me: The benefits of personal control at work.* Research Summaries: People. http://www.hermanmiller.com/DotCom/jsp/research/researchResults.jsp?navId=29&topicId=2

Herman Miller. (2008). *Home sweet home: Comfort in the workplace.* Research Summaries: People. http://www.hermanmiller.com/DotCom/jsp/research/researchResults.jsp?navId=29&topicId=2

Herman Miller. (2010a). *Culture and work styles in the BRIC countries.* Research Summaries: People. http://www.hermanmiller.com/DotCom/jsp/research/researchResults.jsp?navId=29&topicId=2&size=20

Herman Miller. (2010b). *Generations at work.* Research Summaries: Efficiencies. Retrieved on July 7, 2010, from http://www.hermanmiller.com/DotCom/jsp/research/researchResults.jsp?navId=29&topicId=8

InformeDesign. (2010, August 18). "Personal Lighting Control in a Daylit Office." Retrieved on October 1, 2010, from http://www.informedesign.org/Rs_detail.aspx?rsId=3455

InformeDesign. (2010, September 15). "Generational Differences in Response to an Office Redesign." Retrieved on October 1, 2010, from http://www.informedesign.org/Rs_detail.aspx?rsId=3467

InformeDesign. (2009, September 28). "Private Office Environment Preferences Vary Between Genders." Retrieved on XX, from http://www.informedesign.umn.edu/Rs_detail.aspx?rsId=3359

InformeDesign. (2004, May 28). "Lighting Preferences in the Office Environment." Retrieved on July 20, 2010, from http://www.informedesign.org/Rs_detail.aspx?rsId=1672

InformeDesign. (2003, June 4). "Computers are Causing Health Problems." Retrieved on July 20, 2010, from http://www.informedesign.org/Rs_detail.aspx?rsId=1335

International Facility Management Association (IFMA). (n/d). *Definition of facility management.* Retrieved on July 22, 2010, from http://www.ifma.org/what_is_fm/index.cfm

Lancaster, L. & Stillman, D. (2002). *When Generations Collide: who they are, why they clash, how to solve the generational puzzle at work.* New York: HarperCollins.

Levitch, G. (2003). *BlueSpace: The office of the future has a mind of its own.* Steelcase, Inc. Retrieved on July 20, 2010 from www.oneworkplace.com/pdfs/whitepapers/Bluespace.pdf

McLennan, K. J. (2007). *The virtual world of work: How to gain competitive advantage through the virtual workplace.* Charlotte, NC: Information Age Publishing.

Nussbaumer, L. L. (2009). *Evidence-based design for interior designers.* New York: Fairchild Books.

Piotrowski, C. M., & Rogers, E. A. (2007). *Designing commercial interiors* (2nd ed.). New York: Wiley.

Sitmatic. (n/d). *Custom fit measuring.* Retrieved on July 22, 2010, from http://sitmatic.com/Administrivia.html

Steelcase. (2010, May). "Benching: An idea whose time has come…again." *360 White Papers.* Retrieved on February 8, 2010, from http://www.steelcase.com/en/resources/research/360%20white%20papers/pages/main.aspx

CHAPTER 8

Armstrong World Industries (AWI). (2010). *Education – classroom.* Retrieved on October 4, 2010, from http://www.armstrong.com/commceilingsna/article51225.html

Assisted Living Federation of America (ALFA) (2009). "Senior living options." Retrieved August 11, 2010, from http://www.alfa.org/alfa/Assisted_Living_Information.asp?SnID=1161891151

Beane, G. (2010, March 4). "Accessibility watch: Navigating New York's building code." *MetropolisMag.com.* Retrieved on July 28, 2010, from http://www.metropolismag.com/pov/20100304/accessibility-watch-navigating-new-yorks-building-code

Brawley, E. C. (2002). "Therapeutic gardens for individuals with Alzheimer's disease." *Alzheimer's Care Quarterly, 3*(1), p. 7–11.

Calkins, M. P. (2009). "Evidence-based long term care design." *NeuroRehabilitation, 25*, p. 145–154. Retrieved from DOI 10.3233/NRE-2009-0512

Cama, R. (2006). "The opportunity is now." In Marberry, S. O. (Ed.), *Improving Healthcare with Better Building Design*. Chicago, IL: Health Administration Press.

Easter Seals. (n/d). "Facility design." Retrieved on August 18, 2010, from http://www.easterseals.com/site/PageServer?pagename=ntl_cdc_provider_facility

Flegal, K. M., Carroll, M. D. Ogden, C. L., & Curtin, L. R. (2010, January 13). "Prevalence and trends in obesity among US Adults, 1999–2008." JAMA. 2010;303(3):235-241. Published online: http://jama.am–assn.org/cgi/content/full/303/3/235?ijkey=ijKHq6YbJn3Oo&keytype=ref&siteid=amajnls

Hill-Rom® (2010a). Hill-Rom® architectural products. Retrieved on August 4, 2010, from http://www.hill-rom.com/usa/AP_Home.htm

Hill-Rom®. (2010b). Hill-Rom® Art of Care® Manual Bariatric Recliner. Retrieved on August 4, 2010 from http://www.hill-rom.com/usa/Furn_Bariatric_Recliner.htm

Eakens, K. (2009, October 2). "Round rock plans for future park needs: Play for all abilities park." *Impact Newspaper*. Retrieved on February 10, 2010, from http://impactnews.com/round-rock-pflugerville/146-news/5756-round-rock-plans-for-future-parks-needs

InformeDesign. (2007, July 6). "Evaluating nursing home environments." Retrieved on August 5, 2010, from http://www.informedesign.org/Rs_detail.aspx?rsId=2622

InformeDesign. (2007, November 3). "Assessing Classroom Indoor Air Quality." Retrieved on October 1, 2010, from http://www.informedesign.org/Rs_detail.aspx?rsId=2891

InformeDesign. (2009, January 8). "Considering Single-Patient Rooms in Hospitals." Retrieved on August 4, 2010, from http://www.informedesign.org/Rs_detail.aspx?rsId=3207

InformeDesign. (2009, April 15). "Supportive Classrooms for Children with Autism." Retrieved on July 12, 2010, from http://www.informedesign.umn.edu/Rs_detail.aspx?rsId=3296

InformeDesign. (2010, March 31). "Behavioral Interventions for Improving School Ventilation Performance." Retrieved on July 12, 2010, from http://www.informedesign.umn.edu/Rs_detail.aspx?rsId=3411

InformeDesign. (2010, June 18). "Children's Use of Different Playground Features." Retrieved on July 12, 2010, from http://www.informedesign.umn.edu/Rs_detail.aspx?rsId=3439

Joines, S. (2009). "Enhancing quality of life through universal design." *NeuroRehabilitation, 25*, p. 155-167.

Kane, R. A. (2001). "Long-term care and a good quality of life: Bringing them closer together." *The Gerontologist 41*(3),293–304.

KI. (2010). "Arissa." Retrieved on August 6, 2010, from http://www.ki.com/video/Arissa_shapes_sizes.mov

Kliment, S. A. (Ed.). (2004). *Building type basics for senior living.* New York: Wiley.

Nussbaumer, L. L. (2009). *Evidence-based design for interior designers.* New York: Fairchild Books.

Medical-Look. (2010). "Neurological disorders." Retrieved on August 7, 2010, from http://www.medical-look.com/Neurological_disorders/

Medical News. (2010). "One billion battling with neurological disorders." Retrieved on August 7, 2010, from http://www.news-medical.net/news/2007/03/01/22314.aspx

Merriam-Webster, Inc. (2011). Bariatric. In *Merriam-Webster's Collegiate Dictionary.* Retrieved on June 13, 2011, from http://www.merriam-webster.com/dictionary/bariatric

Nussbaumer, L. L. & Rowland, L. (2007). "Transforming nursing homes into…homes?" *Journal of Family and Consumer Sciences, 99*(4), 15-20.

Pacer. (2010). "ADA Q & A: Child care providers." Retrieved on August 18, 2010, from http://www.pacer.org/publications/adaqa/childcare.asp

Pedersen, M. C. (2009, September 16). "Green Rx." *Metropolis.Mag.* Retrieved on August 18, 2010, from http://www.metropolismag.com/story/20090916/green-rx

Perkins, B. & Bordwell, R. (2010). *Building type basics for elementary and secondary schools.* Hoboken, NJ: Wiley.

Piotrowski, C. M., & Rogers, E. A. (2007). *Designing commercial interiors* (2nd ed.). New York: Wiley.

Salter, C. (2002, January 31). "(Not) the same old story." *Fast Company.* Retrieved on August 11, 2010, from http://www.fastcompany.com/magazine/55/newwisdom.html

Stoecklin, V. L. & White, R. (2010). *Designing quality child care facilities.* Retrieved on August 18, 2010, from http://www.whitehutchinson.com/children/articles/designing1.shtml

Thomas, W. H. (1996). *Life worth living: How someone you love can still enjoy life in a nursing home.* Acton, MA: VanderWyk and Burnham.

Thomas, W. H. (2009). *The Eden Alternative®.* Retrieved August 11, 2010, from http://www.edenalt.com

Tisch, C. (2010, March). "Cooper University Hospital." *Interiors & Sources, 26*(2), p. 30–32

USC Architecture (2008, October 14). "The academic work of Victor Regnier, FAIA." Retrieved on August 11, 2010, from http://www.youtube.com/watch?v=OES_ribqW94&feature=channel

Wiens, J. (2009, March). "Design collaborative: Caregiver relief." *Interiors & Sources, 16*(2), p. 22–23

Wiens, J. (2010, April). "Design collaborative: Seating for all." *Interiors and Sources.* Retrieved on August 5, 2010, from http://www.interiorsandsources. com/ArticleDetails/tabid/3339/ ArticleID/9553/Default.aspx

CHAPTER 9

Americans with Disabilities Act (ADA). (2008). *Questions and answers.* Retrieved on June 15, 2011, from http://www.ada.gov/q&aeng02.htm

Crowell, C. (2009, July 13). *Trendlines: ADA/universal design.* Retrieved on July 28, 2010, from http:// www.hotelworldnetwork.com/overall-design/ trendlines-adauniversal-design

InformeDesign (2005, December 7). "Satisfying Environments for Shoppers." Retrieved on July 12, 2010, from http://www.informedesign.umn. edu/Rs_detail.aspx?rsId=2220

InformeDesign. (2009, December 18). "Benefits of Sustainable Hotels." Retrieved on July 28, 2010, from http://www.informedesign.org/Rs_detail. aspx?rsId=3363

Jones, L. M. & Allen, P. S. (2009). *Beginnings of interior environments, (10th Ed.).* Upper Saddle River, NJ: Pearson Prentice Hall.

Levine, D. (2003) *Universal design New York2.* Center for Inclusive Design & Environmental Access, University at Buffalo, The State University of New York. Retrieved on July 28, 2010, from www.nyc.gov/html/ddc/downloads/pdf/udny/ udny2.pdf

Pedersen, M. C. (2005, September 19). "The friendlier skies." *Metropolis Magazine online.* Retrieved on August 11, 2010, from http:// www.metropolismag.com/story/20050919/the- friendlier-skies

Regitz, S. (2009, September). "First, do no harm." *Interiors & Sources, 16*(7), p. 42.

Rygge Sivile Lufthavn (RSL). (2008). "Moss Airport Rygge: About Rygge-Universal Design." Retrieved on August 13, 2010, from http:// www.en.ryg.no/kat/000038.asp

Stoessel, E. (2009, August 18). "Living lab an example of universal design." Retrieved on August 2, 2010, from http://lhonline.com/ design/rossetti_udll_0818/index.html

St. Julien. (n/d). *Environmental commitment.* Retrieved on August 2, 2010, from http://www.stjulien. com/environmental-commitment

Sun Tran. (n/d). *Accessibility.* Retrieved on June 16, 2011, from http://www.suntran.com/ accessibility.php

Szenasy, S. S. (2009, February). "Out of reach? An accessible world may be just around the corner—if we're willing to speak up." *Metropolis Architecture + Design, 28*(7), p. 24.

CHAPTER 10

Center for Inclusive Design and Environmental Access (Center for IDEA). (2009). Danise Levine, AIA. Retrieved on September 10, 2010, from http://www.ap.buffalo.edu/idea/Staff/levine.asp

Hockenberry, J. (2006, October 11). "The re-education of Michael Graves." *Metropolis Magazine.* http://www.metropolismag.com/story/20061011/the-re-education-of-michael-graves

Olson, S. (2010). "An architect with disabilities champions public accessibility for all." *Institute for Human Centered Design.* Retrieved on September 10, 2010, from http://www.adaptenv.org/index.php?option=News&articleid=362

Rosetti Enterprises. (2010). *Rosemarie Rossetti, Ph.D.* September 15, 2010, from http://www.rosemariespeaks.com/biography/index.cfm?bhcp=1

Universal Design Living Laboratory (UDLL). (2009). *The story behind the project.* Retrieved on September 15, 2010, from http://www.udll.com/about/

Basic Metric Conversion Table

DISTANCES	
ENGLISH	**METRIC**
1 inch	2.54 centimeters
1 foot	0.3048 meter / 30.38 centimeters
1 yard	0.9144 meter
METRIC	**ENGLISH**
1 centimeter	0.3937 inch
1 meter	3.280 feet
WEIGHTS	
ENGLISH	**METRIC**
1 ounce	28.35 grams
1 pound	0.45 kilogram
METRIC	**ENGLISH**
1 gram	0.035 ounce
1 kilogram	2.2 pounds

General formula for converting: Number of Units × Conversion Number = New Number of Units

To convert inches to centimeters: [number of inches] × 2.54 = [number of centimeters]

To convert centimeters to inches: [number of centimeters] × 0.3937 = [number of inches]

To convert feet to meters: [number of feet] × 0.3048 = [number of meters]

To convert meters to feet: [number of meters] × 3.280 = [number of feet]

To convert yards to meters: [number of yards] × 0.9144 = [number of meters]

To convert ounces to grams: [number of ounces] × 28.35 = [number of grams]

To convert grams to ounces: [number of grams] × 0.035 = [number of ounces]

To convert pounds to kilograms: [number of pounds] × 0.45 = [number of kilograms]

To convert kilograms to pounds: [number of kilograms] × 2.2 = [number of pounds]

Index

Page numbers in italics refer to images or tables.

entrances/exits, 109–10, 148

ergonomics, 38, 89, 181–82, 184–85

evidence, 54

evidence-based design, 54

exclusion, 37–38

experimentation, 68–69

F

fact finding, 62

Fair Housing Act (FHA), 122

faucet design, 82–83

finishes, 149

Fletcher, Valerie, 278–79

focus groups, 54, 66

food and beverage facilities, 236–38, 239

formaldehyde, 92

Fuller, R. Buckminster, 53

furniture design, 87–90
    bariatrics, 89, 197, 199
    desks, 94, *95*
    office furniture, 90–91, 151
    seating, 94–95, 150–51, 189–90; lift chairs, 87–88
    waiting room/lobby furniture, 89

G

gardens, 209–11

Gehry, Frank, 231

GenXers, 177–78

glare, 102–3

Graves, Michael, 258–59, *260–61*

H

Habitat for Humanity (HH), 134, 136

healthcare design, 196–213
    hospitals, 196–201
    long-term care facilities. 201–13; gardens, 209–11

heating, ventilation, and air conditioning (HVAC), 161

Herman Miller, 38, *40*

high speech intelligibility, 214

historic buildings, 108–9, 160–64

Homes and Communities Agency (HCA), 30

hospitality design, 232–38
    food and beverage facilities, 236–38, 239
    hotels, 232–37

hospitals, 196–201

hot-desking, 175, 193

hoteling, 175

housing, *See* residential design

Housing and Urban Development (HUD), 136

I

inclusive design, 30–37
    accessible, 36, 37, 41
    adaptable, 36, 37, 39–40
    advantages, 43–46
    challenges of inclusivity, 37–38
    childcare facilities, 217, 219, 224, 218–19
    commercial design, 142–70
    criteria, 37, 39–41
    and the design process, 62–73
    educational facilities, 213–17
    healthcare design, 196–213
    hospitality design, 232–38
    and little people, 45–46, 104–7
    office design, 174–93
    playgrounds, 224–28
    principles of, 32–33, 35
    product design, 80–97
    purpose of, 32
    religious facilities, 248–51
    residential design, 100–39
    responsive, 36, 37, 39
    retail design, 238–42
    secure, 37, 41
    and senior citizens, 47–49
    transportation design, 242, 244–46
    and *universal design*, xii, 4, *31*, 34–37